ALL
ABOUT
EVERYTHING

THE ULTIMATE FACT-PACKED ALMANAC

LONDON, NEW YORK, MELBOURNE, MUNICH, AND DELHI

DK LONDON

Senior Art Editor Helen Spencer
Editor Alexandra Beeden
Designers Natalie Godwin, Steve Woosnam-Savage
US Senior Editor Shannon Beatty
US Editor Margaret Parrish

Managing Editor Esther Ripley
Managing Art Editor Karen Self

Publisher Sarah Larter
Art Director Phil Ormerod
Associate Publishing Director Liz Wheeler
Publishing Director Jonathan Metcalf

Pre-Production Producer Nikoleta Parasaki
Senior Producer Gemma Sharpe

Jacket Designer Laura Brim
Jacket Editor Manisha Majithia
Jacket Design Development Manager Sophia MTT

DK INDIA

Senior Editor Monica Saigal
Senior Art Editor Ranjita Bhattacharji
Editor Vibha Malhotra
Art Editors Neha Sharma, Parul Gambhir, Devan Das

Managing Editor Pakshalika Jayaprakash
Managing Art Editor Arunesh Talapatra

Jacket Designer Suhita Dharamjit
Picture Researcher Surya Sankash Sarangi

Pre-Production Manager Balwant Singh
Production Manager Pankaj Sharma
DTP Designers Bimlesh Tiwary, Pawan Kumar, Nand Kishor Acharya

CONTENT PREVIOUSLY PUBLISHED IN *ONE MILLION THINGS*

Senior Editor Julie Ferris
Senior Designer Stefan Podhorodecki
Project Editors Francesca Baines, Hazel Beynon
Designers Katie Knutton, Hoa Luc, Smiljka Surla, Nihal Yesil
US Editor Margaret Parrish

Editors Steven Carton, Jenny Finch, Niki Foreman, Fran Jones, Andrea Mills
Additional Design Jim Green, Spencer Holbrook, Phil Letsu, Johnny Pau, Marilou Prokopiou, Jacqui Swan

Managing Editor Linda Esposito
Managing Art Editor Diane Thistlethwaite

Commissioned Photography Dave King
Creative Retouching Steve Willis
Picture Research Nic Dean

Publishing Manager Andrew Macintyre
Category Publisher Laura Buller

DK Picture Researcher Lucy Claxton, Rose Horridge
Production Editor Andy Hilliard
Production Controller Pip Tinsley

Jacket Design Jacqui Swan, Akiko Kato
Jacket Editor Mariza O'Keeffe
Design Development Manager Sophia MTT
Development Team Natasha Rees, Yumiko Tahata

First American Edition, 2014
Published in the United States by
DK Publishing
4th floor, 345 Hudson Street
New York, New York 10014

14 15 16 17 18 10 9 8 7 6 5 4 3 2 1
001–197381–May/14

Published in Great Britain by Dorling Kindersley Limited.

A catalog record for this book is available from the Library of Congress.

ISBN: 978-1-4654-1746-6

DK books are available at special discounts when purchased in bulk for sales promotions, premiums, fund-raising, or educational use. For details, contact: DK Publishing Special Markets, 345 Hudson Street, New York, New York 10014 or SpecialSales@dk.com.

Printed and bound by Printing Express Limited, Hong Kong

Discover more at
www.dk.com

ALL ABOUT EVERYTHING

THE ULTIMATE FACT-PACKED ALMANAC

Contributors and consultants:
Kim Bryan, Laura Buller, Peter Chrisp, Mike Goodman,
Andrea Mills, Carole Stott, Richard Walker, Claire Watts,
Jon Woodcock, John Woodward

Nature   8

Plants   10
Trees   12
Flowers   14
Fruits   16
Fungi   18
Plankton   20
Insects   22
Insect anatomy   24
Fish   26
Feeding   28
Crustaceans   30
Amphibians   32
Life cycles   34
Attack and defense   36
Reptiles   38
Mollusks   40
Birds   42
Eggs   44
Movement   46
Living together   48
Mammals   50
Sleep   52
Skulls   54
Quick quiz   56
Fast facts   58

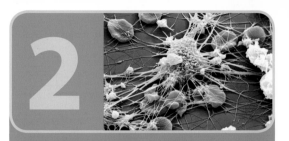

Human body   60

Cells   62
Skeleton   64
Muscles   66
Body systems   68
Respiration   70
Blood   72
Skin, hair, and nails   74
Brain   76
Senses   78
Reproduction   80
Genetics   82
Health   84
Quick quiz   86
Fast facts   88

3

Science and technology 90

Elements 92
Molecules 94
Acids and bases 96
Chemical reactions 98
States of matter 100
Water 101
Materials 102
Gravity 104
Dynamics 106
Magnetism 108
Electricity 110
Electromagnetic spectrum 112
Color 114
Machines 116
Robots 118
Transportation 120
Scientists 122
Quick quiz 124
Fast facts 126

4

Space 128

Universe 130
Galaxies 132
Stars 134
Constellations 136
Sun 138
Planets 140
Moons 142
Comets 144
Meteorites 146
Telescopes 148
Space exploration 150
Space travelers 152
Quick quiz 154
Fast facts 156

CONTENTS

Earth   158

Planet Earth	160
Plate tectonics	162
Volcanoes	164
Earthquakes	166
Mountains	168
Oceans	170
Rocks and minerals	172
Gems	174
Metals	176
Fossils	178
Dinosaurs	180
Weather	182
Erosion	184
Rivers	186
Climate zones	188
Farm crops	190
Environment	192
Quick quiz	194
Fast facts	196

People and places   198

Africa	200
Asia	202
North America	204
South America	206
Europe	208
Australasia	210
Antarctica	212
Flags	214
Maps	216
Economy	218
The state	220
US presidents	222
Religion	224
Festivals	226
Cities	228
Extreme living	230
Quick quiz	232
Fast facts	234

7

History 236

Prehistory	238
First civilizations	240
Classical world	242
Medieval life	244
American civilizations	246
Seafarers	248
War	250
Industrial Revolution	252
Disease	254
Money	256
20th century	258
Quick quiz	260
Fast facts	262

8

Art and culture 264

Art	266
Architecture	268
Symbols	270
Language	272
Literature	274
Media	276
Photography	278
Theater	280
Movies	282
Dance	284
Music	286
Orchestra	288
Sports	290
Quick quiz	292
Fast facts	294

Quiz answers	296
Index	298
Acknowledgments	304

NATURE

ALBATROSS COLONY
Every year, black-browed albatrosses return to the Falkland Islands in the Atlantic Ocean to breed. This albatross colony is the largest in the world, with more than 500,000 birds. Each pair produces a single egg.

PLANTS

All green plants use the energy of sunlight to make sugary carbohydrate food from water and carbon dioxide in the air. This is why they grow well only in sunlit, moist places. The food fuels growth and is used to make cellulose—the tough, fibrous tissue that helps support all the various parts of the plant, from its stems and leaves to its flowers.

3 STEM

The strong stem of the plant supports its leaves in the sunlight. It also contains bundles of tubes or veins. These allow water containing dissolved nutrients to flow up from the roots to the leaves, and also carry sugary food from the leaves to other parts of the plant.

1 GERMINATION

A bean plant begins life as a seed with two halves, called cotyledons. In spring when the weather is mild, the seed starts to absorb water through a minute hole in its outer coating (the testa). The seed swells and about three days later a root grows to hold the plant in place, and a shoot appears above the ground. This process is called germination.

Strong ribs kept rigid by water pressure support the thin, delicate leaf tissue

More leaves are produced as the plant continues to grow

Cotyledons become the first leaves of the plant, once the plant is above the ground

Shoot sprouts from the testa to form a root, with two seed leaves, called cotyledons, at its tip

Seed is covered by a hard coat called the testa, which protects it from fungi and bacteria

2 ROOTS

The plant's roots absorb water from the soil. The water is used by the leaves to make food. The water also contains dissolved mineral salts, such as nitrates and phosphates, which are essential for growth.

4 **LEAVES**

The leaves are the plant's food factories. They act like solar panels, as the green chlorophyll enables the plant to absorb the energy of sunlight and use it for photosynthesis—the process in which the plant takes carbon dioxide from the air and combines it with water drawn up by the roots to make sugar. Oxygen is also produced in the process and released into the air.

Green chlorophyll in leaves absorbs solar energy and uses it for photosynthesis

New leaves sprout from buds that form at the tips of shoots

Growing point of bean plant is at top of main stem, between leaf stalks

Leaves make sugar, which mixes with water to make sap that flows to other parts of plant

Stem is kept upright at first by water pressure, but is gradually stiffened with tough cellulose

Cotyledons contain food that fuels early growth, but fall off after true leaves form

Soil provides the plant with anchorage and is the main source of water and nutrients

Root network anchors plant in the soil as well as absorbing water and nutrients

5 **TRANSPIRATION**

As sunlight warms a plant, water in the leaves is lost as water vapor, through pores called stomata. The leaves then take in water from the stem, which in turn draws more water up into the plant from the roots. The water carries nutrients from the soil with it.

TREES

Trees are the tallest, heaviest, and oldest of all living things. The California giant sequoia known as General Sherman weighs approximately 6,000 tons—30 times as much as the biggest animal, the blue whale. The oldest living bristlecone pine tree, which also grows in California, is nearly 5,000 years old. Yet even these ancient giants can still produce tiny seeds that grow into new trees.

Holly

Hawthorn flowers

English oak

Blue Atlas pine needles

LEAVES

Like all green plants, trees absorb sunlight through their leaves and use its energy to turn air and water into sugar. A tree's leaves are its food factories.

Japanese maple

A monkey puzzle tree has leathery, sharp-pointed scales

NEEDLES AND SCALES

Thin leaves make food efficiently, but they are easily damaged by hot sun or frost. So many trees that grow in very hot or cold places have thicker, tougher needles or scales.

Robina has a pinnate compound leaf

COMPOUND LEAVES

Most trees have simple leaves of various shapes, but some have compound leaves made up of many leaflets. These either sprout from a long stalk (pinnate) or fan out from a single point (palmate).

Horse chestnut has a palmate compound leaf

Arolla pine needles

Oak leaves

Acorns are oak seeds

FRUIT

The flowers of some trees turn into juicy fruits that contain seeds. If birds eat the fruit, the seeds pass through them unharmed and are scattered far away.

Apple blossom

Apples are big, fleshy fruits

Yew berries

FLOWERS

All trees produce flowers, but some may not be obvious because they do not have colorful petals. Other trees, however, such as apples, have showy flowers that attract insects.

Magnolia trees bear some of the biggest flowers

TREE RINGS

Every year a tree adds a layer of new wood to its trunk. If the tree is cut down, each year's growth shows as a visible ring, so the number of rings gives its age.

Closed pinecone

Pinecone seeds

Open pinecone

Nutmeg spice is a seed

SEEDS AND NUTS

Some trees have tiny seeds, but others produce the bigger seeds we call nuts. Animals eat them, but also bury and forget them, so they grow into new trees.

CONES

Coniferous trees such as pines have woody cones that contain small papery seeds. When the cones open up in the sun, the seeds fall out and blow away.

DECIDUOUS LEAVES

Many trees lose their leaves in winter, and grow new ones in spring. Before they fall, the old leaves lose their green color and turn yellow, brown, or even red.

Maple seeds

Horse chestnut

Red maple

FLOWERS

Many plants produce beautiful flowers, often vividly colored and fragrant. These intricate structures form the reproductive parts of plants, and they have evolved so that they attract insects and birds to sip the sugary nectar at the flower's center. While feeding, the insect or bird is dusted with pollen, which is produced by the stamens and contain the male sex cells. The pollen is deposited on the sticky stigma of another flower. This is pollination. A pollen tube then grows down the style to the ovary and fertilizes an ovule. This is fertilization. Some plants, such as grasses and many types of tree, rely on the wind to carry their pollen, and their flowers do not need showy petals or fragrant nectar to attract animals. Since this is a less efficient system, they must produce far more pollen, which can fill the air and cause hay fever.

1

Stamen is made up of an anther and a filament

3

Bright reds and pinks are more attractive to birds than insects, because not all insects can see the color red

FLOWER STRUCTURE

A typical flower develops inside a bud at the end of a stalk. When the bud opens, it reveals a ring of petals, each of which secretes nectar from its base. At the center of the flower lie the male structures that produce pollen. These surround the female structures that hold the ovules, or egg cells. An outer ring of green sepals may protect the flower when it is in bud.

2 CARPEL

An ovary, a style, and a stigma form the main parts of a carpel. At the heart of the flower lie the ovules, enclosed in a case called an ovary. The top of each ovary extends into a style that carries a sticky pad called a stigma. The flowers of some plants have many carpels, each with its own stigma, but this lily has just one.

3 STAMEN

The tiny, dustlike pollen grains that contain the male cells are produced by stamens. These usually form a ring around the central carpel or carpels. Each stamen has a long filament that supports a clublike anther that produces the pollen.

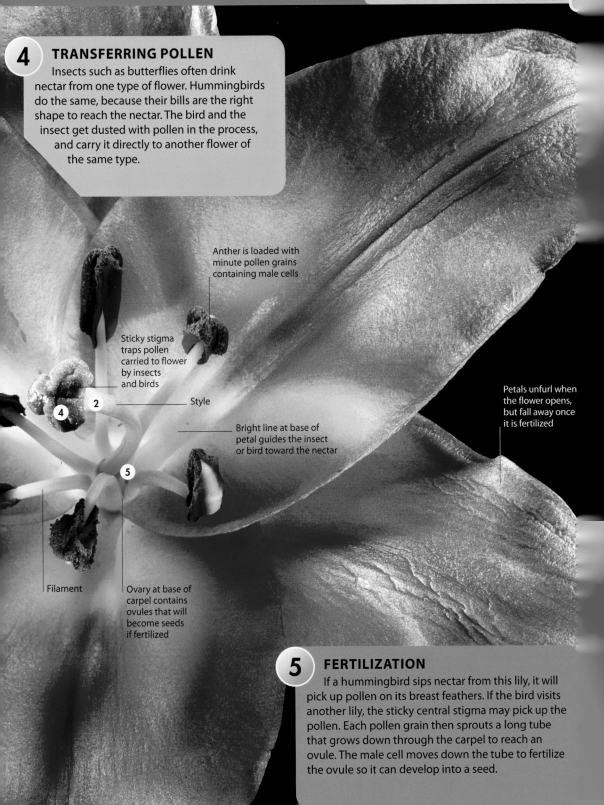

4 TRANSFERRING POLLEN

Insects such as butterflies often drink nectar from one type of flower. Hummingbirds do the same, because their bills are the right shape to reach the nectar. The bird and the insect get dusted with pollen in the process, and carry it directly to another flower of the same type.

Anther is loaded with minute pollen grains containing male cells

Sticky stigma traps pollen carried to flower by insects and birds

Style

Bright line at base of petal guides the insect or bird toward the nectar

Petals unfurl when the flower opens, but fall away once it is fertilized

Filament

Ovary at base of carpel contains ovules that will become seeds if fertilized

5 FERTILIZATION

If a hummingbird sips nectar from this lily, it will pick up pollen on its breast feathers. If the bird visits another lily, the sticky central stigma may pick up the pollen. Each pollen grain then sprouts a long tube that grows down through the carpel to reach an ovule. The male cell moves down the tube to fertilize the ovule so it can develop into a seed.

FRUITS

All plants produce fruits that contain their seeds. Some fruits are dry husks, but others are juicy and tasty. These attract animals, which eat them and carry the seeds in their stomachs. The tough-skinned seeds are not digested, but are scattered far away from the parent plant in the animals' droppings, and grow into new plants. The fruits shown here are cultivated types that have been specially bred for their size and flavor.

Tough skin encloses soft flesh

2

Bananas

Watermelons

Pomelo

Dates

Dragon fruit

1

Oranges

Lemons

Limes

Kiwis

Blueberries

Cantaloupe

Sweet granadilla

Strawberries

Tamarillos

Figs

Honeydew melon

Starfruit

3

1 ORANGE

An orange has very soft, juicy flesh contained in many segments, which are enclosed by a hard rind. Each segment usually contains a seed. An orange is technically a type of berry, which develops over the winter from the single ovary of an orange flower. Green at first, it turns orange as it swells to full size.

2 BANANA

The bananas that are cultivated in the tropics have been bred to be seedless, but the wild bananas of Southeast Asia have small fruits containing many big, hard seeds. They grow in bunches on large plants with huge leaves that sprout straight from the ground.

3 NUTS

All nuts are large seeds, which the plant has equipped with a store of concentrated plant food. This ensures that the seedlings get a good start in life. The nut is surrounded by a hard shell, which is technically a fruit, but tough and fibrous rather than soft and juicy.

4 DURIAN

To attract fruit-eating mammals, many fruits are fragrant. The Southeast Asian durian fruit is famous for its strong aroma, which some people like and others hate. Animals such as forest pigs and orangutans seem to love both its smell and taste.

5 GRAPES

Some fruits such as grapes grow as clusters of soft, edible, thin-skinned berries. Each berry has several seeds embedded in its flesh, although many cultivated varieties of grapes are seedless. Berries are often vividly colored to attract birds, which have excellent color vision.

Papayas

Grapes **5**

Mango

Pineapple

Pomegranates

Coconut

Sharon fruit

6

Guavas Cucumber

4 Durian

Prickly pears Plums

Peaches

Pumpkins

Butternut squash **7** Tomatoes

Physalis

Red kuri squash

Rambutans

Passion fruit

Bell peppers

Raspberries

Eggplant

Quinces

Blackberries

Red currants

Fruit forms pod, protecting big seeds

Fava beans

Baby eggplants

Chile peppers

Nuts

8

Apples

---

6 **PEACH**

The juicy flesh of a peach, plum, or cherry encloses a hard pit that contains a single seed. This type of fruit is called a drupe. The fleshy part is meant to be eaten, so animals spread the seeds, but some animals such as parrots can crack the pits and eat the seeds, too.

7 **TOMATO**

Not all fruits are edible. Some of the wild relatives of tomatoes are extremely poisonous. They include deadly nightshade, which is lethal to humans, although some animals can eat the berries without coming to harm. Tomatoes are also related to chile peppers.

8 **FAVA BEAN**

The edible part of a fava bean plant is its seeds, and its fruit is the entire pod. The wild ancestors of such beans do not attract animals. Instead, their pods dry up and split open with explosive force, so the seeds shoot out and are scattered on the ground.

FUNGI

The mushrooms and other fungi that can appear overnight in damp places are not plants. They belong to a completely separate group of living thing that feeds on dead or living plants and animals. Each fungus forms a hidden network of slender stems called a mycelium, and the visible part is just the "fruiting body" that sprouts like an apple on a tree to spread the spores that grow into new fungi.

1   OAK BOLETE
A typical mushroom has radiating gills beneath its cap that produce millions of spores. Other fungi, like the oak bolete, have spongy undersides that release spores from tiny holes or are covered with spore-producing tufts.

Beechwood sickener

Oak bolete

Inocybe geophylla

Orange birch bolete

Birch brittlegill

Sulfur tuft

Lepiota cristata

Death cap

Inocybe sindonia

False chanterelle

Yellow ramaria

Turkeytail

Sheathed woodtuft

Pearly webcap

Felt saddle

White saddle

Omphaliaster asterosporus

2   DEATH CAP
Some fungi are extremely poisonous if they are eaten. The aptly named death cap has probably been responsible for 90 percent of all known deaths from mushroom poisoning.

3   TURKEYTAIL
Fungi are vital to life because they break down and recycle dead organisms. The turkeytail grows on dead wood, rotting it down so the nutrients it contains can be used by growing plants.

4   SAFFRON MILK CAP
Many fungi grow around the roots of certain plants and provide them with plant foods in exchange for sugars. Saffron milk cap, for example, always grows with pine trees.

5 PARASOL MUSHROOM

Some fungi, like the penny bun and parasol mushroom, are good to eat. But if you are not an expert at identifying them, you could be poisoned by a killer like the death cap.

Bloodred webcap

The ring is part of the veil that covered the cap of the young mushroom

Parasol mushroom

The tough stem and cap contain chitin, which also forms the wings of insects

Fly agaric

Cortinarius rickenianus

Rosso coral

Bearded milk cap

Green brittlegill

Russula maculata

Persistent waxcap

Mealy funnel

Penny bun

Hare's ear

Chanterelle

Saffron milk cap

Collared earthstar

Stump puffball

Pholiota adiposa

Grooved bonnet

6 FLY AGARIC

The fly agaric is one of the best-known "toadstools"—a word often used for inedible or poisonous fungi. The white scales on its red cap are the remains of a thin veil that covered the growing fungus.

7 PENNY BUN

The rootlike fibers attached to the stem are just a tiny part of the penny bun's mycelium. This can cover huge areas. The mycelium of a single honey fungus can extend 1.6 million sq ft (150,000 sq m).

8 STUMP PUFFBALL

Puffballs are named for the way the ripe fungi puff clouds of dustlike spores when they are kicked or hit by rain. Just one giant puffball can contain an amazing 7 trillion (7,000,000,000,000) spores.

PLANKTON

The sunlit surface waters of many oceans teem with life, most of it microscopic, that drifts with the currents. The whole drifting community is called the plankton. It is made up of plantlike phytoplankton, which use the energy of sunlight to make food from carbon dioxide and water, and zooplankton—animals that feed on both the phytoplankton and each other. This image shows the plankton in a splash of seawater, magnified more than 25 times.

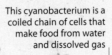

This cyanobacterium is a coiled chain of cells that make food from water and dissolved gas

◄ CYANOBACTERIA

Once known as "blue-green algae," these simple organisms were among the first forms of life to appear on Earth, more than 3.5 billion years ago. They still flourish in the oceans where, like diatoms, they turn carbon dioxide and water into sugary carbohydrates.

The glassy shell of this diatom reveals the green structures that use solar energy to make food

► DIATOMS

The phytoplankton consist of microscopic organisms such as diatoms and cyanobacteria. Diatoms have shells of glassy silica that fit together like tiny boxes with lids, and they exist in a dazzling variety of forms. They thrive in cool seas, where they turn the water gray-green and often multiply into vast cloudy "blooms" that are visible from space.

◄ CRAB LARVA

Among the members of the zooplankton are the eggs and young of animals that have very different shapes and lives when adult. They include the eggs of reef corals and infant fish, mollusks, and crustaceans like this crab larva. Drifting in the plankton provides them with food and helps them disperse through the oceans to find new places to live.

The size of a rice grain, this crab larva is light enough to drift near the surface in the plankton

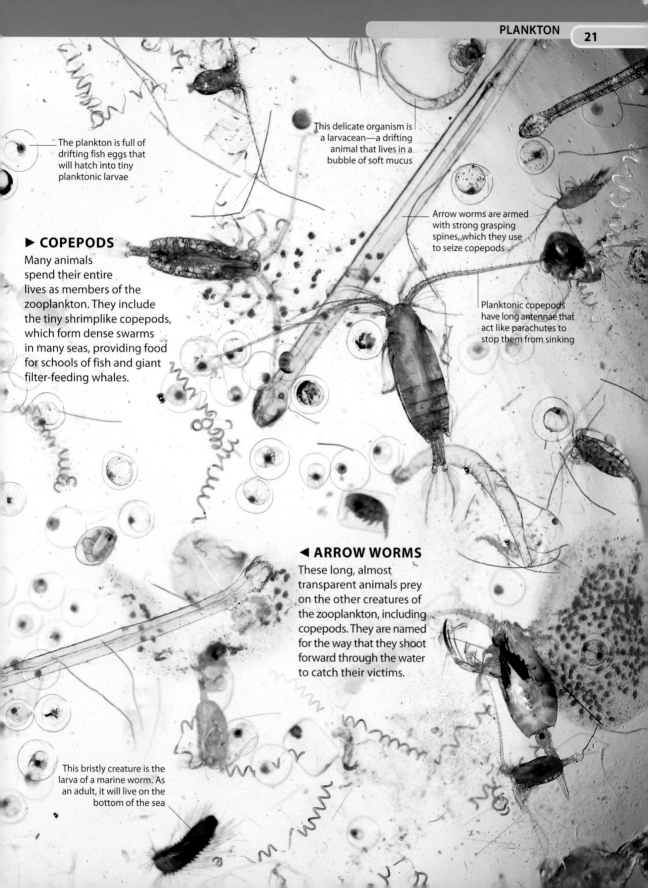

The plankton is full of drifting fish eggs that will hatch into tiny planktonic larvae

This delicate organism is a larvacean—a drifting animal that lives in a bubble of soft mucus

Arrow worms are armed with strong grasping spines, which they use to seize copepods

Planktonic copepods have long antennae that act like parachutes to stop them from sinking

▶ COPEPODS

Many animals spend their entire lives as members of the zooplankton. They include the tiny shrimplike copepods, which form dense swarms in many seas, providing food for schools of fish and giant filter-feeding whales.

◀ ARROW WORMS

These long, almost transparent animals prey on the other creatures of the zooplankton, including copepods. They are named for the way that they shoot forward through the water to catch their victims.

This bristly creature is the larva of a marine worm. As an adult, it will live on the bottom of the sea

INSECTS

Insects are the most successful creatures on Earth. Beetles alone account for almost a third of all known animal species. Many insects are tiny, but others are big enough for us to see the amazing intricacy of their structure. Some may bite or sting, and a few are real pests, but most are harmless, fascinating, and beautiful.

Great eggfly butterfly pupa

Swallowtail butterfly

Red admiral butterfly

Butterfly eggs

Cabbage white caterpillars

BUTTERFLIES

Butterflies start life as leaf-munching caterpillars, then form protective cases and become pupae, before turning into colorful winged beauties that sip nectar from flowers.

Housefly

Oleander moth

Pink barred sallow moth

Dragonfly

Hoverfly

Blowfly larvae

Tortoiseshell caterpillar

Green brindled crescent moth

Polyphemus moth

Cranefly

Oak silkmoth pupa

MOTHS

Moths are basically the same as butterflies, but most moths fly by night on whirring wings. Many are dull brown for camouflage, but a few are brightly patterned.

FLIES

True flies have just two wings for flying, rather than four like other adult insects. Some are biting bloodsuckers, and a few can spread diseases, but others like hoverflies are harmless.

Yellow brimstone moth

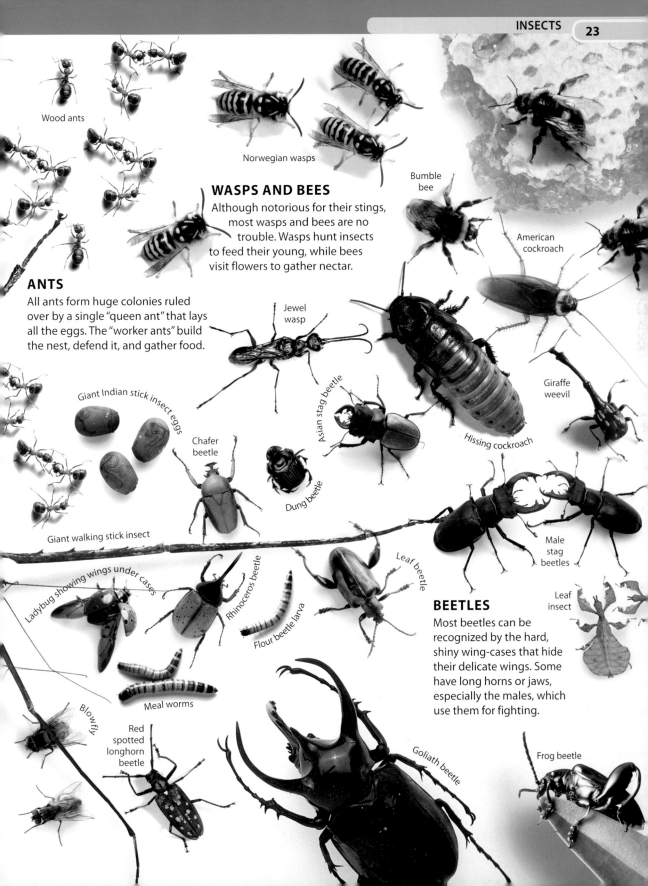

Wood ants

Norwegian wasps

Bumble bee

American cockroach

WASPS AND BEES

Although notorious for their stings, most wasps and bees are no trouble. Wasps hunt insects to feed their young, while bees visit flowers to gather nectar.

ANTS

All ants form huge colonies ruled over by a single "queen ant" that lays all the eggs. The "worker ants" build the nest, defend it, and gather food.

Jewel wasp

Giant Indian stick insect eggs

Chafer beetle

Dung beetle

Asian stag beetle

Hissing cockroach

Giraffe weevil

Giant walking stick insect

Male stag beetles

Ladybug showing wings under cases

Rhinoceros beetle

Flour beetle larva

Leaf beetle

Leaf insect

BEETLES

Most beetles can be recognized by the hard, shiny wing-cases that hide their delicate wings. Some have long horns or jaws, especially the males, which use them for fighting.

Blowfly

Meal worms

Red spotted longhorn beetle

Goliath beetle

Frog beetle

INSECT ANATOMY

Many insects start life as soft-skinned grubs, or larvae, but eventually they all turn into adults with hard, segmented bodies and six jointed legs. Their skin is toughened with a substance called chitin, which is a bit like hard plastic, so it acts as an external skeleton. It is often shiny and brightly colored, but it can look furry or scaly. Most adult insects like this wasp also have wings made from sheets of chitin, powered by muscles inside their bodies.

1 EYES
Like many other insects, an adult wasp has two large compound eyes. Each has hundreds of tiny lenses that see the world as a mosaic of colored dots. A wasp also has three small simple eyes, which are called ocelli, on the top of its head.

2 ANTENNAE
An insect's long antennae help it feel its way, but they are mainly used to detect scent. They are covered with sensitive nerve endings that pick up chemical signals. The antennae of some moths can detect scents from more than half a mile (1 km) away.

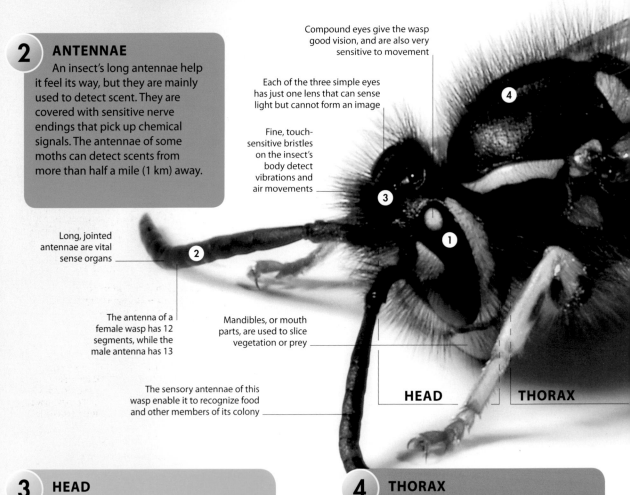

Compound eyes give the wasp good vision, and are also very sensitive to movement

Each of the three simple eyes has just one lens that can sense light but cannot form an image

Fine, touch-sensitive bristles on the insect's body detect vibrations and air movements

Long, jointed antennae are vital sense organs

The antenna of a female wasp has 12 segments, while the male antenna has 13

Mandibles, or mouth parts, are used to slice vegetation or prey

The sensory antennae of this wasp enable it to recognize food and other members of its colony

HEAD

THORAX

3 HEAD
An insect's head contains its brain and carries most of its sense organs. It is also equipped with mouthparts that are specialized to deal with its diet. A mosquito has a sharp needle for sucking blood, while this wasp has stout jaws for chewing other insects.

4 THORAX
The legs and wings of an insect are attached to the front section of its body, the thorax. This is packed with wing muscles, which power the wings a little like someone in a rowboat using a pair of oars. It also contains the insect's crop, used to store food.

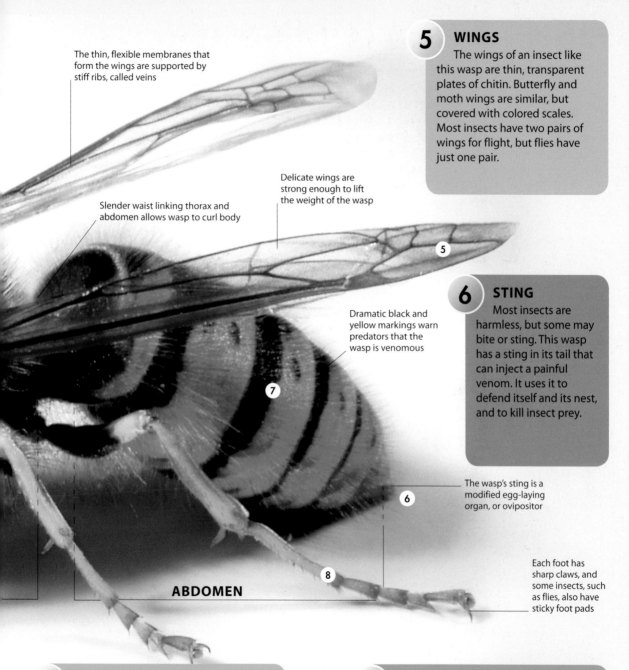

The thin, flexible membranes that form the wings are supported by stiff ribs, called veins

5 WINGS

The wings of an insect like this wasp are thin, transparent plates of chitin. Butterfly and moth wings are similar, but covered with colored scales. Most insects have two pairs of wings for flight, but flies have just one pair.

Delicate wings are strong enough to lift the weight of the wasp

Slender waist linking thorax and abdomen allows wasp to curl body

6 STING

Most insects are harmless, but some may bite or sting. This wasp has a sting in its tail that can inject a painful venom. It uses it to defend itself and its nest, and to kill insect prey.

Dramatic black and yellow markings warn predators that the wasp is venomous

The wasp's sting is a modified egg-laying organ, or ovipositor

Each foot has sharp claws, and some insects, such as flies, also have sticky foot pads

ABDOMEN

7 ABDOMEN

The flexible abdomen contains most of an insect's internal organs, including its digestive system. Tiny holes lead to a system of tubes that supply air to its organs and muscles. The vivid stripes of this wasp warn other animals that it can sting.

8 LEGS

All adult insects have six legs. When they walk, they lift three legs while keeping the other three on the ground—like a tripod—so they have no problem with balance. Each leg is a series of stiff tubes, hinged together and powered by muscles inside the tubes.

FISH

Fish were the first animals with backbones to appear on Earth, about 500 million years ago. They have since evolved into a wonderful variety of forms. From powerful sharks to delicate seahorses, fish now make up more than half of all vertebrate species. Most fish live in the salty oceans, like those shown below, but many—including the fish on the opposite page—live in freshwater lakes and rivers. A few, such as salmon, are able to live in both.

1 RAY

Closely related to sharks, with skeletons made of cartilage, rays are flattened fish that swim by using their lateral (side) fins like wings. They live on the seabed, hunting smaller fish and shellfish.

2 BOXFISH

The curious boxfish are named for their boxlike defensive armor, formed from thick, fused scales. This prevents all body movement, so the fish swim by using their small fins like oars.

3 PUFFERFISH

Pufferfish defend themselves by inflating their bodies with water or air so they are hard for predators to swallow. Some species have sharp spines that add to the effect, and many of their internal organs contain lethal poisons.

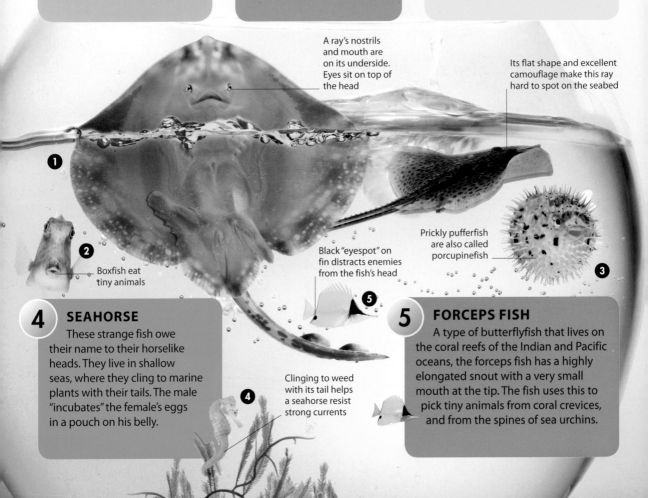

A ray's nostrils and mouth are on its underside. Eyes sit on top of the head

Its flat shape and excellent camouflage make this ray hard to spot on the seabed

❶

Boxfish eat tiny animals

❷

Black "eyespot" on fin distracts enemies from the fish's head

Prickly pufferfish are also called porcupinefish

❸

❺

4 SEAHORSE

These strange fish owe their name to their horselike heads. They live in shallow seas, where they cling to marine plants with their tails. The male "incubates" the female's eggs in a pouch on his belly.

Clinging to weed with its tail helps a seahorse resist strong currents

❹

5 FORCEPS FISH

A type of butterflyfish that lives on the coral reefs of the Indian and Pacific oceans, the forceps fish has a highly elongated snout with a very small mouth at the tip. The fish uses this to pick tiny animals from coral crevices, and from the spines of sea urchins.

6 SALMON

Big, powerful salmon spend most of their lives at sea, but swim upstream to the shallow rivers with gravelly bottoms where they breed. They have adaptations that allow them to move between fresh- and saltwater.

7 CARP

Able to live in water that has very little oxygen, carp are well equipped for life in warm, still lakes and ponds. They feed by using their extendible jaws to root around on the bottom for small animals and aquatic plants.

8 VELVET CICHLID

One of about 650 species of cichlid, mostly found in the tropics, velvet cichlids live in slow-flowing South American rivers. They dig in the riverbeds for small animals such as worms and freshwater shrimp.

9 STICKLEBACK

This fish gets its name from the sharp spines on its back. It lives in ponds, rivers, and lakes, and some shallow seas. In spring, the male makes a nest of plant fiber, and does a dance to attract females to lay their eggs.

10 PIRANHA

Notorious for its sharp teeth and mass attacks on other animals that enter the water, the piranha is a fearsome predator that lives in South American rivers. A large, hungry school can reduce a big animal to a skeleton.

11 PIKE

This powerful hunter lives in lakes and slow-flowing rivers throughout Europe, northern Asia, and North America. Pike hunt fish and waterbirds by lying in wait among aquatic plants and darting out to seize victims.

Three sharp spines help to defend the stickleback from bigger predatory fish

Tough, shiny scales help protect the carp's skin from injury and attack by parasites

The colors of this cichlid are variable, changing as the fish grows older

Long, pointed jaws have big, sharp teeth to give the pike a good grip on slippery prey

An acute sense of smell enables the piranha to detect the slightest trace of blood in the water

FEEDING

All animals get the nutrients they need by eating plants, animals, or other organisms such as bacteria or fungi. Some of these foods are easy to find but hard to digest, like leaves and grass. Others, such as animal prey, can be difficult to find or catch, but are easy to digest and rich in food value. Animals have developed a variety of adaptations for gathering and digesting their food. Some of these are much more specialized than others, and govern the animal's whole way of life.

Gills in long slots at the back of the shark's mouth trap floating food

Sucker surrounds the mouth and sharp teeth

Parrots often use their feet to grip nuts while they crack into them with their bills

1 **BASKING SHARK**
The enormous basking shark has tiny teeth. It feeds by swimming through swarms of tiny drifting organisms with its mouth gaping open, and trapping them in its sievelike gills. Many whales filter feed in a similar way, as do some birds, such as flamingos.

2 **GIRAFFE**
A giraffe's extralong neck allows it to eat leaves that other animals cannot reach. Like many leaf-eaters and grass-eaters, giraffes have bacteria in their digestive system that break down the tough plant fiber to release vital nutrients.

3 **LEECH**
A parasitic leech clings to a living animal, slices into its skin, and sucks its blood. Some leeches may take up to five times their own weight in blood, but only need to feed once or twice a year.

4 **PARROT**
Birds need concentrated food that does not weigh them down, so most birds feed on insects, meat, fruit, or seeds. Many parrots eat nuts, cracking the strong shells with their powerful hooked bills, but some have brush-tipped tongues to lap up sugary flower nectar.

5 GIANT ANTEATER

Many animals eat insects, but few are so specialized for the job as the giant anteater. It has a long, sticky, wormlike tongue that it flicks in and out of its long snout up to 150 times a minute to scoop its tiny prey from their nest.

6 TAPEWORM

This parasite lives in the intestines of another animal—including some people. Since it is surrounded by predigested food it does not need a digestive system of its own, or even a mouth, and it just soaks up nutrients through its thin skin.

A housefly can contaminate food by walking on it

7 LION

Catching large live animals can be difficult and dangerous. A lion relies on its strength and long, sharp canine teeth to kill its prey. It slices the meat into mouthfuls with scissorlike cheek teeth, but swallows it without chewing because meat is easy to digest.

8 EGYPTIAN VULTURE

Many creatures are scavengers that feed on carrion (dead flesh) and other scraps. They include the Egyptian vulture, which clears up remains that would otherwise simply rot. Without scavengers, the world would be a lot less healthy.

9 HOUSEFLY

Many insects, including all flies, can eat only liquid food. Some suck blood, or gather nectar or plant juices. The housefly can also liquefy some solid foods such as sugar by drenching them with saliva and soaking up the result with its moplike mouthparts.

10 BROWN BEAR

Although basically a meat-eater, the brown bear devours many foods, ranging from meat and fish to fruit and honey. This means that it is not specialized for any particular way of feeding, and can change its food with the seasons. Humans have the same "omnivorous" (eat-all) diet.

CRUSTACEANS

This varied group of invertebrates includes more than 40,000 species. Crustaceans take their name from the hard, jointed shells, or exoskeletons, that support and protect their bodies. Most crustaceans live in the sea, or in freshwater lakes and rivers. Only woodlice live on land. Crustaceans have at least four pairs of jointed legs, gills for breathing under water, and sensory antennae that they use to feel and smell the things around them.

3 LANGOUSTINE
Found in the Atlantic Ocean and North Sea, langoustines are also known as Norway lobsters. They come out at night from their seafloor burrows to feed on worms and smaller crustaceans. Their muscular tails are eaten as "scampi."

1 CRAB
Armed with a pair of powerful claws, and protected by a thick shell, a crab is built for both attack and defense. Crabs can creep forward very slowly, but they prefer to scuttle sideways because they can move much quicker that way.

2 BARNACLE
Young barnacles drift in the water like shrimp, but when they become adults they cement themselves to rocks, piers, and even other crustaceans. They feed by extending feathery legs from their shells to catch tiny floating creatures.

Heavy pincers can crack open mollusk shells

Eyes are on the end of short stalks

Mouthparts manipulate and chew food

Hard, armor plates protect barnacle's body

Legs catch food as it floats by

Barnacle cements itself head first to a hard surface

Jointed back legs are used for walking

Tough shield, or carapace, covers crab's head and thorax

Abdomen is tucked away beneath the crab's body

Langoustine can grow up to 6 in (15 cm) in length

4 LOBSTER

Weighed down by their heavy shells, lobsters usually walk on the seafloor, but they can swim backward to escape danger by flipping their tails. Like all crustaceans, they have to molt (shed) their hard exoskeletons several times as they grow.

5 WOODLOUSE

Woodlice are the only crustaceans that are completely at home on land, but they must live in damp places. They have seven pairs of legs and some species can roll themselves into a ball if they feel threatened. Despite their name, they do not damage wood.

6 SHRIMP

Many shrimp swim or drift in the water, but others spend most of their lives searching for food on the seabed. Some specialize in picking bloodsucking parasites off the fish that live on coral reefs, which line up to be cleaned.

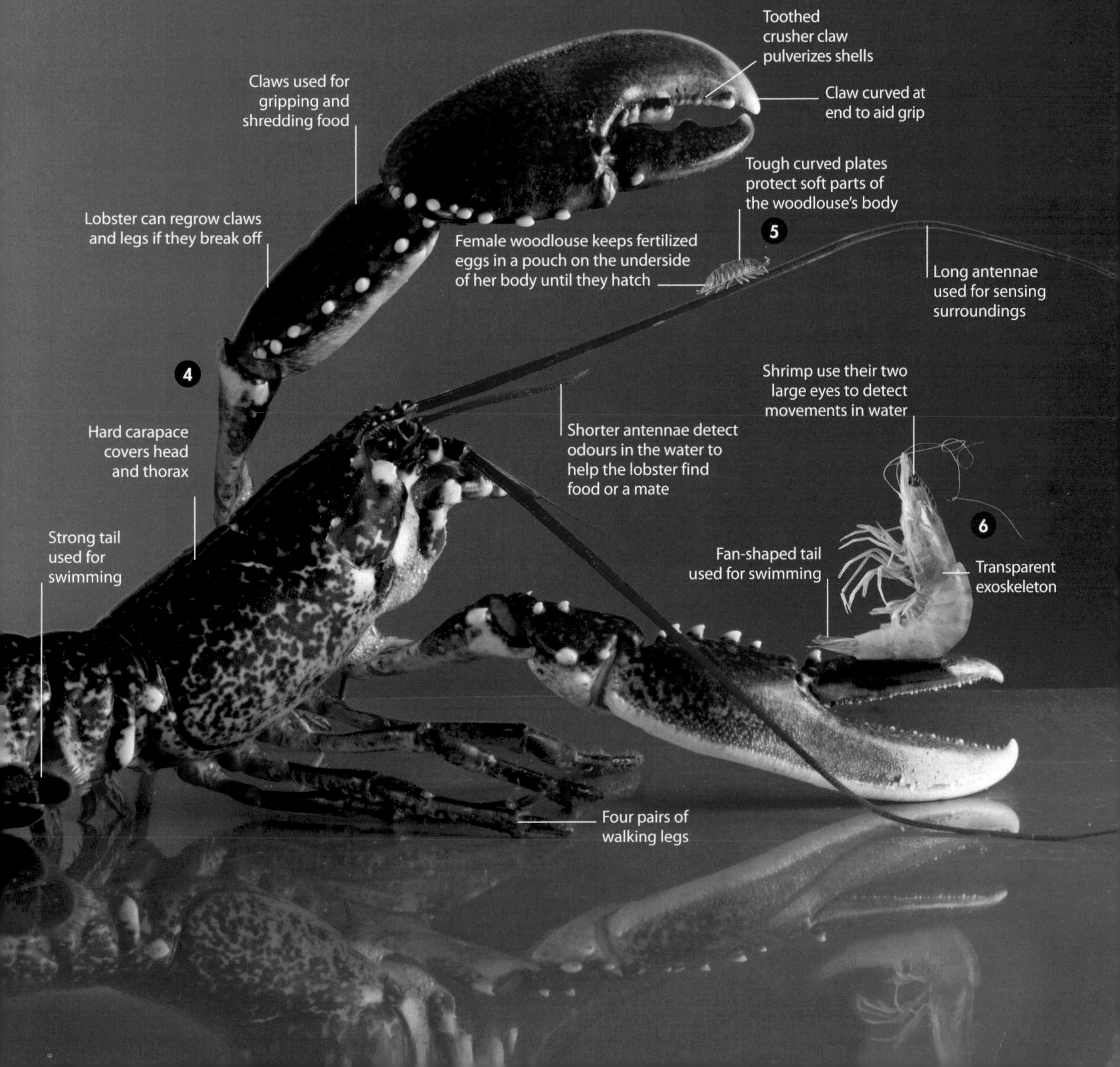

Toothed crusher claw pulverizes shells

Claw curved at end to aid grip

Claws used for gripping and shredding food

Tough curved plates protect soft parts of the woodlouse's body

Lobster can regrow claws and legs if they break off

Female woodlouse keeps fertilized eggs in a pouch on the underside of her body until they hatch

Long antennae used for sensing surroundings

Hard carapace covers head and thorax

Shorter antennae detect odours in the water to help the lobster find food or a mate

Shrimp use their two large eyes to detect movements in water

Strong tail used for swimming

Fan-shaped tail used for swimming

Transparent exoskeleton

Four pairs of walking legs

AMPHIBIANS

Although amphibians look a little like scaly reptiles, they do not have waterproof skin, so cannot live in hot, dry places where they might dry out. Most hide away by day, and emerge only at night. They must also lay their eggs in ponds and other wet places, and many spend their early lives as aquatic tadpoles.

1 COMMON FROG
All amphibians eat live animals, which they hunt by sight. The frog on the left is leaping through the air to catch a ladybug, which it will snap up and swallow alive.

Common frog

Frog's thin, moist skin can absorb oxygen directly from the air

Tinker vine frog

2 MIDWIFE TOAD
Most frogs and toads lay their eggs in water, but the male midwife toad wraps the strings of eggs around his legs and looks after them until they are ready to hatch.

Mandarin salamander

Midwife toad

3 MANDARIN SALAMANDER
Salamanders and newts are a bit like frogs with long tails. Some, like the Asian mandarin salamander, have vividly colored skin that warns enemies that they are poisonous to eat.

Colorful lumps and bumps ooze toxic fluids for protection from predators

Australian tree frog

Big eyes help poison dart frogs see well in the dark forest

Poison dart frog

Madagascan tomato frogs

4 POISON DART FROG
Tiny tree frogs of American tropical forests are protected by powerful poisons on their skin. Some are so deadly that local people use them to make poison darts.

5 AUSTRALIAN TREE FROG
Tree frogs have suckers on the tips of their toes so that they can cling to wet foliage. Most tree frogs only visit pools of water to breed.

6 TOMATO FROG
Many frogs and toads, like these tomato frogs, defend themselves by inflating their bodies with air so that they are harder to eat.

7 TADPOLES
Nearly all frogs start life in the water as tadpoles with long tails and no legs. Gradually they grow legs, hop out of the water, and their tails shrivel away.

8 AFRICAN BULLFROG
A mouse makes a tasty snack for a bullfrog, which will eat almost anything that moves.

9 CAECILIAN
Wormlike caecilians burrow in tropical forests by pushing their bony heads through the soil. They have no legs and are almost blind.

Froglet losing tail

7 Froglet with tail

Tadpoles

Frogs cannot chew, but they have huge mouths so that they can swallow their prey whole

Red-eyed tree frog

Common frogs are able to lighten or darken their skins to blend in with their surroundings

European common frog

8

African bullfrog

Asian painted frog

Foam-nesting frog

11

9 Caecilian

Fire salamander

Covered by tough skin, a caecilian's eyes cannot form clear images but they can detect light

12

10 Chilean four-eyed frog

Bright yellow spots warn off enemies, even at night

10 FOUR-EYED FROG
A four-eyed frog has a pair of big eyespots on its back. If attacked, it turns its back and inflates its body so that it looks like a fierce animal.

11 FOAM-NESTING FROG
Some tree frogs keep their eggs moist by laying them in a nest of wet foam high in the trees.

12 FIRE SALAMANDER
Bright patterns warn predators that this salamander can spray a blinding poison up to 13 ft (4 m) through the air.

LIFE CYCLES

All animals pass through different stages of life as they grow into fully developed adults. The first stage is the start of a new life, and for most animals the final phase is when they breed to start the cycle over again. For some animals, such as most mammals, these stages are very similar. For others, such as many insects, every stage is quite different, and involves a complete transformation, or metamorphosis, from the previous stage.

▶ DOG

A dog's life cycle is typical of many mammals, because it starts life as a smaller version of its parents. As it grows bigger, its internal organs develop so it can eat an adult diet, and eventually produce its own young.

After about two weeks, the puppy can see, but its digestive system can still only cope with milk.

The older puppy can eat solid food provided by its mother, and begins to learn vital skills through play.

For the first two weeks, the puppy cannot see the world around it.

Though not able to breed just yet, this young dog can find its own food.

Blind and helpless, a newborn puppy cannot eat solid food, so it lives on its mother's milk.

The fully grown dog now looks to find a mate to produce puppies of its own.

◀ FROG

Most amphibians, such as frogs, have complex life cycles. A typical frog lays eggs in water, and these hatch as fishlike tadpoles. The tadpoles develop lungs and legs, and hop out of the water as tiny froglets, eventually becoming fully grown adult frogs.

Young tadpole has three pairs of feathery gills, which absorb vital oxygen from the water

Wriggling out of the jelly into the water, the tadpole uses a sticky fluid to cling to an aquatic plant.

As the tadpole grows older, it develops back legs, then front legs, and its body starts to look like that of a frog.

An embryo develops inside the egg and starts to move, using energy supplied by the yolk of the egg.

Tail shrinks to a stump as the froglet learns to use its legs to swim and hop

Lungs develop, the tail shrinks, and the new froglet hops out of the water to live on land, where it hunts small animals.

An adult frog lays frogspawn containing hundreds of eggs protected by jelly, which swells up in the water.

Living mainly on land, the adult frog will return to the water in spring to find a mate and either lay or fertilize eggs.

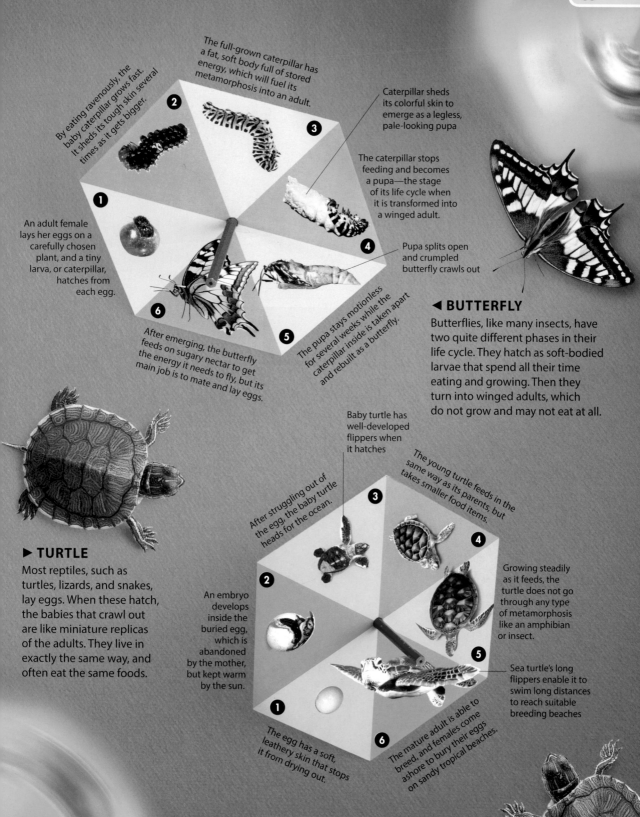

By eating ravenously, the baby caterpillar grows fast. It sheds its tough skin several times as it gets bigger.

2

The full-grown caterpillar has a fat, soft body full of stored energy, which will fuel its metamorphosis into an adult.

3

Caterpillar sheds its colorful skin to emerge as a legless, pale-looking pupa

The caterpillar stops feeding and becomes a pupa—the stage of its life cycle when it is transformed into a winged adult.

1

An adult female lays her eggs on a carefully chosen plant, and a tiny larva, or caterpillar, hatches from each egg.

4

Pupa splits open and crumpled butterfly crawls out

6

After emerging, the butterfly feeds on sugary nectar to get the energy it needs to fly, but its main job is to mate and lay eggs.

5

The pupa stays motionless for several weeks while the caterpillar inside is taken apart and rebuilt as a butterfly.

◄ BUTTERFLY

Butterflies, like many insects, have two quite different phases in their life cycle. They hatch as soft-bodied larvae that spend all their time eating and growing. Then they turn into winged adults, which do not grow and may not eat at all.

Baby turtle has well-developed flippers when it hatches

3

The young turtle feeds in the same way as its parents, but takes smaller food items.

After struggling out of the egg, the baby turtle heads for the ocean.

2

4

Growing steadily as it feeds, the turtle does not go through any type of metamorphosis like an amphibian or insect.

An embryo develops inside the buried egg, which is abandoned by the mother, but kept warm by the sun.

► TURTLE

Most reptiles, such as turtles, lizards, and snakes, lay eggs. When these hatch, the babies that crawl out are like miniature replicas of the adults. They live in exactly the same way, and often eat the same foods.

5

Sea turtle's long flippers enable it to swim long distances to reach suitable breeding beaches

1

The egg has a soft, leathery skin that stops it from drying out.

6

The mature adult is able to breed, and females come ashore to bury their eggs on sandy tropical beaches.

ATTACK AND DEFENSE

Many animals are hunters that prey on other animals. Catching and killing fast-moving prey is hard, so over time hunters have evolved features and tactics to make the job easier. This has made survival harder for the animals that they hunt, so many have evolved defenses that make them difficult, or even dangerous, to catch.

▶ DRIFTING TRAP

The long tentacles of the box jellyfish are armed with thousands of tiny stinging cells. The animal simply drifts with the currents and devours any creature that is unlucky enough to come into contact with its tentacles.

◀ NIGHT HUNTER

Insect-eating bats target their prey using pulses of high-pitched sound. The sounds bounce off the victim, creating a sound image that enables a bat to hunt flying insects in total darkness.

◀ VENOM AND CLAWS

Many animals have venomous bites or stings that they can use to kill their prey and to defend themselves. A scorpion normally uses its claws to hunt and the sting on the end of its tail for defense.

◀ AMBUSH

The praying mantis lurks motionless on a plant, waiting for another insect to come within range. Then it shoots out its spiny front limbs to catch its victim and eats it alive.

▼ TEAMWORK

Lions are equipped with daggerlike teeth and long claws, but their main weapon is teamwork. They encircle their prey so there is no escape.

▶ CONSTRICTOR

A python coils around its prey, squeezing a little tighter every time the victim breathes out, until eventually it cannot breathe at all. A snake's lower jaws are loosely linked to its skull, so it can swallow its prey whole.

▶ POISON GLANDS

If attacked by a hunter, a toad defends itself by inflating its body with air and oozing poisons from its skin. This makes it hard to eat and also makes it taste unpleasant, so its enemy is likely to leave it alone.

▼ CAMOUFLAGE

The best defense is to avoid being noticed at all. Camouflage makes animals hard to see against their background. This mountain hare turns white in winter to match the snow.

▼ SPINES

Some animals have defensive armor. Others, like this porcupine, bristle with long, sharp spines. This can make them almost impossible to attack, and even dangerous to animals that try.

▶ PLAYING DEAD

Many hunters will only eat prey that they have killed themselves. Some animals like this opossum take advantage of this by "playing dead" if threatened. An opossum may keep up the pretence for six hours!

▶ NOXIOUS SMELL

Skunks are notorious for the vile-smelling fluid that they spray from scent glands under their tails if attacked. They can aim accurately for up to 7 ft (2 m), often targeting the faces of their enemies.

▶ SAFETY IN NUMBERS

Solitary animals make easy targets, so many try to confuse their enemies by living in dense schools, flocks, or herds. By staying close together, this school looks like one big fish rather than lots of little ones.

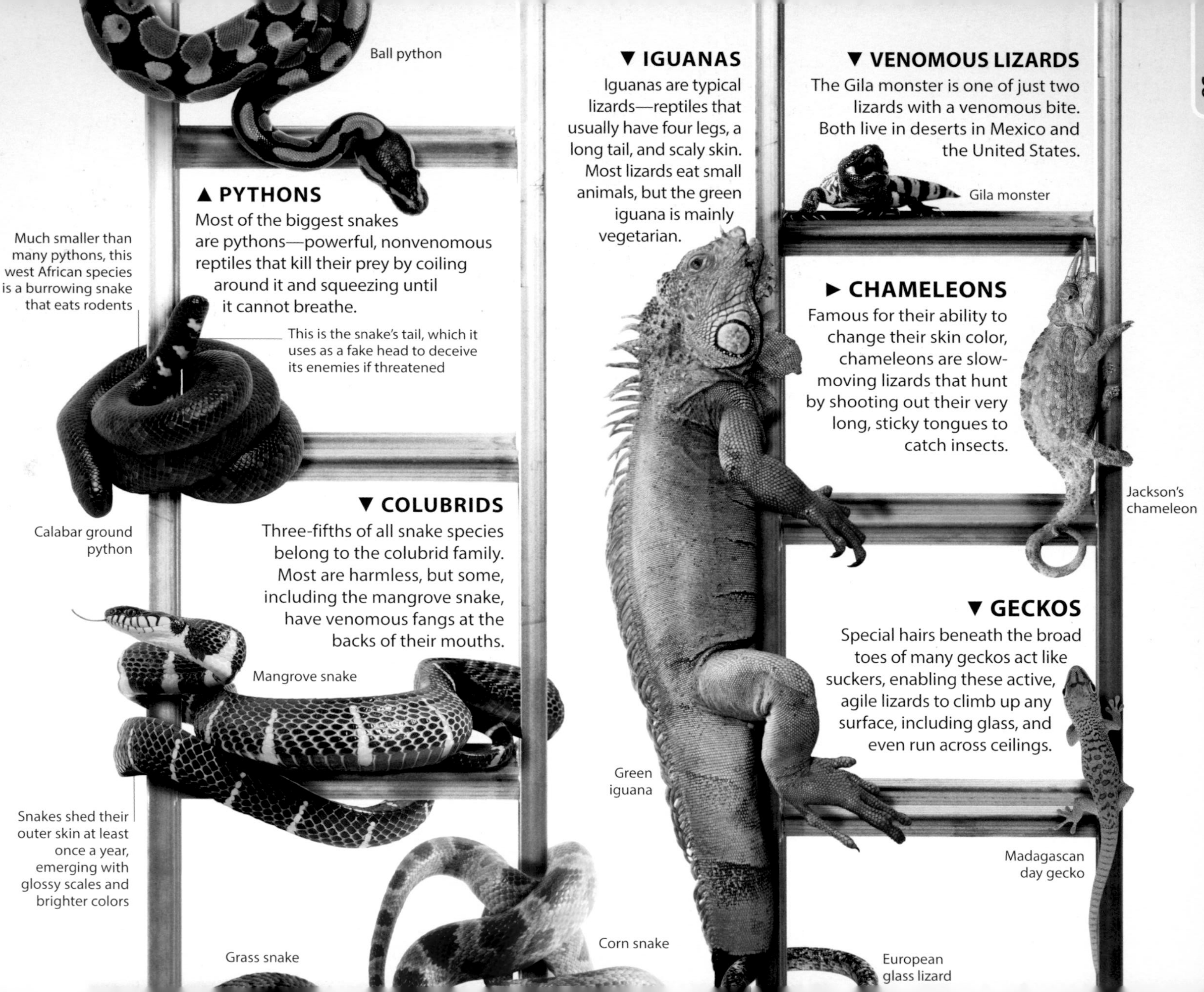

▼ VENOMOUS LIZARDS

The Gila monster is one of just two lizards with a venomous bite. Both live in deserts in Mexico and the United States.

Jackson's chameleon

Gila monster

▶ CHAMELEONS

Famous for their ability to change their skin color, chameleons are slow-moving lizards that hunt by shooting out their very long, sticky tongues to catch insects.

▶ GECKOS

Special hairs beneath the broad toes of many geckos act like suckers, enabling these active, agile lizards to climb up any surface, including glass, and even run across ceilings.

Madagascan day gecko

European glass lizard

▼ IGUANAS

Iguanas are typical lizards—reptiles that usually have four legs, a long tail, and scaly skin. Most lizards eat small animals, but the green iguana is mainly vegetarian.

Green iguana

Corn snake

▲ PYTHONS

Most of the biggest snakes are pythons—powerful, nonvenomous reptiles that kill their prey by coiling around it and squeezing until it cannot breathe.

This is the snake's tail, which it uses as a fake head to deceive its enemies if threatened

Ball python

Much smaller than many pythons, this west African species is a burrowing snake that eats rodents

Calabar ground python

▼ COLUBRIDS

Three-fifths of all snake species belong to the colubrid family. Most are harmless, but some, including the mangrove snake, have venomous fangs at the backs of their mouths.

Mangrove snake

Snakes shed their outer skin at least once a year, emerging with glossy scales and brighter colors

Grass snake

REPTILES

Scaly, creeping, cold-blooded reptiles can seem sinister—especially venomous snakes and snapping crocodiles. Yet many reptiles are glossy, vividly colored creatures with fascinating habits. Most are hunters, but since they do not use any energy keeping warm they do not need to eat much. Crocodiles often go for months without eating, and some big snakes can survive for a year on just one big meal.

▼ TUATARA

Found only in New Zealand, the two species of tuatara are the only survivors of a group of reptiles that mostly died out 100 million years ago, during the age of dinosaurs.

Tuatara

American alligator

▲ CROCODILES

The most powerful of all reptiles, alligators and crocodiles are ferocious predators that ambush, kill, and eat animals as big as zebras.

▲ LEGLESS LIZARDS

Some lizards have no legs, so they look and behave like snakes. The European glass lizard has tiny vestiges of legs, showing that its ancestors were like normal lizards.

The red-tailed racer's slender body is adapted for climbing

Red-tailed racer

Rattlesnake

▼ COBRAS

Among the deadliest of venomous snakes, cobras are armed with a nerve poison that paralyzes their victims so they cannot breathe and they die from suffocation.

▶ VIPERS

Equipped with long poison fangs that hinge forward when they open their mouths, vipers such as rattlesnakes are extremely dangerous. Luckily, rattlesnakes rattle their tails as a warning.

Sensing danger, this grass snake is "playing dead" in the hope that it will be ignored

The grass snake is an excellent swimmer. It ripples its body to move through water in search of frogs to eat

This small turtle has a streamlined shell to help it glide through water

Slider terrapin

Hermann's tortoise

▲ TURTLES

Instantly recognizable by their shells, turtles and tortoises have existed since the first days of the first dinosaurs. Tortoises are famously slow, but turtles can swim quite fast over long distances.

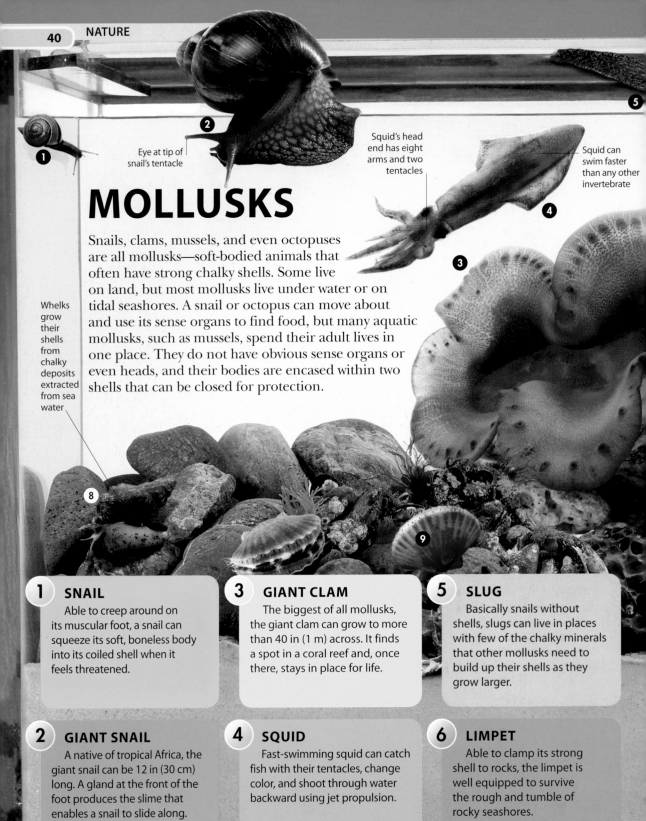

Eye at tip of
snail's tentacle

Squid's head
end has eight
arms and two
tentacles

Squid can
swim faster
than any other
invertebrate

MOLLUSKS

Snails, clams, mussels, and even octopuses
are all mollusks—soft-bodied animals that
often have strong chalky shells. Some live
on land, but most mollusks live under water or on
tidal seashores. A snail or octopus can move about
and use its sense organs to find food, but many aquatic
mollusks, such as mussels, spend their adult lives in
one place. They do not have obvious sense organs or
even heads, and their bodies are encased within two
shells that can be closed for protection.

Whelks
grow
their
shells
from
chalky
deposits
extracted
from sea
water

1 SNAIL
Able to creep around on
its muscular foot, a snail can
squeeze its soft, boneless body
into its coiled shell when it
feels threatened.

3 GIANT CLAM
The biggest of all mollusks,
the giant clam can grow to more
than 40 in (1 m) across. It finds
a spot in a coral reef and, once
there, stays in place for life.

5 SLUG
Basically snails without
shells, slugs can live in places
with few of the chalky minerals
that other mollusks need to
build up their shells as they
grow larger.

2 GIANT SNAIL
A native of tropical Africa, the
giant snail can be 12 in (30 cm)
long. A gland at the front of the
foot produces the slime that
enables a snail to slide along.

4 SQUID
Fast-swimming squid can catch
fish with their tentacles, change
color, and shoot through water
backward using jet propulsion.

6 LIMPET
Able to clamp its strong
shell to rocks, the limpet is
well equipped to survive
the rough and tumble of
rocky seashores.

Limpets use their conical shells to protect themselves from waves

6

Octopus's tentacles dart out to reach prey

Algae living in the giant clam's fleshy lips use sunlight to produce energy-rich food for the clam

Cuttlefish can change color according to their mood

7

Mussels feed by drawing water into the shells and filtering edible particles

12

10

11

---

7 **OCTOPUS**
Like the cuttlefish and squid, an octopus is an intelligent animal with excellent eyesight. It uses the strong suckers on its eight long arms to catch crabs.

9 **SCALLOP**
Like clams, scallops are two-shelled bivalves. By snapping their shells shut, they can shoot through the water when they need to escape danger.

11 **SEA SLUG**
Many sea slugs have flamboyant frills. Bright colors act as a warning to predators to leave them alone.

8 **WHELK**
A type of sea snail, the whelk uses its acute sense of smell to track down dead animals in the water for food.

10 **MUSSEL**
All mussels attach themselves to rocks with strong threads, and live by pumping food-rich water through their bodies.

12 **CUTTLEFISH**
Unlike most mollusks, a cuttlefish has an internal shell. This can be filled with air to make it buoyant, so the cuttlefish can drift through the water after its prey.

Rock pigeon

BIRDS

The only animals with feathers, birds are found in all parts of the world. Many have superb flying skills, with strong chest muscles to power their flapping wings. There is a dazzling diversity of species, from soaring albatrosses and flamboyant peacocks to flightless rheas and tiny hummingbirds.

▶ ZEBRA FINCH

Like many birds, the zebra finch of Australia lives in large flocks that fly and feed together for safety. Its stout bill is adapted for splitting the tough skins of grass seeds to get at their nourishing kernels.

▲ TAWNY EAGLE

Eagles are powerful hunters. They target their prey while soaring high overhead, then swoop down to seize it in their talons. The tawny eagle is also notorious for stealing the victims of other birds of prey.

Immensely strong, sharp-clawed talons are the eagle's main weapons

Penguins' wings are adapted for swimming, not flight

Birds spend hours preening their feathers to keep them in good condition

▲ RHEA

As tall as 5 ft (1.5 m), these large flightless birds roam the grassland of South America. They eat plants, nuts, seeds, and fruits, as well as insects and small animals, such as lizards.

King penguins

Peacock

Farmyard ducks

The male peacock raises its hugely elongated tail feathers to display them

Parrots can crack nuts with their strong bills

Green parakeet

▲ ALBATROSS

The long, narrow wings of an albatross enable it to soar for hours on oceanic winds without moving a muscle. It feeds on marine animals, which it snatches from the ocean with its bill.

Some swifts can keep flying for many months without landing

Swift

► SNOWY OWL

Most owls hunt by night, but the snowy owl is active during the almost continuous daylight of the Arctic summer. It uses its acute hearing to locate small animals such as lemmings feeding beneath the snow.

Soft feathers allow owls to fly in complete silence

Hummingbirds hover on whirring wings to sip flower nectar

Hummingbird

◄ WOODPECKER

Woodpeckers use their powerful bills to carve out nesting holes in trees, and many also hack into soft wood to find insects. This green woodpecker catches ants with its extra-long tongue.

Budgerigars

► TOUCAN

The enormous bill of the toco toucan is much lighter than it looks, because it is a hollow shell of lightweight horny material supported by crisscrossing internal struts. The toucan uses it for display as well as feeding.

Peacock display

Blue tit

► FLAMINGO

Vast wading flocks of flamingos gather tiny animals and algae from warm lakes. Holding their extraordinary bills upside down in the shallows, they use their tongues to pump water through their sievelike bill fringes to trap food.

The flamingo's pink coloring comes from pigments in the bird's food

Great white pelican

► PEAFOWL

The female peafowl, or peahen, looks drab and colorless compared to the dazzling male peacock, with his amazing courtship display of fanned tail feathers.

Webbed feet stop wading birds from sinking in mud

Pelicans use the pouch beneath their bills like fishing nets to catch their food

EGGS

All female birds lay eggs. The young grow inside the eggs, which are kept warm by their parents. To hatch, the baby birds must chip their way through the eggshell. This is not hard for an ostrich chick, but many baby birds hatch at a much earlier stage in their development when they are naked, blind, and almost helpless.

1 GREAT AUK
This beautiful egg is one of the last relics of a big flightless seabird that once lived in the north Atlantic and hunted fish like a penguin. Each pair laid just one egg, and the last known pair was killed in 1844.

2 GOLDEN EAGLE
A female golden eagle lays two eggs a few days apart. She keeps the first egg warm so it hatches earlier. This chick may be the only one to survive if food is hard to find.

3 KING PENGUIN
King penguins breed in huge colonies on windswept rocky islands around Antarctica. Each female lays one egg and both parents take turns keeping it warm by supporting it on their feet beneath their warm bellies.

4 OSTRICH
The ostrich is the world's largest bird, and it lays the biggest eggs. Each one can weigh anything up to 4 lbs (1.9 kg)—the same weight as 27 chicken's eggs.

5 CHICKEN
The egg that everybody recognizes is laid by the domestic chicken. We eat 562 billion of these eggs every year.

6 QUAIL
The quail lays a huge clutch of up to 18 eggs in a nest on the ground. Like many eggs, they have camouflage markings that make them harder to see. The female starts keeping them warm only after she lays the last one. This means they start developing at the same time, so they all hatch at once. The chicks are active as soon as they hatch, just like ostriches.

King penguin ❸

❹

Peregrine falcon

Waxwing

❶

❷

Golden eagle

Great auk

Skylark

Cormorant

Carrion crow

Guillemot

❺

Curlew

Quail

Chicken

❻

❼

Sparrowhawk

Blackcap

Redshank

Song thrush

Coal tit

7 SPARROWHAWK

In the 1960s, sparrowhawks suffered from poisoning by pesticides used in farming. The poisons thinned their eggshells, so they broke when the birds tried to keep them warm. Most of these pesticides are now banned.

8 CUCKOO

Cuckoos lay single eggs in the nests of other birds, and their color varies to match the host bird's eggs. When the cuckoo hatches, it heaves the other eggs out so it can eat all the food its foster parents collect.

9 KIWI

A kiwi is 20 times smaller than an emu, yet their eggs are almost the same size. This means that the egg is huge compared to the kiwi that lays it, at up to a quarter of her weight. That's like a human mother giving birth to a three-year-old child.

Ostrich chick breaking out of shell

Herring gull

Cuckoo

Cetti's warbler

Chough

Meadow pipit

Great northern diver

Nightjar

Emu

Kiwi

Common sandpiper

Elegant tinamou

Red grouse

Yellowhammer

Ruby-throated hummingbird

Tawny owl

Rusty tinamou

Dunnock

Newly hatched ostrich chick

10 COMMON SANDPIPER

Sandpipers are shorebirds that lay their eggs in shallow scrapes on the ground near the water. Their pointed shape allows them to be pushed together in a tight clutch to take up less space. The eggs are camouflaged by speckled patterns, and can be hard to see—but if you do find any birds' eggs, remember it is illegal to collect or disturb them.

11 HUMMINGBIRD

Hummingbirds lay the smallest of all birds' eggs. The bee hummingbird's egg is the size of a pea, because the bird itself is no bigger than a large moth. This ruby-throated hummingbird's egg is bigger, but still tiny compared to the ostrich egg.

MOVEMENT

The feature that makes animals so different from other living things is their ability to move. Some do not move much—a sea anemone, for example, is sedentary (remains in one place) and catches anything that touches its tentacles. Most animals, however, travel to look for food, find breeding partners, or escape from their enemies. They slither, crawl, walk, hop, run, swim, and fly, sometimes at incredible speed. Some have evolved other amazing ways of getting around, like the insects and spiders that walk on water, and the extraordinary sidewinding rattlesnakes.

1 GIBBON

Although gibbons can walk well, they usually move through the forest by using their long, powerful arms to swing from the trees. They hurl themselves from branch to branch with astonishing speed, agility, and elegance.

2 SNAKE

A typical snake slips along by curving its flexible body around plants and stones, and pushing the curves toward its tail. Sidewinders like this desert viper have a more baffling method, looping sideways over the sand like rolling springs.

3 OCTOPUS

An octopus normally hauls itself over the seabed using its long, elastic arms. But it can shoot away from danger by jet propulsion, drawing water into its body and blasting it out at high pressure. Cuttlefish and squid do the same.

4 PENGUIN

All penguins are superb swimmers, using their wings to "fly" through the water, but they walk clumsily. On snowy slopes they often prefer to toboggan on their well-padded bellies, pushing themselves along with their stoutly clawed feet.

5 FISH

Most fish have flexible bodies that allow them to move through the water using their fins for stability and to control their direction. Some fish, such as tuna, propel themselves at high speed using just their tails.

6 STARFISH

A starfish can curl its arms, but it actually creeps over the seabed using hundreds of tiny "tube feet" on its underside. Each tube foot is pumped full of water, and is extended and moved by changes in water pressure.

7 SNAIL

The muscles in a snail's foot contract and expand to create a rippling movement that pushes the snail forward. Glands in the foot produce a slimy mucus to make the track slippery. The slime also protects the snail from debris.

8 WATER STRIDER

The water molecules at the surface of a pool cling together to form an elastic film, strong enough to support tiny animals like this water strider. Its special brush-tipped feet just dimple the surface, so it can skate around without sinking.

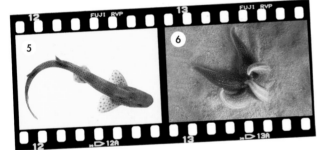

9 CHEETAH

The fastest of all land animals, a cheetah can run at an astonishing 60 mph (95 km/h). It achieves this by flexing its back to extend its stride as it bounds forward on its long legs, but it can only keep up this pace for about 40 seconds.

10 BARN OWL

Birds are the masters of the air. Most, like this barn owl, use their powerful feathered wings to drive themselves forward. Others can travel long distances by soaring on rising air currents like gliders, without beating their wings at all.

11 KANGAROO

A leaping kangaroo uses the elastic tendons in the backs of its legs like the springs of a pogo stick. Every time it lands on its long feet the tendons stretch like rubber bands, then spring back again to catapult the kangaroo forward.

LIVING TOGETHER

Animals and plants often rely on other living things for survival. Food, shelter, and pollination are some of the clearest examples of this. However, some animals and plants have much closer relationships. They can be partners, providing things like food or protection for each other. Some tag along with others without providing anything in return. Many do worse, latching on to other organisms as parasites, which can harm or even kill their often helpless hosts.

The microscopic algae that live in partnership with this coral provide its vivid color

1 CORAL

Corals trap prey in their stinging tentacles. They pass some of the nutrients from their victims to tiny algae living in their tissues. These use the Sun's energy to make sugar, and they pass some of this food back to the corals.

A remora clings to a shark's skin using a special sucker on the back of its head

2 REMORA

Predatory sharks have very sharp teeth that cut their prey to shreds. The scraps are eagerly devoured by fish called remoras, which travel with the sharks by clinging to their skin. They do their hosts no harm, and the sharks seem to ignore them.

Ants protect the aphids from their enemies in exchange for sweet, syrupy honeydew

An impala welcomes the attention of a red-billed oxpecker searching for tasty parasites

This cuckoo chick has outgrown both the host bird and its nest, but it still cries out for food

A strangler vine uses a tree for support, but eventually kills it by competing for food and light

This long, tubular flower is a perfect fit for the long bill of the sword-billed hummingbird

3 ANTS AND APHIDS

Aphids are tiny insects that feed on sugary plant sap. They must eat a lot of it to get enough protein, and they excrete the excess sugar as drops of sweet honeydew. Ants love to drink this, so they "farm" the aphids, protecting them from predators, ensuring a constant supply.

4 OXPECKER

Hoofed grazing animals, such as impalas, are often plagued by tiny bloodsuckers, such as ticks, which they cannot remove by scratching. In Africa, stout-billed birds called oxpeckers do the job for them by picking the parasites off their skin and eating them.

5 CUCKOO

Cuckoos are "brood parasites"—they lay their eggs in the nests of other birds. Each young cuckoo hatches quickly and destroys any other eggs in the nest, so it can eat all the food brought by its foster parents. It soon outgrows its hosts, who often do not seem to notice its massive size.

6 STRANGLER VINE

Some slender rain forest plants, such as figs, grow by encircling a tree and slowly killing it—a process that can take up to 150 years. They steal the tree's nutrients, and eventually the tree dies and decays, leaving the fig plant standing alone.

7 HUMMINGBIRD

Hummingbirds gather flower nectar, and in the process they carry pollen from flower to flower. Some plants have evolved flowers that match the bills of particular hummingbird species, to encourage the birds to visit them and deliver their pollen efficiently.

MAMMALS

Mammals are warm-blooded creatures that feed their babies on milk until the young are able to eat solid food. Most are furry or hairy, unlike all other vertebrates (animals with backbones). Many eat plants, while others prey on other animals. Some, like humans, eat both plants and meat.

▶ ECHIDNA

The echidna and the equally strange platypus are the only mammals that lay eggs. A baby echidna lives on milk produced by its mother for up to six months. The mother eats food such as earthworms, which she digs from the ground with her long snout.

▲ MOUSE

Nearly half of all mammal species are rodents—a group that includes mice, rats, beavers, porcupines, and squirrels. The house mouse is the only mammal, aside from humans, to live on every continent.

◀ ELEPHANT

Elephants use their sensitive trunks to gather coarse vegetation, which they grind to pulp with their massive teeth. They are the biggest land animals and are very intelligent.

▶ KANGAROO

Marsupials such as kangaroos give birth to tiny young that are only half-formed. The newborn crawls into a pouch on its mother's belly to drink milk and grow into a fully developed baby kangaroo, or joey.

▲ BAT

Bats are mammals that can fly. Some eat fruit, but most species, like this long-eared bat, catch insects. They are nocturnal (active at night) and locate prey in the dark by emitting high-pitched clicks and listening for echoes from their target.

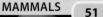

◀ TIGER

Powerful hunters like the tiger eat other mammals and birds. They have long, daggerlike canine teeth for killing their prey, and scissorlike cheek teeth for slicing through hide and meat.

▲ KILLER WHALE

Whales and dolphins, like this killer whale, live in the ocean, swimming with up-and-down movements of their powerful tails. They come to the surface to breathe air.

▲ MOLE

Moles are specially adapted to their underground environment. They have strong claws for digging and very sensitive whiskers, which compensate for their poor eyesight.

◀ GORILLA

Our closest relatives among the mammals are apes like the gorilla—a plant-eater that lives in the rain forests of tropical Africa.

▶ HIPPOPOTAMUS

The hippopotamus spends most of its time wallowing in rivers and lakes. The massively built plant-eater has the largest mouth of any land mammal.

SLEEP

Animals sleep to save energy, rest their muscles, and allow their brains to process the information that they pick up while awake. Some hunting animals sleep a lot, because they devote only a few hours each day to looking for food. Animals that are hunted spend much more of their time awake and alert.

❶ Bats sleep while hanging upside down by their feet in caves, tunnels, cellars, and from trees

1 BATS sleep for about 20 hours a day, often in large colonies.

2 TWO-TOED SLOTHS are awake for only four hours a day. Like bats, they can cling to branches with their claws while fast asleep.

3 LIONS sleep for at least 13 hours a day. While they sleep, other animals feed near them without risking attack.

4 WOLVES may sleep for up to 14 hours a day, especially if they have had a big meal after a successful hunt.

5 HORSES need just three hours of sleep a day.

6 SEALS often sleep on rocks and beaches, but they can also sleep floating upright at sea, or even under water, surfacing to breathe without waking up.

7 PIGS need eight hours of sleep a day, just like adult humans.

8 SHEEP are descended from wild animals that need to stay awake to escape predators, so they sleep for less than four hours a day.

9 HUMAN BABIES need 15 hours of sleep a day. We sleep less as we get older, so adults sleep for an average of eight hours, and elderly people for less than six hours.

10 RABBITS sleep for about eight hours, mainly during the day. They prefer to feed at night when they are not so vulnerable to predators.

Horses can sleep standing up without toppling over because their legs lock in place

11 RED PANDAS, which are like bamboo-eating raccoons, sleep for about 11 hours a day.

12 BABY GORILLAS need about three hours more sleep than their parents. They may sleep or doze for more than 15 hours.

13 CATS often sleep for 15 hours a day. Wild cats are most active during the night.

14 ECHIDNAS are egg-laying mammals that sleep for about 14 hours a day. Scientists believe they do not have phases of dream sleep like other mammals.

15 RED FOXES sleep for about 10 hours a day, mostly during the day. Like many hunters, they are more active at night when they track their prey using their sensitive noses and ears.

16 ELEPHANTS stand up for two of the four hours a day they sleep. They have to lie down for the dreaming stage, when their muscles are too relaxed for them to stay on their feet. Large plant-eating animals tend to get less sleep than smaller animals, because they have to spend so much time looking for food and eating.

17 TIGERS can sleep for up to 16 hours at a stretch because they can catch all the food they need within a very short time.

18 KOALAS eat tough eucalyptus leaves that are hard to digest and provide little energy, so they spend about 15 hours a day sleeping and another five hours dozing.

19 DOGS sleep for 10 hours a day.

20 HEDGEHOGS usually sleep for 10 hours during the day. In winter, they hibernate (spend the cold months in a sleeplike, inactive state).

Dogs have similar sleep patterns to humans

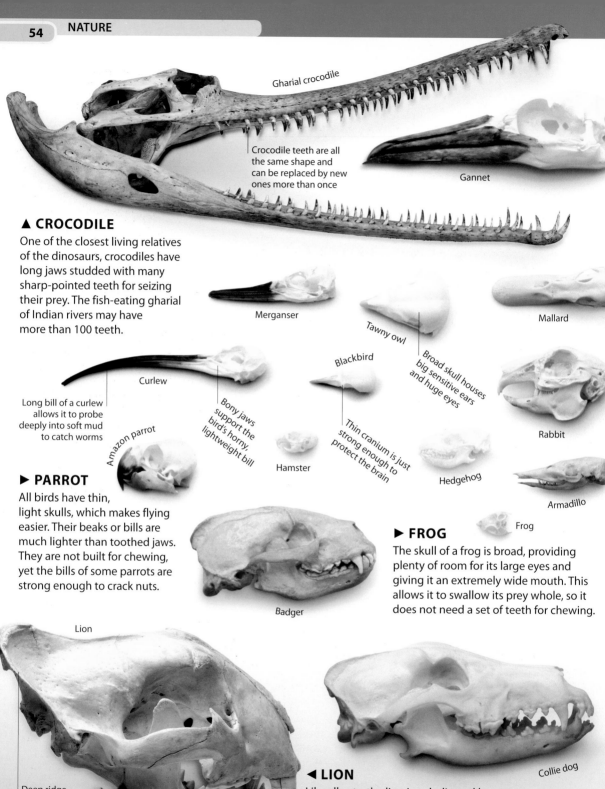

Gharial crocodile

Crocodile teeth are all the same shape and can be replaced by new ones more than once

Gannet

▲ CROCODILE

One of the closest living relatives of the dinosaurs, crocodiles have long jaws studded with many sharp-pointed teeth for seizing their prey. The fish-eating gharial of Indian rivers may have more than 100 teeth.

Merganser

Tawny owl

Mallard

Blackbird

Broad skull houses big sensitive ears and huge eyes

Curlew

Long bill of a curlew allows it to probe deeply into soft mud to catch worms

Bony jaws support the bird's horny, lightweight bill

Thin cranium is just strong enough to protect the brain

Rabbit

Amazon parrot

Hamster

Hedgehog

Armadillo

▶ PARROT

All birds have thin, light skulls, which makes flying easier. Their beaks or bills are much lighter than toothed jaws. They are not built for chewing, yet the bills of some parrots are strong enough to crack nuts.

Badger

Frog

▶ FROG

The skull of a frog is broad, providing plenty of room for its large eyes and giving it an extremely wide mouth. This allows it to swallow its prey whole, so it does not need a set of teeth for chewing.

Lion

Deep ridge on back of skull anchors massive muscles attached to jaw

Collie dog

◀ LION

Like all cats, the lion is a dedicated hunter. It has short, powerful jaws with huge stabbing canine teeth at the front and meat-slicing carnassials at the back.

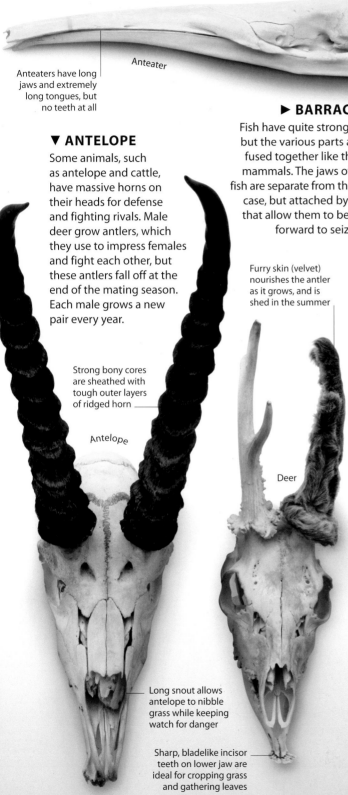

Anteater

Anteaters have long jaws and extremely long tongues, but no teeth at all

The big eyes of this powerful, fast-swimming predator are contained in large sockets

▼ ANTELOPE

Some animals, such as antelope and cattle, have massive horns on their heads for defense and fighting rivals. Male deer grow antlers, which they use to impress females and fight each other, but these antlers fall off at the end of the mating season. Each male grows a new pair every year.

Strong bony cores are sheathed with tough outer layers of ridged horn

Antelope

► BARRACUDA

Fish have quite strong skulls, but the various parts are not fused together like those of mammals. The jaws of many fish are separate from the brain case, but attached by bones that allow them to be thrust forward to seize prey.

Barracuda

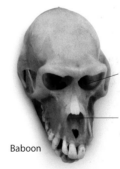

Massive jaws are armed with needle-sharp teeth for a secure grip on prey

Furry skin (velvet) nourishes the antler as it grows, and is shed in the summer

Deer

▼ BABOON

Close relatives of humans, baboons have similar skulls, but longer jaws and bigger back teeth. This is because they eat large quantities of grass, which requires a lot of chewing. They also have long, sharp canines, which they use to kill animals for food and to fight among themselves.

Eye sockets at front of skull allow the baboon to see things in three dimensions

Baboon

Nasal cavity contains thin scroll-like bones, which support the membranes that detect scent

Long snout allows antelope to nibble grass while keeping watch for danger

Sharp, bladelike incisor teeth on lower jaw are ideal for cropping grass and gathering leaves

SKULLS

Most vertebrates (animals with backbones) have strong bony skulls. They are made up of cranial bones that protect their brains, jaw bones that support their teeth or beaks, and face bones that contain their eye sockets and nasal cavities. The whole structure can be quite heavy, and is supported by strong neck muscles.

QUICK QUIZ

What can you remember about Nature?
Jot down your answers, then check them on pp.296–97.

1 The oldest living tree can be found in **California**, but do you know how old it is?
- Ⓐ 100 years
- Ⓑ 500 years
- Ⓒ 1,000 years
- Ⓓ 5,000 years

2 What can you learn by looking at the **rings** in a **tree trunk**?

3 Trees make **sugar** from **air** and what other **substance**?

4 Name this **leaf**.
- Ⓐ Horse Chestnut
- Ⓑ Ash
- Ⓒ Holly
- Ⓓ Oak

5 **Match** the **skin** to the **animal**:

- Ⓐ Tiger
- Ⓑ Iguana
- Ⓒ Octopus
- Ⓓ Salamander

6 Name these **parts** of the **flower**.

7 Leeches are **parasites** that **suck blood**. How often do they **need to feed**?
- Ⓐ Once or twice a day
- Ⓑ Once or twice a week
- Ⓒ Once or twice a month
- Ⓓ Once or twice a year

8 What are **creatures** that feed on dead animals called?

9 Do you know **what I am**?
- Ⓐ Norwegian wasp
- Ⓑ Bumble bee
- Ⓒ Hover fly
- Ⓓ Honey bee

10 Why does a **pufferfish inflate** itself?

- Ⓐ To attack larger prey
- Ⓑ To deter predators
- Ⓒ To improve buoyancy
- Ⓓ To attract a mate

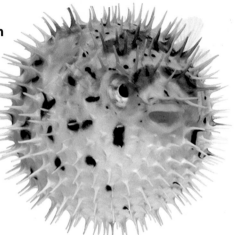

11 What is the biggest bird in the world?

12 Who rules an ant colony?

- Ⓐ The queen
- Ⓑ The king
- Ⓒ The boss
- Ⓓ The antlord

13 Whose bill is this?

- Ⓐ Parakeet
- Ⓑ Kingfisher
- Ⓒ Toucan
- Ⓓ Pelican

14 How many legs does an insect have?

15 Why does the **four-eyed frog** have eyes on its back?

- Ⓐ So it can see in two directions at once
- Ⓑ So it can sleep with two eyes open
- Ⓒ So it can turn its back to look fierce when attacked
- Ⓓ Because it wants to attract a mate

16 Which of these animals uses **jet propulsion** to move when **alarmed**?

- Ⓐ Torpedo ray
- Ⓑ Sparrowhawk
- Ⓒ Sea squirt
- Ⓓ Squid

17 Which of these animals needs **8 hours of sleep a day**, just **like humans**?

- Ⓐ Pig
- Ⓑ Elephant
- Ⓒ Cat
- Ⓓ Wolf

18 Match the **skull** to the **animal**:

❶ ❷ ❸

Ⓐ Armadillo Ⓑ Badger Ⓒ Hamster

19 I love living in **damp places**, have **seven pairs of legs**, and if threatened I might **roll up into a ball**. Do you know what I am?

- Ⓐ Millipede
- Ⓑ Hedgehog
- Ⓒ Woodlouse
- Ⓓ Lobster

20 What makes flamingos turn pink?

- Ⓐ Sunburn
- Ⓑ Embarrassment
- Ⓒ A good joke
- Ⓓ Food

FAST FACTS

A typical bed is home to about ***2 million*** dust mites.

Lichen are only an inch or so tall, but they **live for a very long time** in the coldest places on Earth. Some lichens in **Antarctica** are more than

4,000 years old.

After a **tree dies**, all the carbon dioxide it absorbed when alive is eventually released back into the **atmosphere**. The same amount of **carbon dioxide** is released whether the tree burns or rots.

The **largest water plant** is the Amazonian giant lily. Its leaves are **so big** that a child could run across them and **not get wet.**

Magnolias are the most ancient flowering plants of all. **Fossils** of magnolias have been found that are **20** million years old.

The *nepenthes* is the world's largest *carnivorous* (meat-eating) plant. It catches insects in its huge *vase-shaped* pitcher leaves. It is sometimes called the "monkey cup" because monkeys like to drink out of its *pitchers.*

Fungi live by **feeding** on other organisms or their waste. **Pilobolus** fungi feed on cow dung.

*The **largest fungus** ever found is an Armillaria ostoyae in Oregon, which covers nearly 4 sq miles (10 sq km) of forest floor and is thought to be **8,500 years old.***

The **streaks of color** in cheeses such as **Stilton** and **Danish Blue** are made by **mold**, which is a microscopic fungus.

Many desert plants have **very long roots** to find **water** deep underground. The North American mesquite tree's roots grow up to

150 ft (50 m) long.

In the 1980s, **tiny nanoplankton** were discovered **floating in the oceans**. They are less than 20 millionths of a yard long, and are the most plentiful organisms in Earth's seas.

The smallest flowering plant is the duckweed *Wolffia*, which is just 0.6 mm long. About *25* of these plants would fit on **one fingernail.**

Aphids are born pregnant and can **give birth** just **10 days** after they are born themselves.

Eels lay their eggs in the oceans. The baby elvers then make their way to freshwater rivers. A female eel can lay up to

4 million eggs in one year.

The seeds of the **coco de mer** are the largest of any plant. They can weigh up to 45 lb (20 kg).

*One type of **lungfish can breathe** under water **using gills** and in the air **using lungs.***

The **smallest mammal**, the **bumblebee bat**, weighs just 0.07 oz (2 g)—**lighter** than a penny coin.

A domestic rabbit can give birth to **20** babies a month.

The hummingbird is the only bird that can fly straight up, down, and backward.

Bamboo is the tallest grass. It can grow up to **150 ft (50 m) tall.**

A male walrus's tusks can grow up to **3ft** (1 m) long.

A **male howler** monkey's **howls** can be **heard** up to 8 miles (5 km) away.

Crocodiles that live in saltwater **cry**. They do it to get rid of excess salt in their bodies, not because they are sad.

Sharks have the best sense of smell of any fish. They can detect ***one*** part of blood in ***100 million*** parts of water.

Prairie dogs live in huge burrows called towns. One town in Texas was home to

400,000,000 individuals.

A woodpecker can peck up to **20** times per second.

A **hyena** can produce **hydrochloric acid** in its **stomach** so it can **digest bone**.

Cobras kill 7,000 people every year in India.

An army ant can carry **25** times its own weight.

Octopuses have three hearts—two to pump blood to their gills and one to pump blood around their bodies.

Ants *never* sleep.

There is enough poison in a single *poison dart frog's* skin to kill **10,000** mice.

The **pregnancy** of an Indian **elephant** lasts for about 648 days.

The biggest living cat is the Siberian tiger, which weighs up to 650 lb (300 kg).

A mole can tunnel through **330 ft** *(100 m) of earth in a day.*

Springtails, a kind of **insect**, can survive in temperatures as low as -36°F (-38°C) because their bodies contain **antifreeze**.

A red **kangaroo** can cover **25 ft** (8 m) in a single **hop**.

The world's **largest** living **rodent**, the capybara, can weigh up to **140 lb** (65 kg).

A **termite** queen lays **2,000 eggs** a day.

Whale milk is nearly **50%fat.**

The blue whale is the largest animal that has ever lived. Its heart alone weighs **1,500 lb** (700 kg).

China's earthquake **early warning** system involves the close monitoring of **snakes**, which leave their nests shortly before an **earthquake.**

A pile of **elephant dung** may contain **7,000** beetles.

Male humpback whales sing songs that last **20 minutes** or longer. They may be doing this to *serenade* females.

Camels can go up to **two weeks** without drinking, but when there is **water** around, they can down 40 gallons (200 liters) in 10 minutes.

There are more than **370,000** known species of **beetle.**

Monarch butterflies migrate **2,500 miles** (4,000 km) from North America to Mexico or Butterfly Grove in San Francisco to **hibernate** during winter, even though they have **never been there** before.

A **bee's buzz** is made by its wings, which flap **250 times a second.**

Cows have four stomachs, which they use to **process** hard-to-digest grass and **vegetation.**

A **blue whale's whistle** can be heard more than 62 miles (100 km) away **under water.**

Whales and dolphins put **half their brains** to sleep at a time so that they **don't drown.**

A dog can make about 100 different **facial expressions**, most of them involving its **ears.**

Dogs devote 40 times more brain cells to their **sense of smell** than humans.

Beaver **dams** can be **1,000 ft** (300 m) long and may be **hundreds** of years old.

Spiders occasionally team up to build **huge webs**. A web found in 2007 in Lake Tawakoni State Park in Texas, measured 590 ft (180 m) across. It was built by **lots** of different **species** of spider.

The largest flying bird is the *wandering albatross.* It has a wingspan of up to **11 ft** (3.5 m), which means that each of its wings is *almost as long* as an **adult human** is tall.

A flea can cover **12 in** (30 cm) in one jump—that's 200 times the length of its own body.

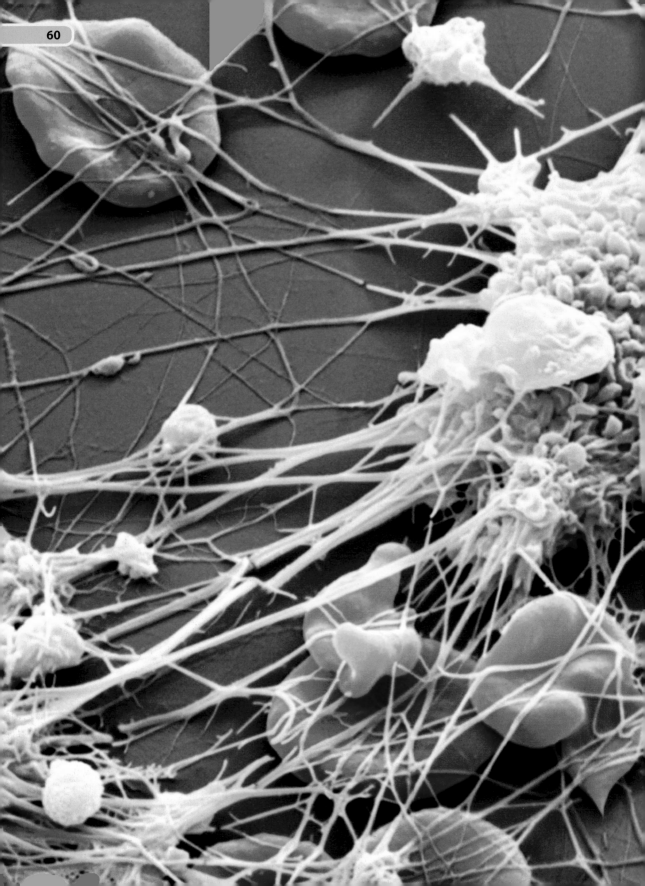

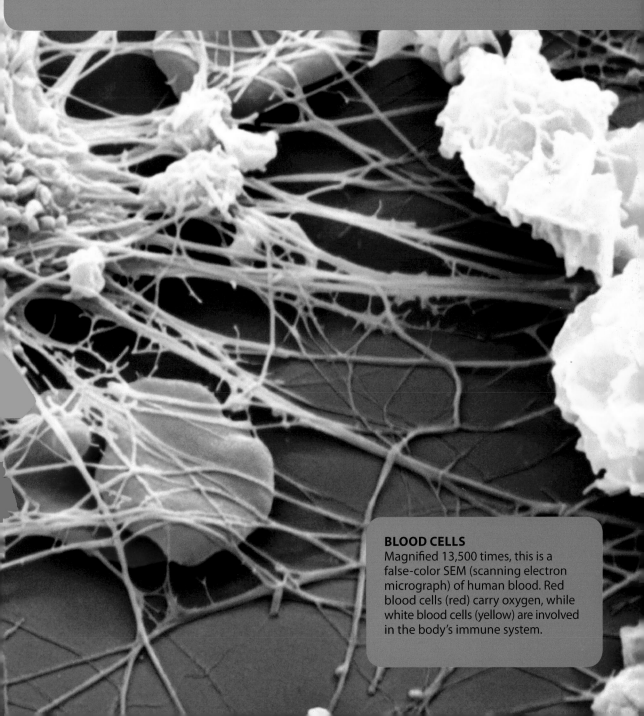

HUMAN BODY

BLOOD CELLS
Magnified 13,500 times, this is a
false-color SEM (scanning electron
micrograph) of human blood. Red
blood cells (red) carry oxygen, while
white blood cells (yellow) are involved
in the body's immune system.

CELLS

The body is constructed from trillions of tiny living units, known as cells. There are more than 200 different types of cell—and each has its own shape, size, and specific job to do. Typically, cells of the same type work together in units called tissues. Each individual cell is surrounded by a thin membrane that regulates the movement of nutrients and other substances in and out of the cell. Cells multiply by continually dividing into two identical "offspring." This division allows the body to grow and to replace cells that are damaged or worn out.

1 NERVE CELLS

Found in the brain, spinal cord, and nerves, nerve cells, or neurons, carry and process high-speed electrical signals, called nerve impulses. These impulses coordinate body processes and enable us to feel, think, and move.

2 WHITE BLOOD CELLS

Circulating in blood, and in a clear fluid known as lymph, white blood cells help defend the body against disease. The cells include macrophages and neutrophils, which eat bacteria and other germs, and also lymphocytes, which release germ-disabling antibodies.

A macrophage "reaches out" to capture bacteria (blue), which it will then digest

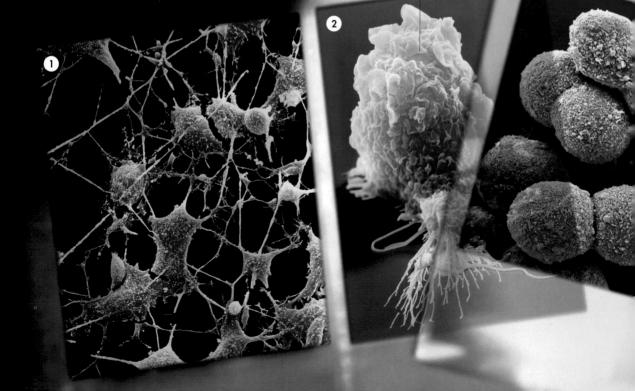

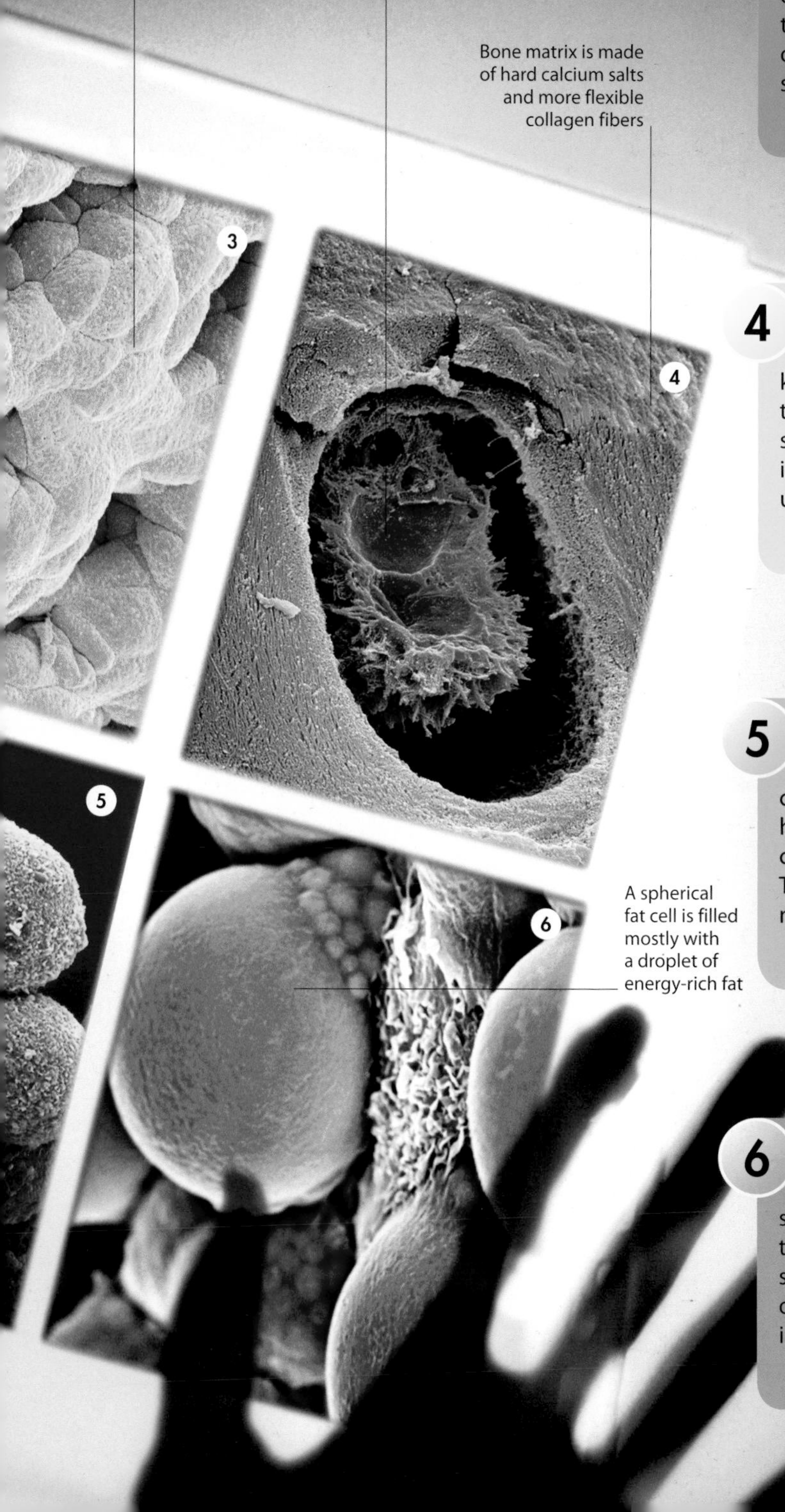

Epithelial cells locked together to form the protective, pitted lining of the stomach

Spiked osteocyte lives in a lacuna, or space, in the bone matrix

Bone matrix is made of hard calcium salts and more flexible collagen fibers

3 EPITHELIAL CELLS

Tightly packed together, these cells provide a barrier to stop harmful chemicals and germs from reaching body tissues. They cover the body, forming the outer layer of skin, and line hollow organs such as the stomach, lungs, and bladder.

4 BONE CELLS

Osteocytes are bone cells that help to keep the bone in good condition. At first, they lay down bone, but later become stranded within a bony space. They keep in touch through tiny threads and pick up supplies from nearby blood vessels.

5 LIVER CELLS

Also known as hepatocytes, liver cells enable the liver to perform many hundreds of roles to control blood composition and keep the body stable. These include processing and storing nutrients (foods), and removing poisons.

A spherical fat cell is filled mostly with a droplet of energy-rich fat

6 FAT CELLS

As their name suggests, fat cells specialize in storing fat. They group together to form adipose tissue, which serves as an energy store, cushions organs such as the kidneys, and insulates the body under the skin.

SKELETON

Constructed from 206 bones, the human skeleton is a strong, flexible framework that supports and shapes the body and produces movement when pulled by muscles. The skeleton also protects soft, internal organs, such as the brain and lungs. Bones, which make up 20 percent of the body's mass, are connected to each other at joints and are held together by strong straps of tissue called ligaments.

1 SKULL

The bones in the skull protect the brain, provide a framework for the face, and anchor the muscles that produce facial expressions. The skull consists of 22 bones, 21 of which are locked together by immovable joints called sutures. Only the lower jaw (mandible) can move.

2 CHEST

The bones of the chest (thorax) consist of the sternum (breastbone), the ribs, and part of the backbone. Together, they form a protective "cage" that protects the lungs and the heart.

3 ELBOW

The bones of the upper arm and forearm meet at the elbow. This joint acts like a door hinge, allowing the arm to bend or straighten. The forearm bones can rotate at the elbow, enabling the palm of the hand to face upward or downward.

4 FOREARM

The forearm is made up of two parallel bones—the ulna and the radius. The ulna curves round the humerus to form the elbow's point, while the radius forms a joint with the carpals (wrist bones).

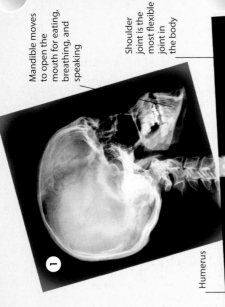

Mandible moves to open the mouth for eating, breathing, and speaking

Shoulder joint is the most flexible joint in the body

Humerus

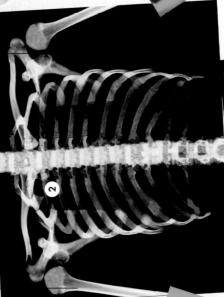

Phalanges are the 14 slender bones that form the fingers and thumb

Sacrum anchors the backbone to the pelvic girdle

Hip joint is where the ball-shaped head of the femur fits into the cup-shaped socket in the hip bone

Radius is the outer bone of the forearm

Ulna is the inner bone of the forearm

5 HAND

Hinged at the wrist, the hand consists of 27 bones and many moveable joints (knuckles), which enable it to perform a wide range of tasks. The human thumb is opposable, which means that it can be rotated to touch the tips of each of the other fingers.

7 KNEE

The knee joint between the femur (thigh bone) and tibia (shin bone) is the strongest and most complex joint in the body. This hinge joint allows the leg to bend or straighten and supports the body's weight during activities such as running, jumping, or kicking.

9 FOOT

Each foot consists of the ankle, sole, and toe bones, which support and move the body's weight. These bones also provide a flexible platform that pushes the body off the ground during movement and absorbs the shock on landing.

6 PELVIS

This strong, bowl-shaped structure consists of the two curved hip bones (pelvic girdle) and the sacrum. The pelvis supports the abdominal organs and attaches the thigh bones to the rest of the skeleton.

8 TOES

The phalanges of the toes are much shorter and less flexible than those of the fingers. The phalanges enable the body to stay upright and to stand on tiptoe. They also help to propel the body forward during movement.

Femur (thigh bone) is the longest bone in the body

Tibia (shin bone) forms joints with the femur and ankle bones

Fibula is the smaller bone of the lower leg

Metatarsals are the five long bones that connect the toes to the middle part of the foot

Tarsals are the seven bones that form the ankle, heel, and part of the arch of the foot

Phalanges are the 14 slender bones that form the toes

MUSCLES

Every body movement, whether it's a leap in the air, a wink of the eye, a rumbling stomach, or a rapid heartbeat, is produced by muscles. Skeletal muscles are attached to bones of the skeleton, which they pull to move us around. Smooth muscle moves food along the intestine. Cardiac muscle keeps the heart pumping. All muscles are made of cells called fibers that contract (get shorter) to produce a pulling force.

1 SKELETAL MUSCLE

Long, cylindrical muscle fibers run in parallel and can reach up to 1 ft (30 cm) in length. They are bundled together to form muscles that are attached to bones by strong cords called tendons. Skeletal muscles move the body when instructed by the nervous system.

2 SMOOTH MUSCLE

Tightly packed into layered sheets, smooth muscle fibers are found in the walls of hollow organs, such as the small intestine, along which they push food, and the bladder, from which they expel urine. Smooth muscle contracts slowly and cannot be controlled voluntarily.

Deltoid muscle raises arm sideways and swings it backward and forward

Rectus abdominis muscle pulls in the abdominal wall and bends the body forward

Sartorius muscle bends the thigh at the hip and turns it inward

Quadriceps femoris is a group of four muscles that straightens the leg at the knee

Tibialis anterior muscle lifts the foot

SURFACE MUSCLES

Diaphragm muscle separates the thorax (chest) from the abdomen and aids breathing

Adductor longus muscle pulls and turns the thigh inward

DEEP MUSCLES

FRONT MUSCLES

Skeletal muscles are arranged in overlapping layers, with surface muscles covering those deeper down. Muscles at the front of the body produce facial expressions, move the head forward and to the side, move the arms forward and bend them at the elbow, bend the body forward and to the side, bend the legs at the hip, straighten the knees, and lift the feet upward.

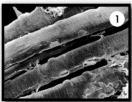

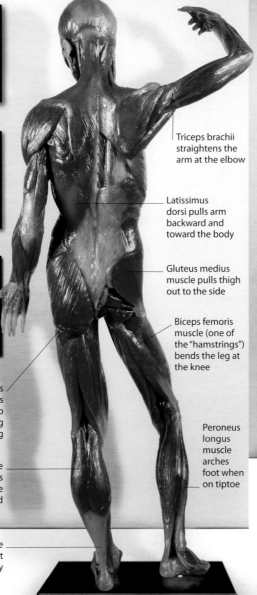

Triceps brachii straightens the arm at the elbow

Latissimus dorsi pulls arm backward and toward the body

Gluteus medius muscle pulls thigh out to the side

Biceps femoris muscle (one of the "hamstrings") bends the leg at the knee

Gluteus maximus muscle straightens the thigh at the hip when standing or climbing

Gastrocnemius muscle pulls the Achilles tendon to bend the foot downward

Peroneus longus muscle arches foot when on tiptoe

Achilles tendon is the thickest and strongest tendon in the body

SURFACE MUSCLES

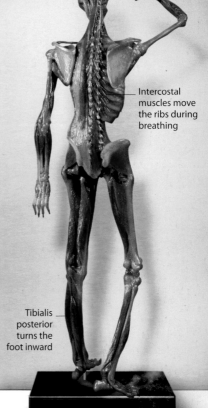

Intercostal muscles move the ribs during breathing

Tibialis posterior turns the foot inward

DEEP MUSCLES

REAR MUSCLES

All muscles are given Latin names that describe their size, location, shape, action, or other feature. Working downward from head to feet, skeletal muscles at the rear of the body keep the head upright, steady the shoulders, keep the back upright to maintain posture, pull the arms backward and straighten them, straighten the thighs at the hip and bend the knees, and point the toes downward.

3 CARDIAC MUSCLE

Found solely in the wall of the heart, cardiac muscle fibers form a branching network that contracts automatically, without stopping or tiring, to pump blood around the body. Stimulation by the nervous system increases or decreases heart rate according to the body's demands.

BODY SYSTEMS

The body's trillions of cells are highly organized. Cells of the same type are grouped together in tissues. Two or more types of tissue are used to build organs that perform specific roles. Linked organs form different systems that each carry out an essential job, such as digestion. There are 12 body systems that cooperate and interact with each other to form the human body. The organs of six body systems are shown here. The other six systems are the integumental (skin), skeletal (bones), muscular, endocrine (hormones), immune (defense), and reproductive systems.

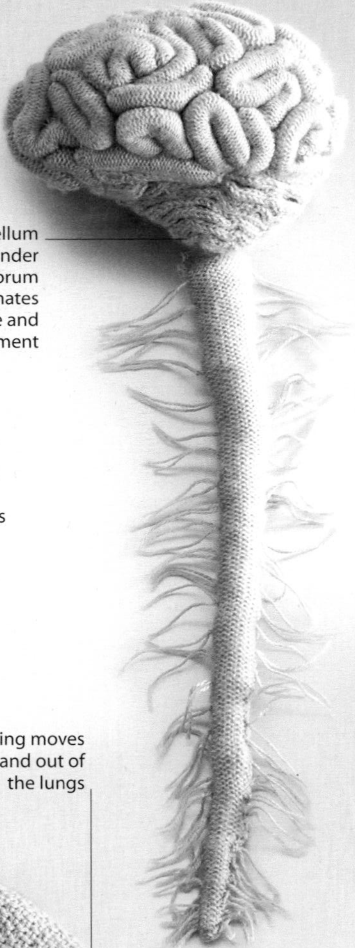

▶ BRAIN

The brain is the center of the nervous system, which is responsible for controlling body activities. It is dominated by the folded cerebrum that enables us to feel, think, and remember, and instructs the body to move. Other brain parts are the cerebellum, tucked under the cerebrum, and the brain stem, which automatically controls breathing and heart rate and links the brain to the spinal cord.

▼ SPINAL CORD

An extension of the brain that runs down the back, the spinal cord relays signals between brain and body through the spinal nerves connected to it. It also controls many of the body's automatic reflex actions, such as pulling the hand back if it touches something sharp. Together the brain, spinal cord, and nerves form the nervous system.

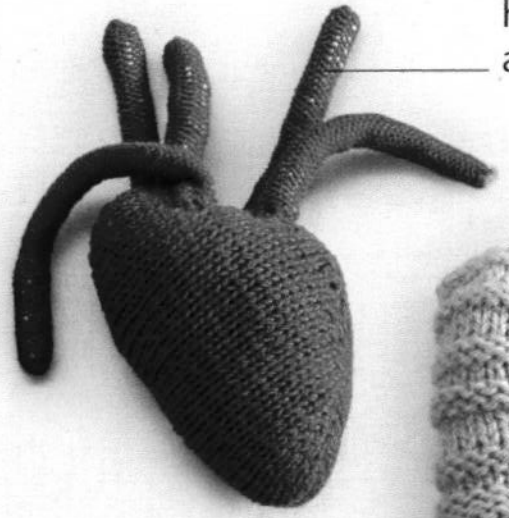

▼ SPLEEN

The spleen is part of the lymphatic system, the body's drainage network. It contains white blood cells, which fight infection by destroying bacteria, and also removes worn-out red blood cells from the blood.

The cerebellum is tucked under the cerebrum and coordinates balance and movement

Blood travels to and from the heart via arteries and veins

Breathing moves air in and out of the lungs

Air travels from the nose and mouth along the trachea to the lungs

▶ HEART

The cardiovascular system moves blood around the body to deliver oxygen and food to all the body's cells, and to remove their wastes. Located between the lungs, the heart is the center of this system—a hollow, muscular pump that contracts without tiring more than 70 times a minute to force the blood around the body along blood vessels.

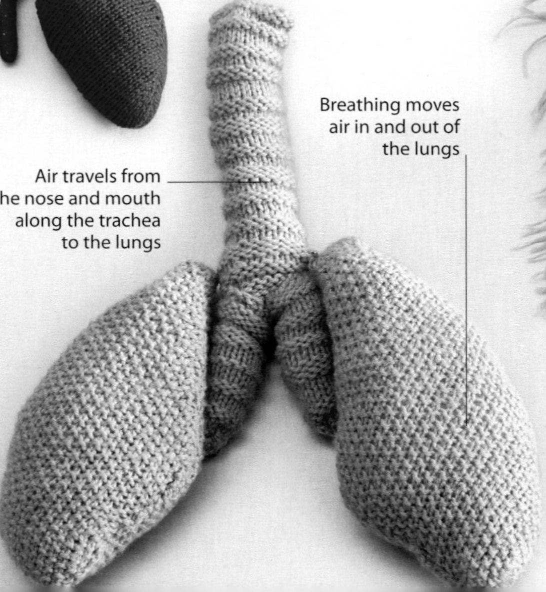

▶ LUNGS

The respiratory system consists of the two lungs and the air passages that carry air from the outside. Each lung contains a network of branching tubes that end in millions of tiny air bags. It is from these bags that oxygen in the air passes into the bloodstream. It is carried to all body cells where it is used to release life-giving energy from food.

▼ STOMACH

This muscular bag expands as it receives and stores food that has been chewed and swallowed. During storage the stomach's walls churn food into a part-digested "soup," which is released into the small intestine.

The large intestine turns waste into feces (poop) and pushes them out of the body

The small intestine is a long tube in which most digestion and absorption occurs

▼ DIGESTIVE SYSTEM

The body needs nutrients for energy, growth, and repair. The digestive system breaks down food to release these essential nutrients. The system consists of the mouth and teeth, the esophagus (a muscular tube leading from the mouth to the stomach), the stomach, and the small and large intestines. Food is digested using mechanical force, such as chewing, and through chemical digesters called enzymes. Nutrients are then absorbed into the blood and carried to the body's cells.

Liver stores excess glucose and releases it when the body needs it

Billions of harmless bacteria digest waste in the large intestine

▼ LIVER

The largest internal organ, the liver controls the composition of the blood, processing nutrients newly absorbed from the small intestine.

▼ PANCREAS

The pancreas releases chemicals called enzymes into the small intestine to aid digestion, and hormones (chemical messengers) into the blood to control levels of glucose—the body's main fuel—in the blood.

The gallbladder stores bile, a fluid that aids fat digestion

Each kidney contains a million tiny filtering units that process blood to make urine

▼ URINARY SYSTEM

Consisting of the kidneys, ureters, bladder, and urethra, the urinary system makes urine and removes it from the body. The kidneys make urine by removing wastes and excess water and salts from the blood, thereby keeping its composition constant. Urine is stored in the bladder and expelled through the urethra at its base.

Ureter has muscular walls that squeeze urine downward to the bladder

Bladder is a muscular bag that, when filled, pushes urine out through the urethra

RESPIRATION

The body's trillions of cells require an uninterrupted supply of oxygen to release the energy they need to stay alive. They get this by means of a process called respiration. Air containing oxygen is breathed into the body by the respiratory system. Oxygen enters the bloodstream through the lungs and is carried to body cells. Waste carbon dioxide is carried by the blood to the lungs and breathed out.

RESPIRATORY SYSTEM

Located in the head, neck, and chest, the respiratory system consists of the lungs, which fill most of the chest, and the air passages—nasal cavity, throat, larynx, trachea, and bronchi— that carry air. This X-ray shows the parts of the respiratory system located in the chest.

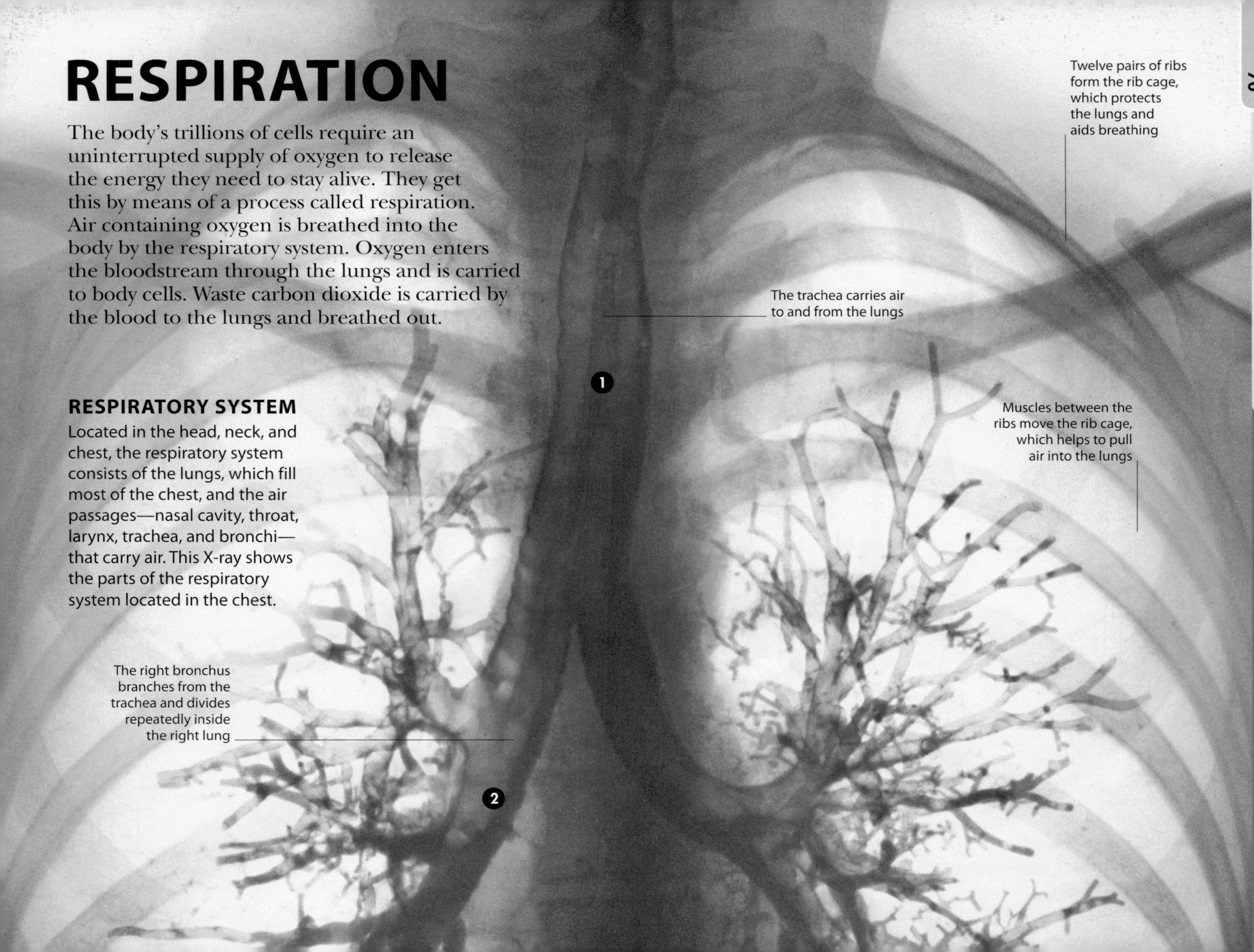

Twelve pairs of ribs form the rib cage, which protects the lungs and aids breathing

Muscles between the ribs move the rib cage, which helps to pull air into the lungs

The trachea carries air to and from the lungs

The right bronchus branches from the trachea and divides repeatedly inside the right lung

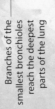

Branches of the smallest bronchioles reach the deepest parts of the lung

The diaphragm is a domed sheet of muscle that separates chest from abdomen

1 TRACHEA

Also called the windpipe, this flexible tube carries air between the larynx (voice box) at the base of the throat and the two bronchi that arise at its lower end. Up to 20 C-shaped rings of cartilage that encircle the trachea hold it open during breathing in. Mucus lining the trachea cleans the incoming air by trapping dirt and germs, a process that began in the nasal cavity.

2 BRONCHIAL TREE

Once inside a lung, each bronchus divides into smaller bronchi that then split even further. These, in turn, divide repeatedly to form smaller branches called bronchioles. This arrangement is often called "the bronchial tree" because its structure looks like an upside-down tree with the trachea as the trunk, bronchi as branches, and bronchioles as twigs.

3 BRONCHIOLES AND ALVEOLI

The narrowest bronchioles end in 300 million air-filled bags called alveoli that fill most of the lungs and are surrounded by blood capillaries. Oxygen passes through the wall of each alveolus into the bloodstream in exchange for carbon dioxide, which moves in the opposite direction. The alveoli provide a large surface across which this exchange can take place efficiently.

4 DIAPHRAGM

Situated just below the lungs, the diaphragm plays a key role in breathing. When breathing in, the diaphragm contracts and flattens as muscles pull the ribs upward and outward. This increases the space in the chest so that air is sucked into the lungs. When breathing out, the relaxed diaphragm is pushed upward, and the ribs move downward and inward, squeezing air from the lungs.

BLOOD

Flowing all around your body, blood delivers food, oxygen, and other essentials to trillions of cells and removes their wastes. Blood also distributes heat around your body and defends it against infection. Blood is made up of a yellow liquid called plasma in which float blood cells. Red blood cells pick up oxygen in the lungs and deliver it to your body's cells. White blood cells defend the body against disease-causing germs. Blood also contains platelets, which enable it to clot to seal damaged blood vessels. The heart pumps blood around the body along three types of blood vessel. Arteries carry blood away from the heart, while veins return blood to the heart. Microscopic capillaries link arteries and veins and supply blood to cells.

Circulating around the average body are 9 pints (5 liters) of blood. Oxygen-rich blood in arteries is bright red in color. Oxygen-poor blood in veins is dark purple-red.

Blood is 55 percent plasma and 45 percent blood cells. One drop of blood contains 250 million red blood cells, 375,000 white blood cells, and 16 million platelets.

Plasma is 90 percent water and contains more than 100 different dissolved substances including food, waste, hormones, and salts.

White blood cells called neutrophils and macrophages eat germs. Lymphocyte white blood cells disable germs by releasing chemicals called antibodies.

Unraveled and stretched out, one adult's blood vessels would encircle the Earth twice. Capillaries would make up 98 percent of the total length.

Each as broad as a thumb, the largest artery and vein (the aorta and vena cava) are 2,500 times wider than a capillary, which is just one-tenth the width of a hair.

Oxygen-carrying red blood cells make up 99 percent of all blood cells. Every second, two million new red blood cells are made by jellylike red marrow inside bones.

During a lifespan of 120 days, a red blood cell travels around the body 170,000 times—once each minute. It is then dismantled and recycled by the spleen and liver.

Packed into every red blood cell are 250 million red-colored hemoglobin molecules. Each one carries four oxygen molecules, so a single red blood cell can transport one billion oxygen molecules.

The heart is made largely of cardiac muscle, which does not tire. Over a lifetime of 70 years, the heart beats 2.5 billion times without taking a rest.

The heart beats, on average, 70 times a minute. Heart rate can double or triple during exercise to get extra oxygen to your muscles.

Each person belongs to one of four blood groups—A, B, AB, or O. Blood groups are determined by tiny "markers" carried by red blood cells.

More than 80 million units of blood are donated around the world every year. Blood transfusions replace blood lost during surgery and are used to treat some medical conditions.

SKIN, HAIR, AND NAILS

Skin is the body's protective overcoat, forming a barrier between vulnerable body tissues and the harsh, changing conditions of the outside world. It prevents water loss, blocks invasion by germs, repairs itself when damaged, helps us keep warm, and enables us to sense our surroundings. The uppermost layer of the skin is made from dead cells filled with a tough, waterproof substance called keratin. Hair and nails, both derived from skin, are also made from dead, keratin-filled cells.

The epidermis consists of cells that migrate upward, dying, flattening, and filling with keratin as they do so

Flat, scaly cells in the upper epidermis are constantly worn away as skin flakes

Cells in the base of the epidermis divide constantly to replace those lost from the surface

The dermis contains living cells and fibers that allow skin to stretch and recoil

1 SKIN CROSS-SECTION
A section through the skin reveals that it has two parts. The epidermis is a germ-proof, waterproof barrier that protects against harmful rays in sunlight. The thicker dermis contains blood vessels, sensory receptors, and sweat glands.

2 SWEAT
This salty liquid is produced by sweat glands in the dermis. In hot conditions, sweat is released onto the skin's surface. It then evaporates, cooling the body and helping to maintain a constant body temperature of 98.6°F (37°C).

3 SKIN COLOR
Special cells in the epidermis produce the brown pigment melanin, which filters out harmful ultraviolet rays from sunlight before they can damage skin cells.

Surface of the epidermis on the back of a person's hand

Skin surface is not smooth but covered with ridges into which sweat spreads

Melanin, along with blood flowing through the dermis, gives the skin its color

Sweat is a watery solution, filtered from blood and containing salts and wastes, that oozes from small openings called pores

4 FINGERNAIL

Ideal for gripping objects and scratching itches, fingernails are clear plates that protect the sensitive upper parts of the fingertips. The cells that make nails die, flatten, and fill with keratin as they are pushed forward from the nail's root.

Fingernail is formed from layers of dead, flattened cells from the epidermis

Hair shaft is made of dead cells packed with keratin, pushed up from the hair bulb

Skin covering the fingertips is sensitive because it contains many touch receptors

Hair follicle is a hollow space in the skin from which a hair grows

Hair bulb, deep in the dermis, contains living, dividing hair cells

Sebaceous gland secretes oily sebum that keeps hair and skin flexible and soft

5 HAIR

Millions of hairs grow from the skin covering most body areas. Scalp hairs protect the skin from sunlight and reduce heat loss. Finer, shorter body hairs sense the presence of insects on the skin before they can sting or bite us.

6 TOUCH RECEPTORS

The dermis contains a range of receptors that respond to soft touch, firmer pressure, and vibrations, and send signals to the brain so we can feel our surroundings. The dermis also has receptors that detect pain, heat, and cold.

BRAIN

Safely inside the skull, the brain allows us to sense, think, learn, remember, and move. It also automatically regulates vital functions such as breathing. The cerebrum, the main part of the brain, has two halves, or hemispheres. The left hemisphere controls the right side of the body and is in charge of language, math, and problem solving, while the right side controls the body's left side and deals with creativity, music, and art. The cerebrum's many tasks are carried out by its outer layer, or cortex. This has distinct areas that have different roles. Motor areas trigger movement, sensory areas deal with the senses, while association areas interpret information.

1 PREFRONTAL CORTEX
The most complex part of the cerebrum, the prefrontal cortex makes us what we are. It determines our personality and intellect, and enables us to reason, plan, create and learn complex ideas, and have a conscience.

2 BROCA'S AREA
Named after Paul Broca, the 19th-century doctor who discovered it, Broca's area is normally found in the left hemisphere. It plans what a person wants to say and sends instructions to muscles in the throat, tongue, and lips that produce speech.

3 PREMOTOR CORTEX
Learned movement skills, such as playing tennis, are controlled and coordinated by the premotor cortex. It tells specific muscles to contract either through the primary motor cortex or, in some cases, directly.

4 PRIMARY MOTOR CORTEX
Most movements we make are controlled by the primary motor cortex. Guided by information from the cerebellum and other brain parts, it sends instructions to muscles that move the skeleton instructing them when, and in what sequence, to contract.

5 PRIMARY SENSORY CORTEX
Receptors in the skin for touch, pressure, vibration, heat and cold, and pain send signals to the primary sensory cortex enabling us to feel those sensations. Our lips and fingertips have high concentrations of receptors, hence their sensitivity.

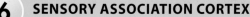

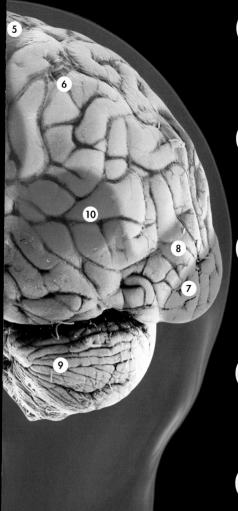

6 SENSORY ASSOCIATION CORTEX

Basic information about touch, pressure, and other skin sensations is passed on by the primary sensory cortex to the sensory association cortex. Here sensations are analyzed, stored, and compared with previous experiences. It enables us to identify objects by touch.

7 PRIMARY VISUAL CORTEX

When light hits the retina at the back of each eye, its light detectors send signals to the primary visual cortex. Here those signals are interpreted as basic shapes, colors, and movements before being passed on to the visual association cortex.

8 VISUAL ASSOCIATION CORTEX

This is where information from the primary visual cortex about seen objects is interpreted and compared with previous visual experiences. The visual association cortex identifies what we are looking at and where it is in space, enabling us to "see" it.

9 CEREBELLUM

The cerebellum is responsible for producing smooth, coordinated movements of the body. It analyzes incoming information about the body's current position and movement, then interacts with the primary motor cortex to precisely time muscle contractions.

10 WERNICKE'S AREA

Usually located in the left hemisphere, Wernicke's area gives meaning to words that have been heard or read. Named after the German doctor Karl Wernicke, it has a direct link to Broca's area, enabling us to speak the words we hear or see.

11 PRIMARY AUDITORY CORTEX

When sounds are detected by the two ears they send signals to the primary auditory cortex. Here the loudness, pitch (whether high or low), and rhythm of sounds are identified. That information is passed on to the auditory association area.

12 AUDITORY ASSOCIATION CORTEX

Sounds are "heard" in the auditory association area. Using information received from the primary auditory cortex, it pieces together the complete sound, and by comparing it with sounds stored in memory, identifies it as, for example, music, speech, or thunder.

SENSES

Our senses make us aware of the world around us and the changes that are happening in it. Our eyes detect light waves, and our ears sound waves, enabling us to see and hear. Our tongue and nose detect dissolved chemicals so we can taste, smell, and enjoy flavors. Our skin allows us to feel the texture and warmth of objects.

Ear flap captures sound waves and funnels them into the ear canal

Ear canal leads to the inner ear where sounds are detected

Spiky papilla enables the tongue to grip food

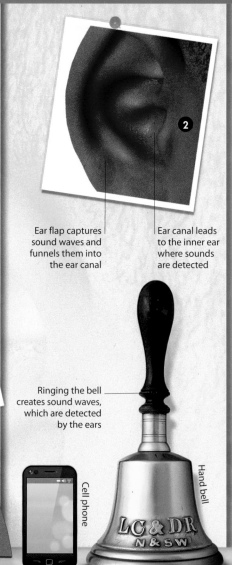

Iris controls the amount of light entering the eye

Candy tastes sweet because it contains a lot of sugar

Ringing the bell creates sound waves, which are detected by the ears

Shapes, color, and movement are all detected by the sense of vision

Cell phone

Hand bell

1 VISION

Vision is the most important sense, providing the brain with an immense amount of information about the body's surroundings. Light reflected from, or produced by, outside objects is automatically focused onto a layer of light receptors that lines the back of the eye. In response, these receptors send signals to areas at the back of the brain. From there, we can determine what we are looking at and where it is, thus enabling us to "see" moving, 3-D images in color.

2 HEARING

The ears detect waves of pressure, called sound waves, that travel through the air. Sound waves are produced by objects, such as a ringing cell phone or bell, which move or vibrate. The waves pass into the inner ear, which is enclosed in bone on the side of the skull. Here, receptors convert pressure waves into signals. The signals travel to the brain, which identifies the pitch, volume, and direction of the sound.

Taste buds housed in mushroom-shaped papilla

Feathers feel soft and ticklish

Skin ridges in the fingertips help us grip the objects we touch

3 TASTE

Small projections on the tongue, called papillae, house taste receptors called taste buds. Food molecules dissolved in saliva are detected by the taste buds. These can distinguish between five basic tastes—sour, sweet, salty, bitter, and umami (savory and meaty). In addition to helping us to enjoy food, our sense of taste enables us to detect foods that may be poisonous.

Lemons and most other citrus fruit taste sour

Citrus fruit

A cactus spine puncturing the skin stimulates a pain receptor

Fresh flowers

Some cheeses emit a strong smell

4 TOUCH

The skin acts like a sense organ. It contains several different types of receptors that enable us to "feel" our surroundings. Most are touch receptors that send signals to the brain when the skin comes into contact with objects. Some detect light touch, some detect heavier pressure, and some detect vibrations. Other receptors in the skin pick up temperature changes or detect pain.

5 SMELL

The nose can detect more than 10,000 different smells. When air is breathed into the nose, odor molecules dissolve in watery mucus and are detected by odor receptors high in the roof of the nasal cavity. Together, the senses of smell and taste enable us to detect flavors. Smell is more important, however, which explains why food lacks flavor when we have a blocked nose. Some smells, such as those produced by burning, can warn us of danger.

REPRODUCTION

Human beings have a limited lifespan but are able, through reproduction, to produce a new generation to succeed them. Male and female reproductive systems produce specialized sex cells—called sperm and eggs—that unite during fertilization and combine their genetic instructions to make a new, unique human. After fertilization the embryo—later called a fetus—grows and develops inside its mother's uterus (womb) for the nine months of pregnancy.

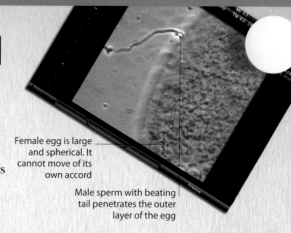

Female egg is large and spherical. It cannot move of its own accord

Male sperm with beating tail penetrates the outer layer of the egg

▲ FERTILIZATION

Inside a woman's reproductive system, sperm swim toward and surround an egg and attempt to penetrate its outer layer. Eventually one succeeds, loses its tail, and its head fuses with the egg's nucleus, thereby combining two sets of genetic instructions (DNA).

72 hours after fertilization the pre-embryo is a ball of 16 cells

◀ CELLS MULTIPLY

As the fertilized egg, or pre-embryo, is swept toward the uterus it divides repeatedly, producing first two cells, then four, then eight, and so on. Six days after fertilization it embeds itself in the uterus lining.

The liver makes the embryo's blood cells until bone marrow can take over

The head becomes more erect and the ears, including the organs of balance, develop

Dark retina of a developing eye on the side of the embryo's head

▲ FOUR WEEKS

This pea-sized, four-week-old embryo—its head is on the left—is growing in its mother's uterus. Its tiny heart is beating and the nervous system and vital organs are forming.

▲ FIVE TO SIX WEEKS

The embryo's brain continues to develop, as do other organs, such as the intestines. Its skull and face are taking shape, and limbs, in the form of buds, are starting to grow. The embryo floats within a sac filled with protective fluid.

▲ SEVEN WEEKS

The bones of the grape-sized embryo start to harden and muscles develop and get stronger. Wrists and ankles are now visible and fingers and toes are just starting to appear. Internally, the kidneys start to remove waste to make urine.

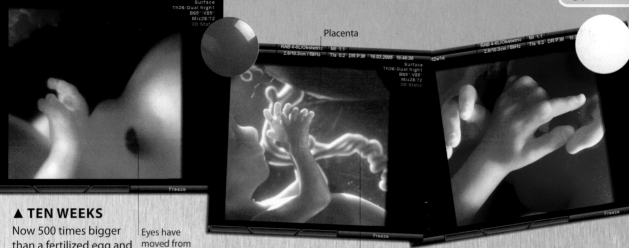

Placenta

▲ TEN WEEKS

Now 500 times bigger than a fertilized egg and consisting of billions of cells of different types, the fetus, as it is now called, has all its basic organs in place and is growing rapidly. Its large head accommodates a fast-expanding brain. Fingers have formed and fingernails are growing.

Eyes have moved from the side of the head, and eyelids are forming

▲ TWELVE WEEKS

Since their implantation, the cells have been growing and specializing and the tiny individual they have molded is now recognizably human. It has facial features, and fingers and toes have separated. The internal organs are in place, and the heart is beating.

The fetus receives food and oxygen through the umbilical cord, which is connected to the mother via an organ called the placenta

▲ TWENTY WEEKS

Fingers and ears clearly visible, the fetus' movements can be felt by its mother inside her expanding uterus. The fetus blinks and swallows and follows phases of sleeping and waking. The ridges that produce fingerprints appear on its fingertips.

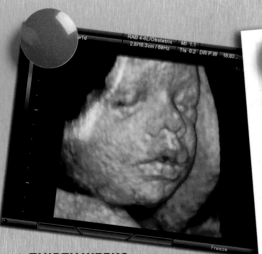

▲ THIRTY WEEKS

Ultrasound scanning, shown here, is a safe method used to monitor the development of a fetus, and it can also reveal whether it is a girl or boy. At this stage, the brain is still growing rapidly. The fetus can hear sounds and its eyes respond to light. Its lungs can now potentially breathe air.

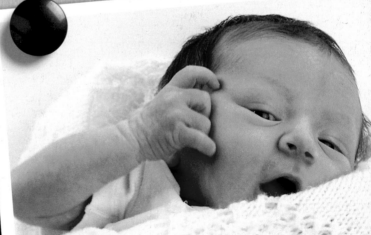

NEWBORN

As pregnancy comes to an end, the uterus contracts to push the fully grown fetus into the bright, noisy outside world. The newborn baby takes its first breath and the umbilical cord is cut. In the next phases of its growth and development the baby is completely dependent on its parents for food, warmth, and protection.

GENETICS

Though all humans share the same basic body plan, each of us (except for identical twins) has a unique mixture of features. That is because the set of instructions—called genes—required to construct a human varies slightly from person to person. Genetics is the study of how the genes we inherit from our parents shape the way we are.

Eye color is controlled by specific genes, and different versions of those genes produce a range of colors

1 **DNA**

Long molecules of DNA (deoxyribonucleic acid) are found in every body cell. When magnified, DNA resembles a twisted ladder with "rungs" made from four types of chemicals called bases (shown in color). The sequence of bases along a section of DNA forms an instruction—a gene—for making one of the proteins that build and run a cell.

2 **CHROMOSOMES**

A cell's DNA molecules are packaged into 23 pairs of chromosomes, which are found in the nucleus, the cell's control center. Normally they are long and thin, but when a cell prepares to divide into two new cells, each chromosome shortens—as its DNA coils up—and duplicates, taking on the X-shape shown here.

3 INHERITANCE

We inherit half of our chromosomes from each of our parents. A set of 23 chromosomes contains about 25,000 genes. Maternal and paternal chromosomes carry matching pairs of each gene—such as the gene that controls eye color—but not necessarily the same version. If two versions are present, only one—the dominant gene—has an effect.

4 GENETIC SIMILARITY

Because brothers and sisters inherit a selection of genes from the same two people, their parents, they are more likely to resemble each other than they would a nonrelative. The same applies to nonidentical twins. Identical twins share exactly the same genes, so they look the same and are the same sex.

HEALTH

A healthy body is one that is fit, strong, supple, and working well. Disease and injury prevent the normal working of the body. While it is not always possible to avoid illness, the chances of developing a disease are reduced by adopting a healthy lifestyle, including getting regular exercise and eating a good, mixed diet of fresh foods. If a person does become sick, a doctor has to figure out exactly what the problem is, and then decides on a suitable course of treatment. This might include drugs, surgery, or other means to return the person to full health.

DRUGS

Chemicals that are used to treat and prevent disease, by changing some aspect of the way the body works, are called drugs. Antibiotics, which kill harmful bacteria, and analgesics, which reduce pain, are both examples of drugs. They may be given to a patient in a number of ways—by injection, as pills and syrups that are swallowed, or as a vapor that is inhaled into the lungs.

Cough syrup

Inhaler is used to introduce drugs, such as those that treat asthma, into the lungs

Hypodermic syringe is used to inject drugs into the bloodstream, skin, or a muscle

Pills

Laryngeal mirror is placed in the mouth to check the larynx (voice box)

Thermometer

Otoscope has a lens and a light and is used to look into a patient's ear

Ophthalmoscope enables a doctor to examine the inside of a patient's eye

Stethoscope is used to listen to chest sounds such as breathing and heartbeat

FIRST AID

The initial treatment to a person who is sick or injured is called first aid. It is often performed by someone who is not medically qualified, but has been trained to use simple yet effective treatments. In more serious cases, first aid may keep a person alive until medical help arrives. A first-aid kit contains essential items such as disposable gloves, scissors, antiseptic cream and wipes, adhesive bandages, sterile dressings, and bandages.

Caterers use blue adhesive bandages because they are easy to see

DIAGNOSIS

If a person is ill their doctor first needs to determine exactly what is wrong with them. This is called making a diagnosis. The doctor asks about symptoms—the features of the disease or injury the patient has noticed—and considers the patient's medical history. Next, the doctor looks for signs to help identify the illness, for example, using a thermometer to check body temperature. The patient may require further tests, such as blood tests or X-rays.

Running shoes are ideal footwear for running and other exercises that improve fitness

Dumbbell weight

Chicken is a meat that is rich in protein, but low in harmful fats

PREVENTION

Regular exercise, such as running, walking, or playing sports, improves fitness by making the heart and body muscles more efficient. It is also important to eat a balanced diet made up of a wide range of foods—including pasta and rice, fruits and vegetables, lean meat, and oily fish—and low in salt, sugar, and in the unhealthy fats found in red meat. Not only does a healthy diet reduce the risk of becoming overweight, but it can also help protect against certain diseases.

Oranges, like all fruits, contain vitamins that are essential for good health

Fish, especially oily fish, contain fatty acids that can reduce the risk of heart disease

Elasticated bandages support joints, limit swelling, and secure dressings that control bleeding

SURGERY

Performed by a doctor called a surgeon, surgery involves cutting into a patient's body to repair, remove, or replace tissue damaged by disease or injury. Surgery takes place in an operating room. To reduce the risk of infection, staff wear gowns and masks, and everything is sterile (free of germs). During an operation the patient is given an anesthetic—a drug or gas that stops them from feeling any pain.

Sterile surgical instruments are the "tools" used by a surgeon to perform operations

Scalpel is a sharp blade for cutting through skin and other tissues

Antiseptic cream

Sterile dressing

Coarse forceps

Fine scissors

Coarse scissors

Probes

Fine forceps are used to grip and lift tissues during an operation

Disposable gloves

QUICK QUIZ

What can you remember about the Human Body?
Jot down your answers, then check them on pp.296–97.

1 **White blood cells** circulate in the **blood** in a **clear fluid**. What do white blood cells do?

A Keep a check on blood loss in case of an injury
B Fight disease-causing germs
C Ensure that the blood flows smoothly through the veins

2 **Where** in the **body** do you find **osteocytes**?

3 What are these **bones** of the **foot** called?

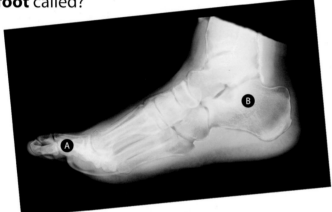

4 How much of the **body's mass** is made up of **bones**?

A 30 percent
B 40 percent
C 20 percent
D 15 percent

5 How many **pairs of ribs** form the **rib cage**?

A Thirteen
B Twelve
C Eight
D Ten

6 How does a **fetus** receive **food and oxygen** in the **womb**?

A The fetus does not need food and oxygen until it is born
B They are carried in blood through the umbilical cord
C The fetus absorbs them from the amniotic fluid
D Cells in the womb help feed the fetus

7 What are you more likely to call your **trachea**?

8 We **produce every body movement**, whether it's **a leap** in the air, **a wink** of the eye, or **a rapid heartbeat**. What are we?

A Ligaments
B Bones
C Muscles
D Cells

9 **Match** the **images** to the correct **body parts**:

A Hair   **B** Fingernail   **C** Skin

10 **Match** the **instruments** to their **names**:

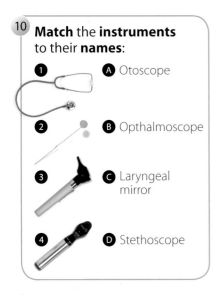

1   **A** Otoscope

2   **B** Opthalmoscope

3   **C** Laryngeal mirror

4   **D** Stethoscope

11 What does the **image** on the right **show**? (clue: they are found in the brain)

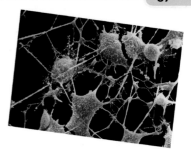

12 A baby starts life with just **two cells**. How many cells does the **pre-embryo** have after **72 hours**?
- **A** Eighteen
- **B** Eight
- **C** Sixteen
- **D** Twelve

13 Can you **name** these parts of the **digestive system**?

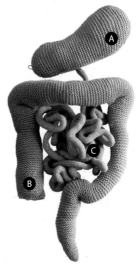

14 In which **sensory organ** would you find **small projections** called **papillae**?
- **A** Nose
- **B** Ears
- **C** Eyes
- **D** Tongue

15 What gives each one of us our **unique mix** of **features**?
- **A** The mood we are in
- **B** The side we slept on when we were in the womb
- **C** Our genes
- **D** Our blood group

16 Which colored **area of the brain** plans what you want to **say** and sends **instructions to the muscles** that you use to **speak**? What is it called?

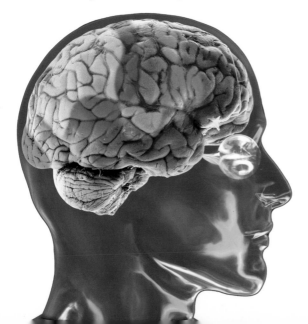

17 **Unraveled** and **stretched** out, an adult's **blood vessels** would **encircle** the **Earth** how many times?
- **A** Two
- **B** Twelve
- **C** Eight
- **D** Ten

18 Our **blood** is made up of **55 percent plasma**. What makes up the other **45 percent**?

FAST FACTS

Your body sheds tens of thousands of **skin flakes** every minute. Over a lifetime, a body loses 44 lb (20 kg) of skin flakes.

You lose **100,000** brain cells every day.

Your brain weighs about 2 percent of your total body weight, but uses 20 percent of your blood supply.

The brain of an adult is **three times heavier** *than that of a newborn baby. From the age of 20, the brain loses* **0.03 oz (1 g)** *a year as* **brain cells die** *and are not replaced.*

Eyes stay the same size from age eight, but **noses** and **ears** never stop growing.

Nose hairs act like a net to trap and remove nasty particles from the air.

Your skin cells fall off at a rate of 40,000 per minute. Dead human skin cells make up about 70 percent of household dust.

The liver handles more than **500** *different jobs, including the disposal of dead blood cells, making proteins, and storing sugars.*

There are 100 trillion cells in your body. A billion of them die every 20 seconds.

The largest human cell is the female ovum.
The smallest is the male sperm.

At rest, you **breathe** about once **every four seconds**. This rises to once every second during exercise.

We make 2 pints (1 liter) of saliva in our mouths every day.

Tiny bacteria make up 3 percent of your body weight.

There are more muscles in a caterpillar than there are in a human body.

You spend *half an hour* every day blinking.

The left lung is smaller than the right lung to make room for the heart.

It takes your stomach up to six hours to process a meal. The food then takes about six more hours to pass through the small intestine.

Everyone has a unique tongue print.

Women's hearts are smaller than men's, but they beat on average 75 times per minute compared to 70 times for men.

About **a third** of adults snore.

Stretched out straight, the small intestine is about 19 ft (6 m) long.

Food spends up to six hours in your stomach being digested.

The smallest muscle in the human body is the stapedius. It is inside the ear and is less than 0.08 in (2 mm) long.

There are more than

600

muscles in the human body. Muscles are 40 percent of the body's total weight.

Blood travels 12,000 miles (19,000 km) every day. That's half way around the world.

After the age of **60** you will lose about half your taste buds.

The **stomach** continually produces new layers of mucus to protect the lining and stop the stomach from digesting itself.

There are around 1,000 trillion bacteria in your body—10 times more than the number of body cells.

The average person eats **30 tons** of food in a lifetime—that's the weight of **80 horses.**

The loudest snore ever recorded was more than 80 decibels, as loud as a pneumatic drill.

The average human head has 100,000 hairs growing on it, but redheads have only 90,000.

An **adult man** normally needs to **eat** about **2,500 calories** (10,000 kilojoules) a day. *Arctic explorers* need about *three times* that much to keep them going in the **cold.**

A fingernail would grow 90 ft (28 m) long if never cut. The middle nail grows fastest, the thumb slowest.

There are the same number of hairs on the body of a human being as on a chimpanzee.

The longest beard ever measured was more than

16 ft
(5 m) long and belonged to Norwegian

Hans Langseth.

Babies start dreaming before they are born.

The average human blinks 23 times a minute. That's 12 million times a year.

A body releases 4 pints (2 liters) of gas per day as burps or farts.

When you sleep, you lose up to 1.4 oz (42 g) in weight every hour.

Common colds can be caused by one of more than 250 types of virus.

A cough releases air at speeds up to *60 mph* (100 km/h).

A single sneeze might contain up to 100,000 viruses.

The **oldest** person ever documented was French woman *Jeanne Calment*, who **died** in **1997** aged **122 years** and **164 days.**

The largest organ is the skin, which has a surface area of about 20 sq ft (2 sq m) and weighs about 22 lb (10 kg).

Babies don't have bony kneecaps, which appear between the ages of two and six.

73 percent of babies' bodies are water. This drops to 60 percent in adult men and 55 percent in adult women.

The most common time of birth is between **3 a.m.** and **4 a.m.**

There are 250,000 sweat glands in a pair of feet. They can produce half a pint (a quarter of a liter) of sweat in one day.

More people died during the flu pandemic at the end of World War I than were killed during the war.

19th-century British surgeon Robert Liston could cut off a leg in *28 seconds.*

Life expectancy at birth in Andorra is 83.5 years—the highest in the world.

Standing upright burns up 140 calories (600 kilojoules) of energy in an hour.

One in **2,000 babies** is born with a **tooth.**

In an average lifetime, you will walk the equivalent of five times around the equator.

You cannot *sneeze* with your eyes open.

The first successful heart transplant took place in 1967. There are now six heart transplants every day in the US alone.

The largest artery, the **aorta**, is about **$1\frac{1}{3}$ in** (3.5 cm) in diameter. That's as wide as a **hose pipe.**

During puberty, boys can grow $3\frac{1}{2}$ in (9 cm) in a year.

Children grow faster in spring.

In a whole lifetime, a human passes **12,000 gallons** (45,000 liters) of urine. That's enough to fill a **swimming pool.**

In your lifetime, you will drink about 18,500 gallons (70,000 liters) of water.

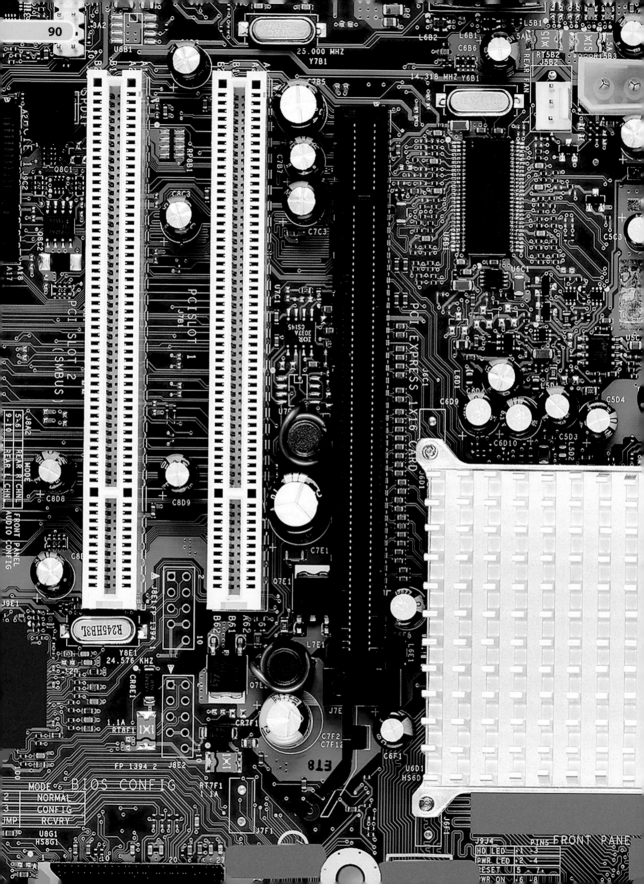

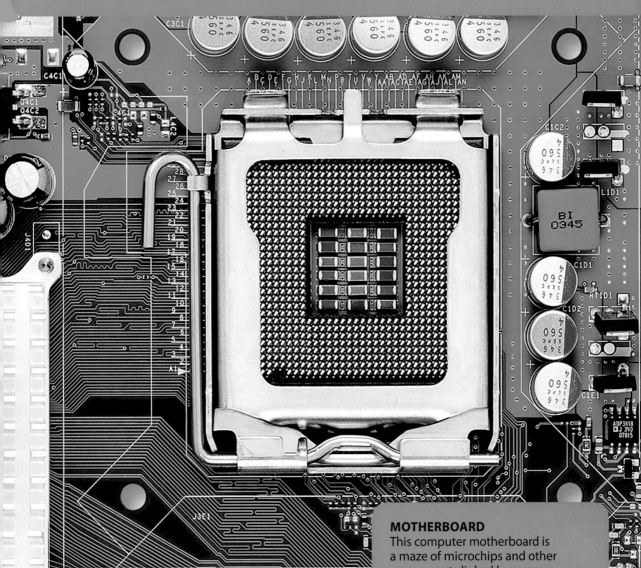

SCIENCE AND TECHNOLOGY

MOTHERBOARD
This computer motherboard is a maze of microchips and other components linked by copper wires. It connects all the computer's components, passing on instructions and data with incredible speed.

ELEMENTS

Everything in the world is made from elements—pure substances that cannot be broken down into anything simpler. Elements can be grouped according to the properties they have in common, such as their appearance, how they conduct electricity, and how they react with other substances. There are nine main groups and the element hydrogen, which is unique.

The Orion Nebula, a vast cloud of gas and dust, is made mainly of hydrogen

HYDROGEN

Hydrogen makes up 90 percent of all atoms in the universe. Pure hydrogen is an invisible gas on Earth. It is not considered part of any one group. Hydrogen powers the nuclear reactions inside stars, including our Sun, and is found on Earth in the compound H2O, or water.

Magnesium is a silvery substance that burns with a dazzling white flame

ALKALINE-EARTH METALS

Alkaline-earth metals react with water and are found in minerals in the Earth's crust. In pure form, they are silvery-white. They are similar to alkali metals, but less reactive. Calcium, found in chalk, milk, and bones, is a member of this group.

Potassium is an alkali metal found in minerals in Earth's crust

3 ALKALI METALS

Sodium, contained in salt, is an alkali metal. These elements are characterized by their vigorous reaction with water. On contact, they will zoom all over the water's surface or even explode. Alkali metals are not found in a pure form in nature because they react so strongly with water.

4 LANTHANIDES

These soft, reactive metals were known as rare earths, because they were wrongly believed to occur only scarcely in nature. Silvery-white in appearance, they tarnish easily on contact with air. Holmium, the element with the greatest magnetic strength, is in this group.

5 ACTINIDES

The elements in this group are radioactive metals mostly created synthetically in nuclear reactors or nuclear explosions. They have unstable atoms that break up and give out radiation particles. Uranium and plutonium are examples of actinides.

6 NONMETALS

Around one-sixth of elements are nonmetals. They are poor conductors of electricity and met at low temperatures. Carbon, nitrogen, and oxygen are all examples of nonmetals, as are the halogens, a group of highly reactive elements that combine with other elements to form salts.

4

Gadolinium, like the other lanthanides, reacts easily with air

5 Radioactive sign is used to show elements that emit radiation

8

After hydrogen, helium is the lightest element, and is used to fill balloons and airships because it is lighter than air

6

The halogen bromine is a red-brown liquid at room temperature, but evaporates quickly to form a choking, poisonous gas

7

Tin is often made into alloys—mixing it with copper makes bronze, while combining it with lead forms pewter

9

Copper is a good conductor of heat and electricity

10

Silicon is often used to make microchips for electronic devices

7 POOR METALS

Metals that are fairly soft and melt easily are known as poor metals. They are readily found as ores (minerals) in the Earth and can be very useful, especially when made into alloys (two metals mixed together to make a harder metal). Aluminum and lead are both poor metals.

8 NOBLE GASES

There are six noble gases—also called rare or inert gases because they do not readily react with anything or combine with other elements to make compounds. They are helium, neon, argon, krypton, xenon, and radon. Except for radon, they are all used in lighting.

9 TRANSITION METALS

This group is the largest and includes iron, silver, gold, nickel, platinum, and titanium. Transition metals are considered typical metals— they are hard and shiny, conduct electricity and heat well, and have high melting points.

10 SEMIMETALS

These elements have some properties of metals and some of nonmetals. Arsenic, for example, is shiny like a metal, but not a good conductor. Some semimetals are semiconductors, behaving as conductors or insulators depending on what other substances are added to them.

MOLECULES

An atom is the smallest possible particle of an element (a substance that consists of atoms of only one kind). Atoms often join in groups of two or more to form molecules. Atoms bond to create molecules by sharing or exchanging particles called electrons. Some molecules, called compounds, are made up of different elements.

Oxygen atom

◄ OXYGEN (O_2)
Some elements can bond in several ways to form different substances. Atoms of the element oxygen (O) bond together in pairs to form molecules of oxygen gas. High in the atmosphere, however, oxygen atoms bond in threes to form the gas ozone.

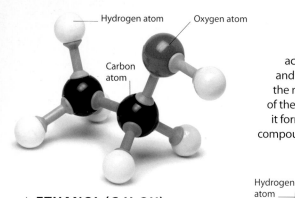

Hydrogen atom   Oxygen atom

Carbon atom

► VITAMIN C ($C_6H_8O_6$)
Like ethanol, vitamin C (ascorbic acid) contains carbon (C), hydrogen (H), and oxygen (O) atoms. However, because the molecule contains different quantities of the elements arranged in a different way it forms an entirely different substance—a compound that is solid at room temperature.

Carbon atom

Hydrogen atom

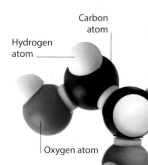

Oxygen atom

▲ ETHANOL (C_2H_5OH)
Ethanol is a compound with molecules containing two carbon (C) atoms, six hydrogen (H) atoms, and one oxygen (O) atom. At room temperature, it is a colorless liquid used as a disinfectant, preservative, and the alcohol in drinks.

Hydrogen atom

◄ METHANE (CH_4)
Molecules of the gas methane contain four hydrogen (H) atoms bonded to a carbon (C) atom. Compounds of carbon and hydrogen are called hydrocarbons. They include fuels, such as methane, oil, and coal, and artificial materials, such as polystyrene.

Carbon atom

Sodium and chlorine atoms always join up in the same way to form cubic crystals

Chlorine atom

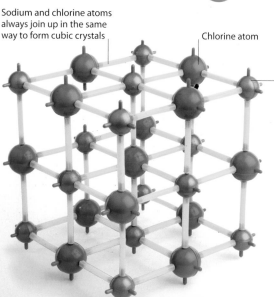

Sodium atom

◄ SALT (NACL)
Table salt, or sodium chloride, is made of equal numbers of sodium (Na) and chlorine (Cl) atoms. Salt does not form as small individual molecules containing one atom each of sodium and chlorine. Instead, many atoms of the two elements link to form a rigid lattice called a crystal.

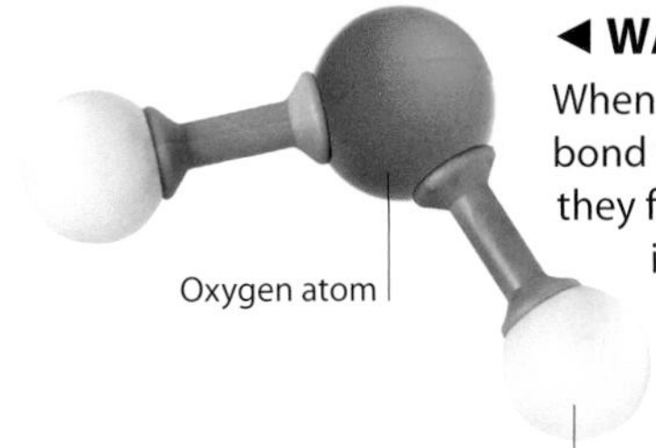

◄ WATER (H₂O)

When two atoms of the gas hydrogen (H) bond with one atom of the gas oxygen (O), they form molecules of liquid water. Water is the most common compound on Earth and is essential for life.

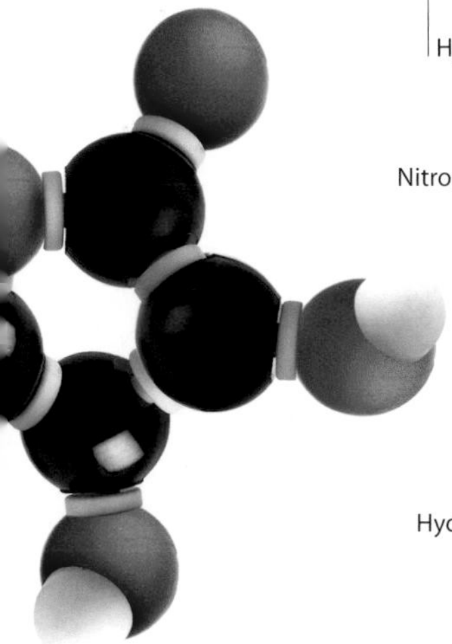

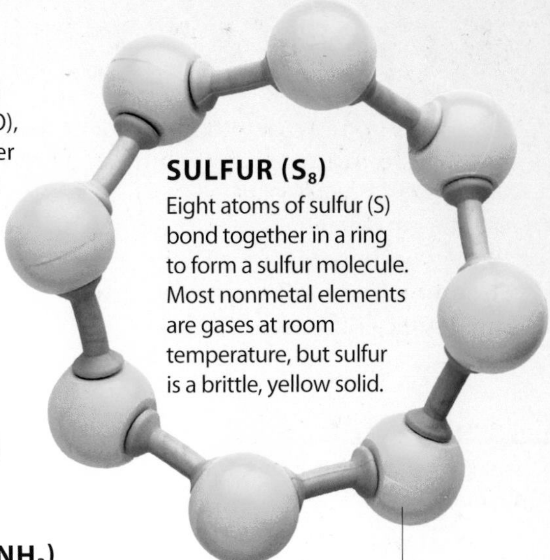

Oxygen atom

Hydrogen atom

SULFUR (S₈)

Eight atoms of sulfur (S) bond together in a ring to form a sulfur molecule. Most nonmetal elements are gases at room temperature, but sulfur is a brittle, yellow solid.

Sulfur atom

Nitrogen atom

▲ AMMONIA (NH₃)

The colorless gas ammonia is made up of one nitrogen (N) atom bonded to three hydrogen (H) atoms. Plants get the nitrogen they need to grow from ammonia and other nitrogen compounds within the soil.

Hydrogen atom

► DIAMOND (C)

A diamond can be thought of as a single giant molecule. It is formed from atoms of carbon (C) bonded in a strong crystal lattice. However, if carbon atoms join in flat sheets of hexagonal tiles, they form graphite, a brittle substance used to make pencil leads.

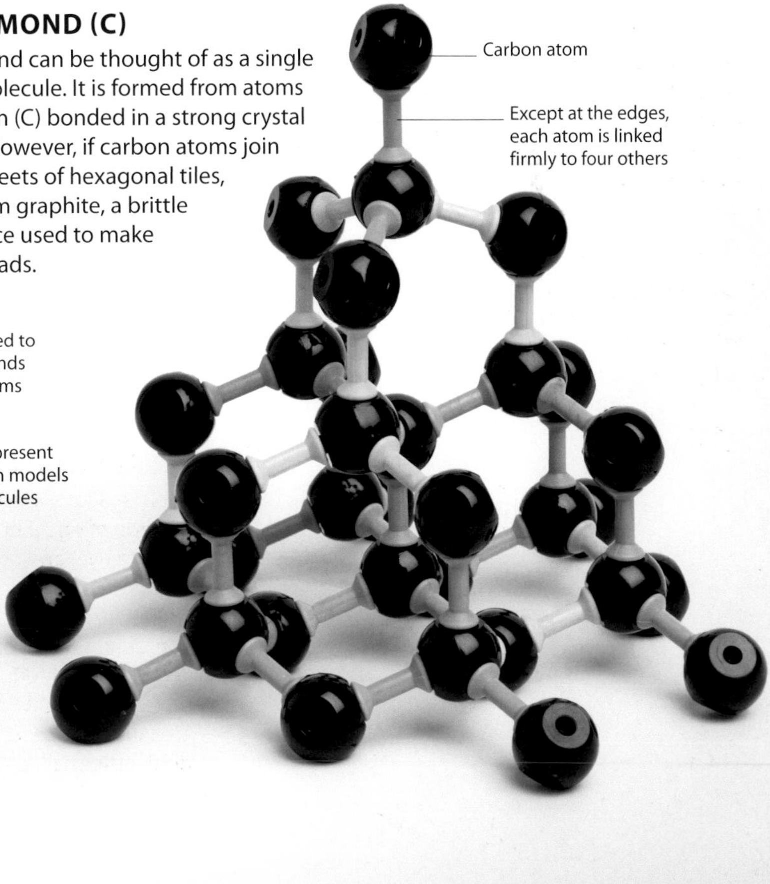

Carbon atom

Except at the edges, each atom is linked firmly to four others

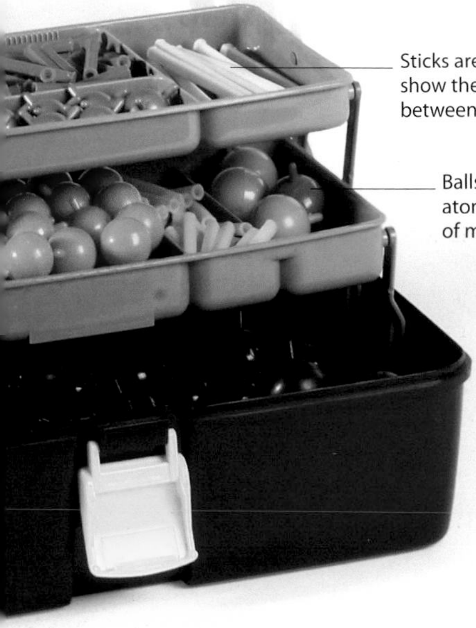

Sticks are used to show the bonds between atoms

Balls represent atoms in models of molecules

ACIDS AND BASES

An acid is a substance that produces positively charged particles of hydrogen, called hydrogen ions, when dissolved in water. The more hydrogen ions an acid contains, the stronger the acid is. A base is the chemical opposite of an acid. Bases produce negatively charged particles in water, called hydroxide ions. The more hydroxide ions a base contains, the stronger it is. Bases that dissolve in water are called alkalis.

▲ CITRIC ACID

The sharp taste in citrus fruit such as lemons and grapefruit is due to the citric acid they contain. Citric acid is often artificially added to manufactured foods and drinks to give a tangy sensation that tastes refreshing.

▼ INDICATOR PAPER

When a strip of indicator paper is dipped into a liquid, the paper changes color. The color can be compared to a pH scale to find out the acidity of the solution. pH stands for "potential of hydrogen," and measures how many hydrogen ions the solution contains.

◀ VINEGAR

The sour taste of vinegar comes from the acetic acid it contains. Every step on the pH scale is 10 times less acidic than the previous step, so acetic acid with a pH of 4 is 1,000 times less acidic than hydrochloric acid.

◀ HYDROCHLORIC ACID

The lower the pH value, the stronger the acid. Hydrochloric acid, created when hydrogen chloride gas dissolves in water, has a pH of about 1. It is highly corrosive, capable of eating through metals.

◀ STINGER

When a bee stings, it injects a mild acid into a person's flesh, which causes a stinging sensation. Washing the sting with alkaline soap may relieve the pain by neutralizing the acid.

◀ CHEMICAL HAZARD

Strong acids and bases have to be stored in containers that will not be corroded by the chemical within. These containers are labeled with chemical hazard symbols that show the potential dangers.

All bases tend to feel slippery like soap

Vinegar is made when bacteria convert the ethanol in alcohol into acetic acid

▶ LIQUID SOAP

Soap is a weak base. It is made by combining a weak acid with a strong base, making it only mildly alkaline with a pH of about 8. An indicator paper dipped into liquid soap turns blue.

▶ LIMESTONE

Calcium carbonate, or limestone, is a type of rock formed from the remains of dead sea creatures over millions of years. It is an important base, which is quarried and crushed to make fertilizers, paints, ceramics, and cement.

◀ WATER

Pure water is neither acid nor alkali, but neutral, with a pH of 7. Rainwater is slightly acidic, with a pH of 5 to 6, while seawater is slightly alkaline, with a pH of between 8 and 9.

▶ CLEANING FLUID

The strongest bases have a pH of 14 or more. Alkaline solutions with a high pH are used as cleaning materials as they dissolve fats. Cleaning fluids such as bleach and caustic soda have a pH of around 10.

The pH of tap water is usually between 6 and 8 depending on the gases and minerals that are dissolved in it

▶ HYDRANGEAS

The hydrangea shrub produces different colored flowers depending on the acidity of the soil. On acid soils, it produces blue flowers, on alkaline soils, it produces pink or purple flowers, and on neutral soils, it has creamy white blooms.

Chalk and vinegar
fizzes vigorously as
the acid breaks
down the chalk

CHEMICAL REACTIONS

The atoms within a molecule are held together with
links called chemical bonds. In a chemical reaction,
the bonds between a molecule's atoms break, and the
atoms bond in a different way to form new molecules.
In some reactions, elements combine to create a
compound. In others, compounds break down
into elements or simpler compounds. All the
atoms from the original substance exist in
the changed substance, but in different places.

Silver metal clings to
the copper coil

Burning is a nonreversible
reaction—the wick cannot be
remade from the ash and smoke

The energy produced when
sulfur and iron react causes
the mixture to glow

The explosion caused by
igniting thermite produces
a temperature of around
4,350°F (2,400°C)

When chemicals in
an apple's cells that
contain substances
called phenols are
exposed to the
air, they oxidize
and turn brown

1 REACTION

When vinegar
(acetic acid) and chalk
(calcium carbonate)
are mixed, a chemical
reaction takes place.
The acidic vinegar
breaks down the chalk
to release carbon and
oxygen as bubbles
of carbon dioxide.
The starting materials
in a chemical reaction
are called reactants.
The materials that
exist after are
called products.

2 DISPLACEMENT

In a displacement
reaction, the metal
that forms part of a
compound is removed
and replaced by another
metal. When a coil of
copper is dipped into a
clear solution of silver
nitrate, the copper
displaces the silver from
the solution to form a
blue solution of copper
nitrate and needles of
solid metal silver.

3 BURNING

When the wick
of a candle burns,
it is reacting with
oxygen in the air to
produce ash and
soot. The burning
also produces energy
in the form of heat
and light. In all
reactions, energy
is used up when
bonds between
atoms break, and
energy is released as
new bonds are made.

4 REACTION RATES

The rate of a chemical
reaction is affected
by factors such as
temperature, pressure,
light, surface area, and
concentration. It is
possible to change
the rate of a reaction
by varying one of
these factors. For
example, increasing
the concentration
of dye in a solution
will dye the material
more quickly.

5 REVERSIBLE

A few reactions are reversible. The molecules created by the reaction can be re-formed into the original materials. The initial reaction is called the forward reaction and the reverse is the backward reaction. Dinitrogen tetraoxide breaks down into nitrogen dioxide when heated, but reverts when cooled.

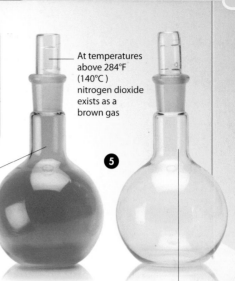

At temperatures above 284°F (140°C) nitrogen dioxide exists as a brown gas

If heated again, brown nitrogen dioxide re-forms

Concentrated dye contains more dye particles to collide with the cloth

At lower temperatures the nitrogen dioxide molecules pair up to make clear dinitrogen tetraoxide

As crystals of potassium permanganate begin to dissolve, purple trails spread through the water, until an even purple solution is formed

When a bread dough mixture is left in a warm place, carbon dioxide bubbles appear, making the bread rise

10 CATALYST

A catalyst is a molecule that helps bring about and speed up a chemical reaction, but does not change itself during the reaction. Natural catalysts are called enzymes. Bread dough rises because enzymes in yeast cause a reaction that produces bubbles of carbon dioxide when it is mixed with water and sugars.

6 APPLYING HEAT

When a mixture of yellow powder sulfur and silver-gray iron filings is heated to a high temperature, a chemical reaction takes place and iron sulfide is formed. Without heat, the substances would not react with each other. Heat speeds up most reactions, and cold slows reactions down.

7 EXOTHERMIC

Thermite is a mixture of aluminum and iron oxide. When it is ignited at a high temperature there is an explosion, as the chemical reaction produces a sudden release of energy in the form of light, heat, and noise. Reactions that produce heat are known as exothermic reactions.

8 OXIDATION

Some chemical reactions happen around us naturally. One of the commonest reactions is oxidation—when substances gain oxygen. Oxidation is happening when metals rust, when wood burns, and when we breathe. In all these reactions, substances are reacting with oxygen from the air.

9 SOLUTIONS

A solution is a mixture in which the molecules are mixed so evenly and completely that it seems like a single substance. In a solution, however, a chemical reaction has not taken place. Neither the solute (the substance being dissolved) nor the solvent (the substance that it is dissolved in) have changed.

STATES OF MATTER

Everthing you can smell, touch, or taste is made from matter, including living things such as yourself and nonliving things such as this book. Matter is made up of atoms and anything that is not made of matter is energy. Heat, light, and sound are forms of energy. You cannot smell, touch, or taste energy, and they are not made from atoms. All matter on Earth exists in one of three states: solid, liquid, or gas.

SOLID

A solid, such as this ice sculpture, has a fixed volume and a shape that is not easy to change. Strong links hold atoms together and do not allow them to move around, as they can in a liquid and in a gas. The atoms in most solids are arranged in regular patterns that form three-dimensional shapes, such as cubes and prisms, called crystals.

GAS

A gas does not have a fixed shape or a fixed volume. It expands to fill all the space around it. Atoms in a gas can move freely in every direction. They whizz around far too fast to ever stick together.

3 LIQUID

A liquid does not have a fixed shape, but does have a fixed volume. Its atoms can move past each other, allowing the liquid to flow so that it takes the shape of its container. Atoms in a liquid are linked together more strongly than in a gas, but not as strongly as in a solid.

4 STATE TO STATE

Matter changes from one state to another when it is heated or cooled. Heating melts solids into liquids and boils liquids to form gases. Cooling condenses gases to form liquids and freezes liquids into solids. As matter changes from one state to another, the atoms within it remain the same but become arranged differently.

5 CHANGING SHAPE

Solids do not always have a fixed shape. Some solids, such as ice or glass, are brittle and will break if you hammer or crush them. Other solids, such as rubber or metals, are malleable and can be hammered, stretched, or squashed into different shapes without breaking.

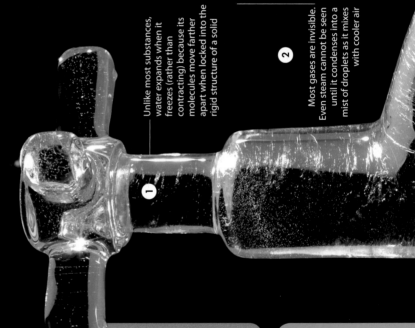

1 Unlike most substances, water expands when it freezes (rather than contracting) because its molecules move farther apart when locked into the rigid structure of a solid

2 Most gases are invisible. Even steam cannot be seen until it condenses into a mist of droplets as it mixes with cooler air

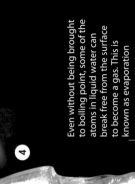

Even without being brought to boiling point, some of the atoms in liquid water can break free from the surface to become a gas. This is known as evaporation

WATER

ater is a tasteless, odorless liquid. Although it appears to be colorless, in fact, it very pale blue. Each molecule of water is made up of two hydrogen atoms and e oxygen atom, giving it the chemical formula H_2O. Water is the Earth's most mmon compound, found everywhere, from the oceans that cover 71 percent the planet to each cell of every living organism.

- Jnlike most compounds, water can exist in all three states of matter—olid, liquid, and gas—within the arth's normal range of temperatures.

- At sea level, water is liquid between 2 and 212°F (0 and 100°C), but elow 32°F (0°C), it solidifies into ce, and above 212°F (100°C), it ecomes gaseous water vapor.

- Jnlike most other substances, water s denser when it is liquid than when t is solid—that is why ice floats on he top of water instead of sinking.

- When water freezes into ice, it xpands by nine percent of its volume with a force that can urst pipes and split rock.

- Water is essential for life, so astronomers look for it when searching for life on other planets.

- Earth is the only planet in the solar system where conditions allow water to exist in liquid form today. All the others are either too hot or too cold.

- The body of an average adult man contains more than 70 pints (40 liters) of water.

- You need about 2 quarts (2 liters) of water every day to keep healthy.

- Twenty percent of the world's population does not have access to clean, safe drinking water.

- Water is not a resource that can be used up like oil. Water from the Earth evaporates into the air, forms clouds, and falls back to Earth as rain. In areas of Earth that receive little rainfall, water can be a scarce resource.

MATERIALS

Almost everything around us is made from some sort of material. Each has different properties, such as strength or flexibility, which makes it useful for making particular products. Some materials, such as wool or stone, grow or occur naturally. Synthetic materials are manufactured. Composite materials combine the properties of two or more materials to achieve the best possible product.

Kevlar is used to reinforce helmets, so that they are light but very strong

► KEVLAR

A light, flexible, synthetic material, Kevlar is used for protective clothing, such as bulletproof vests. Kevlar molecules are arranged in long chains with strong bonds between them, which makes Kevlar five times stronger than steel.

► SILK

This natural fiber is made from the cocoon of the silkworm. Each cocoon may produce 2 miles (3 km) of silk. Silk can be woven into an extremely fine fabric and is prized for its texture and its shiny appearance.

◄ WOOL

This natural material comes from the fleece of sheep. The structure of its fibers means wool has a tendency to shrink, so it is often mixed with synthetic fibers to make easy-care fabrics.

▼ GLASS

This transparent ceramic is made by fusing sand, limestone, and soda at high temperatures, or by recycling old glass. Molten glass can be shaped in many ways, such as into windows, lenses, and threads for optical fibers.

Concrete is the main material used for modern buildings

► CONCRETE

Concrete is made by mixing sand, gravel, cement, and water. It is a liquid when freshly made, so it can be poured into a mold, where it sets to form an extremely hard and durable material.

► CARBON COMPOSITES

These materials are strong and light and can be turned into complex shapes, such as sports equipment. They are made from the carbon by-products of coal, oil, and natural gas.

Plastics can be molded into almost any shape or size

Most metals are malleable and can be bent without breaking

◄ METAL

When heated, metals can be shaped into anything from a paper clip to an aircraft. They are also good conductors of heat and suitable for carrying electricity.

◄ PLASTIC

This group of synthetic materials is made from petrochemicals. They are strong, light, cheap to make, and can be molded or shaped into flexible sheets, films, or fibers.

▼ NYLON

Developed in 1938, nylon was the first synthetic fabric. It can be produced in extremely fine threads, is cheap to manufacture, and was first used as a replacement for silk in stockings and parachutes.

Nylon rope lasts longer than one made of natural fibers

▶ RUBBER

Natural rubber is an elastic material made from latex, a milky fluid from the rubber tree. Synthetic rubber is made from petrochemicals. Rubber is used in tires and for waterproofing fabrics.

▲ CERAMIC

Ceramic materials are made by heating different types of clay to a high temperature. China, bricks, tiles, cement, and glass are all ceramics. These materials are hard, brittle, and resistant to heat.

▼ LYCRA

Synthetic fabrics are designed to have better properties than natural materials, such as cotton. Lycra is a stretchy fabric that keeps its original shape, making it perfect for sports clothes.

▼ WOOD

Wood is a strong material compared to its weight and is a good building material. It is also used for furniture and art objects because of its attractive texture. It is referred to as hardwood or softwood, depending on the type of tree it comes from.

Wood can be cut, carved, and sanded into shape

Cotton fibers are spun into threads and then woven into fabric

Hand-carved granite makes a durable kitchen tool

▶ STONE

Stone is a natural material quarried from the ground. It is hard and heavy and can withstand great pressure. Stone may be cut using diamond saws or extremely high-pressure jets of water.

▲ COTTON

Cotton is a natural material produced from the long, flexible fibers in the fluffy seedpods of the cotton plant. The fabric is soft, comfortable to wear, and there is no static buildup as there is with some synthetic fabrics.

GRAVITY

The force of gravity is a force of attraction that exists between all objects with mass, from microscopic atoms to stars and planets. On Earth, gravity can be seen when objects fall to the ground, pulled by an invisible force. In space, the force of gravity keeps the Moon in its orbit around the Earth, keeps planets in orbit around the stars, and holds huge clusters of stars together as galaxies.

NEWTON'S DISCOVERY

An apple falling from a tree is said to have inspired English scientist Isaac Newton (1642–1727) to explore the force of gravity. He developed a theory stating that every mass attracts every other mass by a force between both masses. The more massive an object is and the nearer it is, the greater its gravitational attraction.

BIRTH OF A STAR

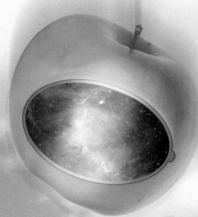

A star is born inside a cloud of dust and gas in space called a nebula. The dust and gas begin to clump together, forming a core. The clump's gravitational attraction increases as its mass increases, dragging in more and more matter. The center, or core, becomes so massive and dense that nuclear fusion begins, and the star begins to shine.

MOON AND TIDES

As the Moon orbits the Earth, its gravity tugs at the water in the oceans, making a mass of water bulge toward the Moon. The force of the Earth's spin creates a matching bulge on the other side of the Earth. These bulges cause the regular rise and fall of the water level at the sea's edge that we know as tides.

MASS AND WEIGHT

These are not the same. An object's mass is the amount of matter it contains. An object's weight is the force exerted on its mass by gravity. This means that on the Moon, where gravity is just one-sixth of Earth's gravity, an astronaut will weigh one-sixth as much as he weighs on Earth, although his mass is the same.

ZERO GRAVITY

In orbit around Earth, astronauts become weightless and float around their spacecraft as if gravity did not exist. In fact, gravity is still pulling the astronauts and their spacecraft toward Earth, but as the spacecraft travels forward, it is also continually "falling" as it follows the curve of the Earth. The craft and astronauts are in a state of free-fall, but falling without ever reaching the ground.

CENTER OF GRAVITY

An object's center of gravity is the point at which it balances. An object with a low center of gravity is more stable—so a sports car is more stable than a double-decker bus. The secret to driving a car on two wheels is to ensure that the center of gravity remains above the wheels—any farther over and the car will tip over.

EINSTEIN'S THEORY

German-born scientist Albert Einstein (1879–1955) developed a theory of relativity to explain how gravity works in space. He compared space and time to a sheet of flexible rubber that everything in the universe rests on. Massive objects like stars make a big dip in the rubber. Less massive objects like planets fall into these large dips and so are trapped orbiting stars. The dips create the effect we call gravity.

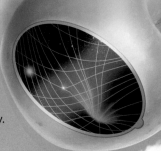

AIR RESISTANCE

In a vacuum, gravity causes everything to fall at the same speed. However, if an apple and a feather are dropped from the same height in the Earth's atmosphere, the apple will fall faster. As they fall, objects are slowed down by air resistance, created by friction between the air and the object. The speed an object falls depends on the balance between gravity's pull and the air's resistance.

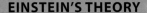

BLACK HOLES

When a massive star dies, its core may collapse. As it shrinks, the core becomes ever denser and forms a region of space called a black hole. The force of gravity in a black hole is so strong that anything entering it is swallowed up, including light. Although invisible, black holes can be identified by the effect their gravity has on everything around them. Material being sucked into the hole heats up, emitting X-rays that can be detected by X-ray telescopes.

DYNAMICS

Every object tends to resist any change in its speed or direction. This property is called inertia. An object's motion is only changed when a force, such as a push or pull, is applied. A heavy, fast-moving object is described as having lots of momentum. The more momentum something has, the more difficult it is to stop. A moving object also possesses kinetic (movement) energy. The principles of dynamics, or how forces make things move, were explained by scientist Isaac Newton (1642–1722) in his three laws of motion.

NEWTON'S FIRST LAW

The first law states that an object will stay still or continue to move at the same speed and in the same direction unless a force acts upon it. When cars approach each other in a crash-test laboratory, they move forward steadily. The dummies inside each car are carried along at the same speed as the car.

❶ INERTIA

If the dummy has no seatbelt, inertia will keep it moving forward at the same speed until it is stopped by part of the car that has been slowed down by the impact—such as the windshield.

NEWTON'S SECOND LAW

This states that when a force acts on an object, it makes the object change speed or direction. As the two cars collide, the front of each car exerts a force on the other car, slowing it down. The dummies inside are slowed down as they experience the force of the seatbelt.

NEWTON'S THIRD LAW

The third law of motion says that when a force acts on an object, the object reacts by pulling or pushing back with equal force, but in the opposite direction. So, it is impossible for one car to push on the other without experiencing a push back with equal force.

❷ COLLISION

When two cars collide, kinetic energy is converted to other forms of energy, such as heat and sound, as the fronts of the cars crumple. This is called an inelastic collision.

❸ MOMENTUM

If a heavy truck collides with a car, the lorry's greater momentum pushes the car along for some distance, but cars of equal weight and speed are halted, as their equal but opposite momenta cancel out.

MAGNETISM

Magnetism is an invisible force that attracts (draws toward itself) or repels (pushes away) certain materials. Any object that can attract or repel magnetic materials is classed as a magnet. The area around a magnet that is influenced by its magnetism is referred to as its magnetic field. It is strongest at the "poles" (usually the ends) of the magnet. Opposite magnetic poles will attract each other, while like magnetic poles repel each other. Planet Earth has its own magnetic field, driven by the molten material that circulates beneath the surface.

The two silver ends of a horseshoe magnet are the north and south pole

Near this magnet the scissors are temporarily magnetic so there is attraction

The magnetic north pole is in northern Canada, about 1,000 miles (1,600 km) from the geographic North Pole

1 **MAGNETIC MATERIALS**

When an unmagnetized magnetic material is placed in a magnetic field it becomes a magnet itself, either temporarily or permanently. Materials such as nickel and iron are easily magnetized and demagnetized and are known as soft magnets. Alloys (mixtures) of iron, nickel, and aluminum are difficult to demagnetize and are referred to as hard, or permanent magnets.

2 **MAGNETIC STRENGTH**

The strength of the attraction that holds all these objects together can also be used in industry. Large cranes with a lifting magnet are used to move tons of scrap metals and old cars, as well as to load heavy machine parts.

3 **MAGNETIC EARTH**

Electric currents circulating inside Earth as the planet rotates cause it to act like a giant magnet, with a magnetic field that extends thousands of miles into space. Earth has magnetic poles, which are near, but not the same as, the geographic North and South poles.

4 **MAGNETIC SCAN**

In a magnetic resonance imaging (MRI) scan, a patient is placed in a magnetic field and radio waves are passed through the body, causing molecules within body tissues to vibrate. Different tissues vibrate in different ways, allowing each part to be seen clearly.

This MRI scan shows soft tissues as well as bones

Steel pins are attracted by the magnetic force of the lodestone

Iron filings push away because like poles repel

North pole

North pole

North pole

South pole

Iron filings join because opposite poles attract

The red needle on this compass points to the magnetic north pole

5 LODESTONE

Nearly 3,000 years ago, people discovered that a strange type of rock could attract iron objects. This rock, called lodestone or magnetite, is a form of iron oxide with strong natural magnetism. The first compasses were made from lodestone.

7 ATTRACTION

Iron filings sprinkled around a magnet will reveal the magnetic force field in action. If you bring two magnets together so that a north pole is facing a south pole, then the filings will bridge the gap, showing attraction.

6 REPULSION

If you bring two magnets together with their two north poles or two south poles facing, you can feel the pushing force between them as their magnetic fields come into contact and the like poles repel each other.

8 COMPASS

In use from around the 12th century, a compass contains a magnetic needle, which is free to rotate on a pivot. The compass needle will always align itself with the Earth's magnetic field, so that its needle points toward the magnetic north pole.

- Electricity is generated when coils of wire are rotated in a magnetic field. This forces electrons along the wire to form an electric current.

- A current only flows if it has a circuit to travel around. A current needs a conductor to flow through, something to power, and, usually, an energy source to drive the current.

- All conductors have a certain resistance to the flow of an electric current. When a conductor resists the current, the electrical energy is turned into heat.

- Materials with electrons that cannot move are unable to conduct electricity and are known as insulators. Electric wire is insulated with plastic or rubber.

- In power plants, the force to rotate the coils is provided by water power (hydroelectricity), or by steam heated by oil, coal, gas, or the process of nuclear fission.

ELECTRICITY

From running a home computer to lighting up the world's cities at night, electricity powers almost everything that we use. Electricity is one of the most useful forms of energy because it can be readily converted into other types of energy such as light, heat, or movement. Electricity results from the behavior of tiny particles, called electrons, each of which possesses an electric charge. When an electric charge builds up in one place it is called static electricity. If the charge flows from place to place it is known as current electricity.

1 NORTH AMERICA

With only five percent of the world's population, the US uses almost 25 percent of the world's electricity, mostly coal-driven. In Canada, hydroelectric generators use moving water to create electricity.

2 SOUTH AMERICA

Some countries in this continent produce electricity using ethanol, a renewable "green" fuel made from the by-products of sugar cane.

3 ANTARCTICA

Electricity here is provided by diesel-powered generators at each research base. As the windiest place on Earth, some bases have begun to install windmills to generate additional electricity.

- Electricity leaves power plants through metal cables on tall pylons. The power is sent out at a much higher voltage than is used in most homes.

- Before arriving in a city, the voltage is reduced by a transformer at a substation. It then travels across the city in cables under the streets.

- In some earthquake-prone cities, such as Tokyo, Japan, electricity is carried in overhead cables. Underground cables would be too prone to earthquake damage.

- The human body is full of electricity. The 100 billion nerve cells in each person's brain work by sending messages in bursts of electricity (impulses).

- A flash of lightning is a giant spark of electricity driven by static electricity (charge) that builds up inside a cloud from a collision of ice crystals and water droplets.

- Static electricity also occurs when you comb your hair or take off a synthetic sweater. It is caused by two things rubbing together and creating a charge.

NIGHT LIGHT

This image was compiled from pictures taken by a military weather satellite. It shows how light from the world's cities is visible from space.

4 EUROPE
Many European countries now rely on nuclear power for electricity. France leads the way, with 78 percent of its electricity coming from nuclear power.

5 AFRICA
Only 10 percent of Africa's population have a regular supply of electricity. Instead, millions of people gather wood and dung to burn for cooking and heating.

6 ASIA
China is the second largest consumer of oil, and the country relies on hydroelectric power from the Three Gorges Dam project as an alternative energy source.

7 AUSTRALIA
Energy consumption in Australia is dominated by coal, which fuels most of the country's electricity. The majority is mined in Queensland and New South Wales.

ELECTROMAGNETIC SPECTRUM

Energy spreads in waves of electromagnetic radiation, like the ripples on a pond. It travels through space at the speed of light, around 185,000 miles/sec (300,000 km/sec). Although energy always travels through space at the same speed, its wavelength (the distance between any two peaks or troughs of the waves) can vary. Short waves, such as X-rays, carry high amounts of energy that can penetrate the human body, while longer, lower energy waves, such as light, cannot. Aside from visible light, all electromagnetic waves are invisible. Together, these waves make up a continuous band of energy known as the electromagnetic spectrum.

GAMMA RAYS

Gamma rays are produced by radioactivity, such as a nuclear explosion. They have a short wavelength and carry large amounts of energy. They are very harmful to humans, but are used to treat cancer by killing damaged cells.

X-RAYS

These high-energy waves can pass through materials such as flesh and suitcase plastic, but not through bone or metal objects. This makes them a valuable tool for examining bones in hospitals and searching for weapons in airports.

ULTRAVIOLET RAYS

With a slightly shorter wavelength than visible violet light, ultraviolet rays also carry more energy than visible light. Ultraviolet rays emitted by the Sun and tanning beds can damage skin not protected by sunblock, causing sunburn.

VISIBLE LIGHT

The Sun emits most of its energy as visible light, which can be split into the colors of the rainbow. Earth's atmosphere allows visible light through, while blocking more harmful wavelengths. Visible light is vital for life. Without it, plants could not grow.

WAVELENGTHS

The difference between wavelengths at either end of the electromagnetic spectrum is immense. The wavelength of gamma rays is only a fraction of the size of an atom, while radio waves at the opposite end of the spectrum can be thousands of miles long.

INFRARED RAYS

Just beyond the visible red in the spectrum is infrared, which can be felt as heat. Often, when heat energy moves it is transported by infrared waves. Infrared satellite images of the Earth's surface are used by weather forecasters to determine temperatures.

MICROWAVES

These have much longer wavelengths than visible light. Longer wavelength microwaves are used in a microwave oven. Shorter wavelength microwaves are used in radar systems that help ships and planes navigate by locating traffic and obstacles.

RADIO WAVES

These are the longest in the spectrum. Many forms of communication, such as TV, cell phones, and radio, use radio waves, with different wavelengths carrying different signals. Radio waves from outer space are picked up by radio telescopes and used in studies of the universe.

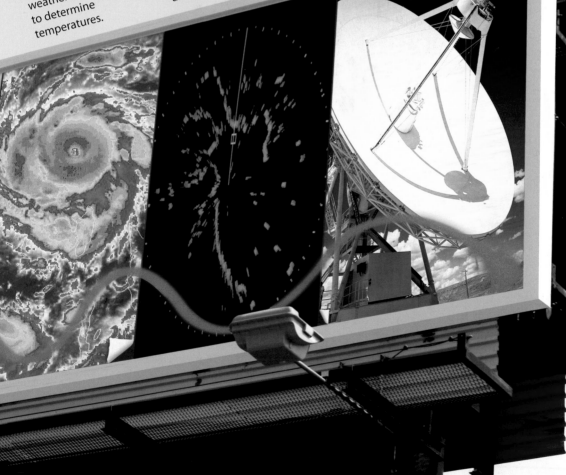

VIOLET

Light at the violet end of the visible spectrum has a shorter wavelength and higher frequency than light at the red end of the spectrum.

SYMBOLISM

We use colors as symbols to represent different ideas in culture and religion. However, the meaning of colors may vary. For example, in some cultures brides wear red, whereas in others they wear white.

Gifts of money are given in red packets at Chinese New Year, because red is the color of luck

COLOR

Light is the visible part of the electromagnetic spectrum. We see different wavelengths of light as different colors. The surfaces of objects absorb some wavelengths and reflect others. A white object looks white because it reflects all the wavelengths that fall on it. A black object absorbs all the wavelengths, so it appears dark.

Red food packaging is believed to cause feelings of hunger

COMPLEMENTARY COLORS

If the colors of the spectrum are arranged in order on a color wheel, colors located opposite each other, such as orange and blue, are called complementary colors. When complementary colors are presented side by side, they appear at their brightest.

Yellow New York taxis are easy to spot in the distance

REAL COLORS

The light from most objects is made up of a range of wavelengths. An object that looks yellow might reflect 80 percent of the light at the yellow wavelength, but also smaller amounts of other color wavelengths.

COLOR BLINDNESS

Our ability to detect colors depends on cells on the eye's retina, which are sensitive to specific wavelengths of light. The cells that detect certain parts of the spectrum are missing or inactive in a color-blind person.

A yellow object absorbs all the wavelengths except yellow, which it reflects back to our eyes. The band of visible colors that make up light is known as the spectrum. Each shade blends into the next, but we usually divide the spectrum into seven colors: red, orange, yellow, green, blue, indigo, and violet.

INTENSITY

On a sunny day, things appear colorful because our eyes can see differences in the wavelengths of light. On a dark day, less light enters the eyes, so we cannot distinguish wavelengths as easily and colors look dull.

SPLITTING WHITE LIGHT

When white light passes through a block of glass called a prism, different wavelengths refract (bend) different amounts, so the light splits showing the colors of the spectrum. When light passes through raindrops this effect creates a rainbow.

Green plants contain a green pigment called chlorophyll

MACHINES

Simple machines make it easier for people to perform tasks, such as lifting or pulling, which would be difficult to do with muscle strength alone. There are six types of simple machines: the wheel, the screw, the lever, the pulley, the inclined plane, and the wedge. These machines change a force into a bigger or smaller force, or alter the direction in which a force acts. The most basic tools, such as crowbars or shovels, are simple machines.

WHEEL (GEAR)

Gears are toothed wheels that mesh and turn together, changing the strength, speed, or direction of a force. A force on the axle of a small gear driving a large gear will lead to a bigger turning force on the axle of the large gear.

SCREW

The spiral thread on a screw changes a turning force into a much stronger up or down force. The screw has to be turned many times to create just a small up or down movement.

LEVER

Most levers magnify the force applied to them, making it easier to move a load. A lever turns around a fixed point called a pivot. The farther from the pivot the force is applied, the easier it is to move the load.

PULLEY

A pulley is a rope looped around a wheel to make a load easier to lift or move. The more ropes and wheels are used, the less force is needed to lift the load, but the farther the rope has to be pulled.

Pivot

As the screw turns, the longer end of the lever is forced down

As the large gear wheel moves, it turns the screw

The rope pulls the cart up to the highest point on the inclined plane

Turning the smaller gear wheel turns the larger wheel, which winds in the rope

5 INCLINED PLANE

This is a flat surface with ends at different heights. Moving an object up an inclined plane reduces the amount of force needed to lift it up, but increases the distance it has to travel.

6 WEDGE

This triangular object is used as a blade to split something or, inserted under an object, to lift it. As a downward force is exerted on the wedge, its widening shape produces a sideways force on the object.

7 CART WHEELS

These wheels allow the cart to move smoothly up the ramp. Unlike gear wheels (1), these are not classified as machines, because they do not change the size of the force applied to them to help do something.

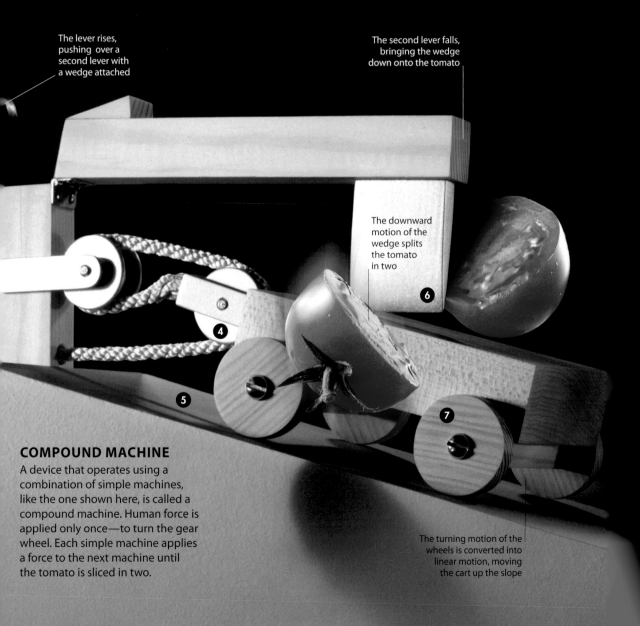

The lever rises, pushing over a second lever with a wedge attached

The second lever falls, bringing the wedge down onto the tomato

The downward motion of the wedge splits the tomato in two

COMPOUND MACHINE

A device that operates using a combination of simple machines, like the one shown here, is called a compound machine. Human force is applied only once—to turn the gear wheel. Each simple machine applies a force to the next machine until the tomato is sliced in two.

The turning motion of the wheels is converted into linear motion, moving the cart up the slope

ROBOTS

A robot is a machine that appears to think and act for itself. The simplest type of robot is a mechanical toy, or automaton, which has been programmed to perform a series of actions that usually have no real function. Some robots are remote-controlled devices, guided at a distance by a human operator. The most complex robots have artificial intelligence—an ability to make decisions for themselves, solve problems, and learn.

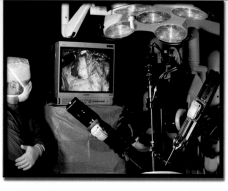

▲ SURGEON ROBOT

Surgical robots, such as da Vinci, can insert minute instruments and a viewer called an endoscope into an incision less than a half inch (1 cm) wide. The surgeon studies the operation site on a screen and moves the robot's instruments by remote control.

The ASIMO robot uses a camera in its head to detect obstacles in its path

▼ HUMANOIDS

Few robots look like the humanoid robots, or androids, of science fiction. Making a machine that can balance and move on two legs over a variety of surfaces is a technical challenge, and not necessary for most functions we need robots to perform.

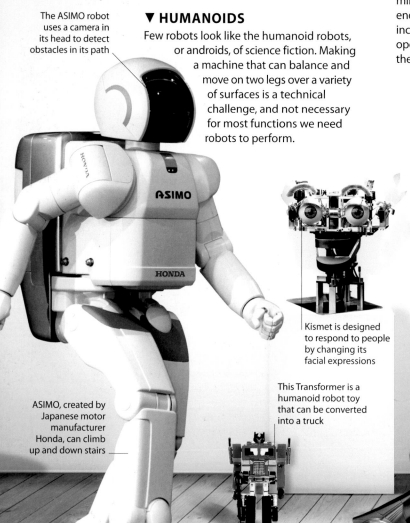

ASIMO, created by Japanese motor manufacturer Honda, can climb up and down stairs

Kismet is designed to respond to people by changing its facial expressions

This Transformer is a humanoid robot toy that can be converted into a truck

Mitsubishi's seabream fish mimics the energy-efficient motion of a real fish

▲ ANIMAL ROBOTS

Robots that imitate the way different types of animals move and behave are vital steps in the development of ranges of movement that may be needed in robots of the future.

Spinybot II has spiny feet to grip onto walls, imitating the actions of climbing insects

Sony's AIBO has complex software that makes it move and behave like a dog

▶ INDUSTRIAL ARMS

Most industrial robots are computer-controlled mechanical arms. They do jobs that would be difficult or dangerous for humans, or jobs that require constant repeated actions. A robot can do all these jobs more quickly or accurately than a human—and without needing to rest.

The task of welding in a car factory is carried out by robots

▲ SPACE TRAVELERS

In space, robot spacecraft and surface vehicles called rovers are sent to explore places that are too dangerous to send human astronauts. The movements of these robots are preprogrammed or directed from Earth, though the rovers also use camera data to avoid obstacles.

▶ HELP AT HOME

Although no one yet has an android servant doing all the domestic chores, some robots are at work in homes, performing repetitive jobs such as vacuuming floors and mowing lawns. These robots are programmed to avoid hazards in their paths.

The Roomba Intelligent FloorVac has sensors to plot its vacuuming route

▼ EXPLORERS

Robot explorers are sent to investigate places on Earth where no human could survive. These robots work in searing temperatures inside volcanoes, under extreme pressure deep in the ocean, and in highly radioactive or toxic sites.

▶ MILITARY ROBOTS

Robot vehicles are useful in warfare because they can enter dangerous situations without risking lives. Robot devices conduct surveillance over enemy land and can find and dispose of bombs and landmines while the operator remains at a safe distance.

HOBO (Hazardous Ordnance Bomb Operator) carries equipment to diffuse an explosive device or explode it safely

iRobots's CoWorker Office robot takes pictures with a camera on its rotating neck

Robug III's legs allow it to cross uneven surfaces to investigate hazardous situations with an onboard camera

TRANSPORTATION

The world today is constantly on the move. It is impossible to imagine life without the planes, trains, ships, and cars that transport people and goods every day. Each of these incredible machines has been specifically designed to travel over land, through the air, and under or over the water.

▼ BY AIR

To travel through the air, aircraft must overcome the force of gravity, which pulls them toward the ground. They achieve this with the help of curved wings and rotors, which produce an upward force called lift as they pass through the air.

As the rotor blades turn they generate lift to pull the helicopter upward

Front landing wheels

Boeing 777-300ER

Elevator flaps control the up-and-down movement of the plane

Rudder flap on the back of the tail fin balances plane as it turns

Hinged surfaces, called ailerons, tilt the plane to make it turn

▼ BY ROAD

Most road vehicles have an internal-combustion engine that burns fuel to make the power that turns the wheels. In a car, the engine is usually in the front and drives either the front or the back wheels. In a motorcycle, the engine is placed between the two wheels.

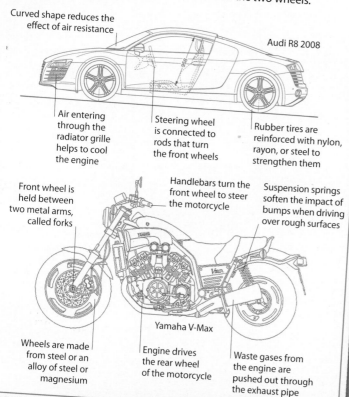

Curved shape reduces the effect of air resistance

Audi R8 2008

Air entering through the radiator grille helps to cool the engine

Steering wheel is connected to rods that turn the front wheels

Rubber tires are reinforced with nylon, rayon, or steel to strengthen them

Front wheel is held between two metal arms, called forks

Handlebars turn the front wheel to steer the motorcycle

Suspension springs soften the impact of bumps when driving over rough surfaces

Yamaha V-Max

Wheels are made from steel or an alloy of steel or magnesium

Engine drives the rear wheel of the motorcycle

Waste gases from the engine are pushed out through the exhaust pipe

Arm, called a pantograph, picks up electric power from overhead cables

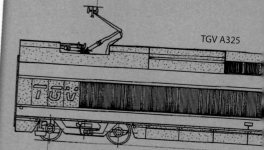

TGV A325

Trucks have four or more wheels, and large shock-absorbers to give a smooth ride

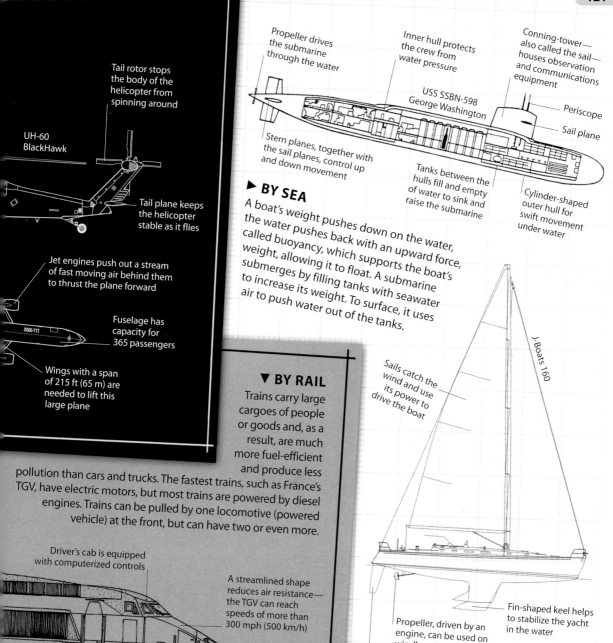

Tail rotor stops the body of the helicopter from spinning around

UH-60 BlackHawk

Tail plane keeps the helicopter stable as it flies

Jet engines push out a stream of fast moving air behind them to thrust the plane forward

Fuselage has capacity for 365 passengers

Wings with a span of 215 ft (65 m) are needed to lift this large plane

Propeller drives the submarine through the water

Inner hull protects the crew from water pressure

Conning-tower—also called the sail—houses observation and communications equipment

USS SSBN-598 George Washington

Periscope

Sail plane

Stern planes, together with the sail planes, control up and down movement

Tanks between the hulls fill and empty of water to sink and raise the submarine

Cylinder-shaped outer hull for swift movement under water

▶ BY SEA

A boat's weight pushes down on the water, the water pushes back with an upward force, called buoyancy, which supports the boat's weight, allowing it to float. A submarine submerges by filling tanks with seawater to increase its weight. To surface, it uses air to push water out of the tanks.

▼ BY RAIL

Trains carry large cargoes of people or goods and, as a result, are much more fuel-efficient and produce less pollution than cars and trucks. The fastest trains, such as France's TGV, have electric motors, but most trains are powered by diesel engines. Trains can be pulled by one locomotive (powered vehicle) at the front, but can have two or even more.

Driver's cab is equipped with computerized controls

A streamlined shape reduces air resistance—the TGV can reach speeds of more than 300 mph (500 km/h)

Sails catch the wind and use its power to drive the boat

J-Boats 160

Fin-shaped keel helps to stabilize the yacht in the water

Propeller, driven by an engine, can be used on windless days

Rudder is used to steer the boat

SCIENTISTS

Scientists study the universe in order to find out how and why things happen. There are many different branches of science, such as physics, chemistry, and astronomy. Scientists make careful observations of the phenomena they are studying. They construct possible explanations for their observations, known as theories or hypotheses. Then they experiment to test whether their theories are accurate.

1 SIR ISAAC NEWTON

English physicist and mathematician Newton (1642–1727) proposed the laws of motion that explain how forces move objects, and went on to devise a theory of gravity. Newton also studied optics, the science of light, and explained how white light is made up of many colors.

2 MARIE CURIE

Marie Curie (1867–1934) was born in Poland, but carried out her investigations into radioactivity in Paris with her French husband, Pierre. She discovered the elements (substances) polonium and radium in 1898 and won two Nobel Prizes. Marie Curie died of leukaemia, probably due to long exposure to radiation.

3 LUIGI GALVANI

Italian scientist Galvani (1737–98) studied the role of electrical impulses in animal tissue by experimenting on frogs. Although his theory that the electricity was coming from the animal tissue was wrong, his discoveries lead to the invention of the battery by Alessandro Volta.

4 ALBERT EINSTEIN

Einstein (1879–1955) was born in Germany but after Hitler came to power, he fled to the United States. Einstein revolutionized physics with his studies of relativity, which show how matter, energy, space, and time are connected. Einstein was awarded the Nobel Prize for Physics in 1921.

In 1610, Galileo improved the newly invented telescope and used it to discover Jupiter's moons, Io, Europa, Ganymede, and Callisto

Pascal's mechanical calculator could only add up, and was not very accurate

The Bunsen burner, an adjustable gas burner used in science experiments, is named after German scientist Robert Bunsen (1811–99)

The unit of electric current known as ampère or amp is named after French scientist André Marie Ampère (1775–1836)

5 ALEC JEFFREYS

British geneticist Jeffreys (born 1950) discovered that each individual has certain distinctive patterns of DNA and worked out how to make images of these DNA sequences. He pioneered DNA fingerprinting, used by forensic scientists in criminal investigations to identify people from traces of DNA.

6 BLAISE PASCAL

Frenchman Pascal (1623–62) explored many practical applications of science and mathematics. He invented a mechanical calculator, a device made up of dials and gears, as well as a type of syringe. He also did experiments with air pressure.

7 GALILEO

Italian astronomer and mathematician, Galileo (1564–1642) was the first person to use a telescope for studying the sky. He discovered the four largest satellites of Jupiter, today known as the Galilean moons.

8 COPERNICUS

Polish astronomer Copernicus (1473–1543) is considered to be the founder of modern astronomy. His studies of the orbits of the planets revealed that the Sun is at the center of the solar system. At the time, the predominant view was that the Earth was the center of the universe.

9 ALESSANDRO VOLTA

In 1800, research into electric currents led Italian physicist Volta (1745–1827) to invent the battery. Volta's battery, or "voltaic pile" was the first reliable means of producing an electric current, and so made it easier to perform further experiments with electricity.

10 BENJAMIN FRANKLIN

US statesman, writer, and scientist Franklin (1706–90) conducted research into electricity. He proved that lightning is an electrical current and suggested the use of lightning conductors to protect buildings from lightning strikes.

3 **4**

DNA fingerprinting reveals a broken pattern which varies between individuals

5

The voltaic pile was constructed from a pile of metal and brine-soaked cardboard disks

Copernicus used an armillary sphere like this to demonstrate his theory that the Sun is at the center of the solar system

8

9

Franklin proposed that a kite flown in a thunderstorm would become electrically charged, proving that lightning was electricity

10

QUICK QUIZ

What can you remember about Science and Technology?
Jot down your answers, then check them on pp.296–97.

1 **Magnesium** is a silvery alkaline-earth metal. If you burn it, what **color** would the **flame** be?
- Ⓐ Yellow
- Ⓑ White
- Ⓒ Blue
- Ⓓ Red

2 The **hydrangea shrub** in your yard has **blue flowers**. What does this tell you about the soil?
- Ⓐ It is acidic
- Ⓑ It is poisonous
- Ⓒ It is neutral
- Ⓓ It is alkaline

3 **Helmets** need to be light but **very strong**. Which **material** is commonly used to **reinforce** them?

4 If you are **stung** by a **bee**, you may be advised to wash the sting with an **alkaline soap**. How does it help?
- Ⓐ Alkali neutralizes the acid injected by the bee
- Ⓑ Washing distracts you from the pain
- Ⓒ It stops the bee from stinging you again
- Ⓓ Washing kills any germs that may infect the wound

5 When **two oxygen (O) atoms** bond together, they **form** molecules of **oxygen (O_2)** gas. Which gas forms when **three oxygen atoms** bond together?

6 Why did the **apple** you cut in the morning **turn brown** by the evening?

7 What does a **radar** system use to help **ships** and planes **navigate**?
- Ⓐ Radio waves
- Ⓑ Ultraviolet rays
- Ⓒ Gamma rays
- Ⓓ Microwaves

8 What **color** is **water**?
- Ⓐ Colorless
- Ⓑ Pale blue
- Ⓒ Sea green
- Ⓓ Gray

9 If you bring **two magnets together** and they **repel each other**, what does it **indicate**?
- Ⓐ You are bringing like poles together
- Ⓑ You are bringing opposite poles together
- Ⓒ One of them is not a magnet
- Ⓓ The magnets are dirty

10 Which **Polish scientist** is known as the founder of **modern astronomy**?

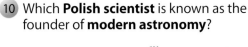

11 Why is **helium** used to fill **balloons**?
- Ⓐ It smells nice
- Ⓑ It prevents the balloon from bursting
- Ⓒ It is heavy and prevents the balloon from floating away
- Ⓓ It is lighter than air, so the balloon floats upward

12 What can you find in the **fuselage** of an **airplane**?
- Ⓐ Fuel
- Ⓑ Passengers
- Ⓒ Spare wheels
- Ⓓ Poisonous gases

13 **Match** the **molecules** to the **elements**:

- ❶
- ❷
- ❸
- ❹
- Ⓐ Sulfur
- Ⓑ Ammonia
- Ⓒ Methane
- Ⓓ Water

14 How can **scientists spot** a **black hole**?
- Ⓐ By observing the light, which can be seen getting sucked into the black hole
- Ⓑ By using an X-ray telescope to detect the X-rays the black hole emits
- Ⓒ With naked eyes; any exceptionally dark area in the night sky is a black hole
- Ⓓ It is impossible to detect a black hole

15 A **silkworm's cocoon** is made of a single continuous thread of **raw silk**. How long is it?
- Ⓐ 0.6 miles (1 km)
- Ⓑ 1.2 miles (2 km)
- Ⓒ 2 miles (3 km)
- Ⓓ 3 miles (5 km)

16 If you see the following **symbol** on a container, what does it tell you about the **substance** inside?

17 Which **color** food packaging is thought to make you **feel hungry**?
- Ⓐ Red
- Ⓑ White
- Ⓒ Blue
- Ⓓ Yellow

18 On the **Moon**, an **object** weighs **one-sixth** as much as it **weighs on Earth**. If John weighs 132 lb (60 kg) on Earth, how much will he weigh on the Moon?

19 What is said to have inspired **Isaac Newton** to explore the **force of gravity**?
- Ⓐ The ebb and flow of ocean tides
- Ⓑ Watching a Moon landing
- Ⓒ An apple falling from a tree
- Ⓓ The first balloon flight

FAST FACTS

The **smallest particle** scientists have found is the **quark**, which is less than **0.00000000000000001 m** across. It is **so small** that no one has seen one, and we only know it is there because of its **effect** on things **around it.**

The number **zero** was first used in India around 875 BCE.

The **smallest** Standard International (SI) **unit of weight** is the **yoctogram**, which was added to weigh **subatomic particles**. The **largest unit**, the **yottagram**, is used to **weigh stars** and planets—Earth weighs in at 6,000 yottagrams.

A jiffy is a *unit of time* equal to one hundredth of a second.

The **official** 1 kg weight is a **cylinder** made in 1899 from **platinum and iridium**, which is kept in Sèvres, near Paris, France.

The supercomputer Blue Gene/L operates at a speed of 596 teraflops—that's 596 trillion calculations per second.

There are **six** kinds of *quarks*, which scientists have named up, down, top, bottom, *charm*, and *strange*.

One byte in a computer's **memory** is made up of eight **bits**. A group of four bits is called a *nibble.*

With the help of **computers**, more recorded data has been produced in the last **three years** than in all of previous recorded history.

*Hydrogen is the lightest, simplest, and by far the most **common element** in the Universe—**93 percent** of all atoms are hydrogen atoms.*

Google processes more than 1 billion searches every day.

Atoms are mostly made of *empty space*. If the *nucleus* were a fly in the middle of a football field, the *electrons* would be like dust particles *flying around* in the stands.

A proton is **1,836** times **heavier** than an electron.

The **densest element**, osmium, **weighs** 13.07 oz/in³ (22.61 g/cm³).

The most powerful laser is 10 sextillion times brighter than sunshine.

Thomas Babbage came up with his idea for a *computer* when he was just *19 years old.*

Tungsten has the **highest melting point** of any metal. It remains a **solid** until the **temperature** reaches **6,192°F** (3,422°C), when it finally melts.

The internet domain name *business.com* was bought by Marc Ostrofsky in 1999 for *$7.5 million.*

Airships **float** because they are filled with **helium**, a gas that is many times **lighter** than air.

At atmospheric pressure, **carbon dioxide** turns from a **solid** into a **gas**, without melting, at -108°F (-78°C).

When a **gas condenses** into a liquid, it takes up, on average

1,300

times less space.

*The **metal lithium** is so light that it floats on water.*

Diamonds are formed from **carbon** that is **compressed** 90 miles (150 km) below the Earth's surface.

The study of large numbers is called googology.

Acid rain caused by industrial **pollution** was first noticed in the Midlands, UK, in the **19th century.**

Pure water has a **neutral pH of 7**, but **rainwater** is **acidic**, with a **pH of 6 or less.**

The *first email* was sent by American Ray Tomlinson in 1971. The *message was* sent from one *computer* to another right *next to it.*

There is the **same** amount of **water** on **Earth** now as there was **2 billion years ago.**

Sound can damage **your hearing** at 90 decibels (dB), the volume of very **heavy traffic**. It starts to become painful when it exceeds 130 dB, a **plane taking off.**

Noise is a mixture of different frequencies of sound. Musical notes have one dominant frequency. Middle C has a frequency of 256 hertz.

The scale used to measure *light intensity* uses a unit called a **candela**. It was originally based on the amount of light given out by a candle. A **flash of lightning** gives off 7.5 million candelas per sq ft (80 million per sq m).

In a vacuum, light travels at a speed of

983,571,056 ft
(299,792,458 m) per second.

On a **sunny day**, 1,000 trillion **photons** (light particles) hit an area the size of a pinhead every second.

*A normal **lightbulb** turns just five percent of the electrical energy it is powered by **into light.***

*Red is the longest visible **wavelength** of light at about 0.7 micrometers.*

Blue light travels farther through **water** than **colors** with a longer **wavelength**, such as red or green. This is why everything **looks blue** under water.

Ultrasound scans use high-frequency sound at around 10 million hertz to give **an image** of a baby in the womb.

X-ray
technology has shown that there are **three different versions** of Leonardo da Vinci's *Mona Lisa* under the visible one.

The *first ever robot* was probably built in *ancient Greece* by Archytas of Tarentum *2,500* years ago. It was a *mechanical bird* powered by *steam*.

Maglev trains are powered by **strong magnets**. The first commercial Maglev train line is in **Shanghai**, China. It covers the 19 miles (30.5 km) from the airport to the city center in just **7 minutes 20 seconds**, reaching a top speed of 268 mph (431 km/h).

The world's largest airliner, the Airbus **A380 "Superjumbo,"** can carry up to 853 passengers.

There are **5,000 robots** in the US military. They carry out dangerous work such as **bomb disposal.**

*The maximum speed (terminal velocity) of a **skydiver**, if they pull their limbs in, is **200 mph (320 km/h).***

The pocket calculator was invented in 1966 by Texas Instruments.

Wilhelm Conrad Roentgen won the first **Nobel Prize** for physics in **1901** for his discovery of **X-rays.**

Mercury is the only metal that is **liquid** at room temperature.

*Two-thirds of the **water** used in the home is used in the **bathroom**.*

It is not safe to **skate** on **ice** until it is at least **5 in** (13 cm) **thick.**

More than two-thirds of the energy stored in **fossil fuels** is lost when those fuels are burned in **power plants** to make electricity. Most of the energy is **lost** as heat.

*A plane's flight data recorder, or **black box**, is actually bright **orange** so that it is easy to spot after a crash. It can withstand temperatures of more than 2,000°F (1,000°C).*

*The world's **smallest guitar** is just 10 millionths of a meter long. It was made by Cornell University and produces **notes** 17 octaves **higher** than a normal guitar.*

English scientist Sir Isaac Newton's dog *Diamond* knocked over a **candle** and started a fire that destroyed *20 years'* worth of his work.

*The first instant camera was made by **Polaroid** in 1948.*

Newton was one of the **greatest** scientists in history. He also invented the **cat flap.**

Any **Rubik's Cube** can be solved in **26** moves or fewer.

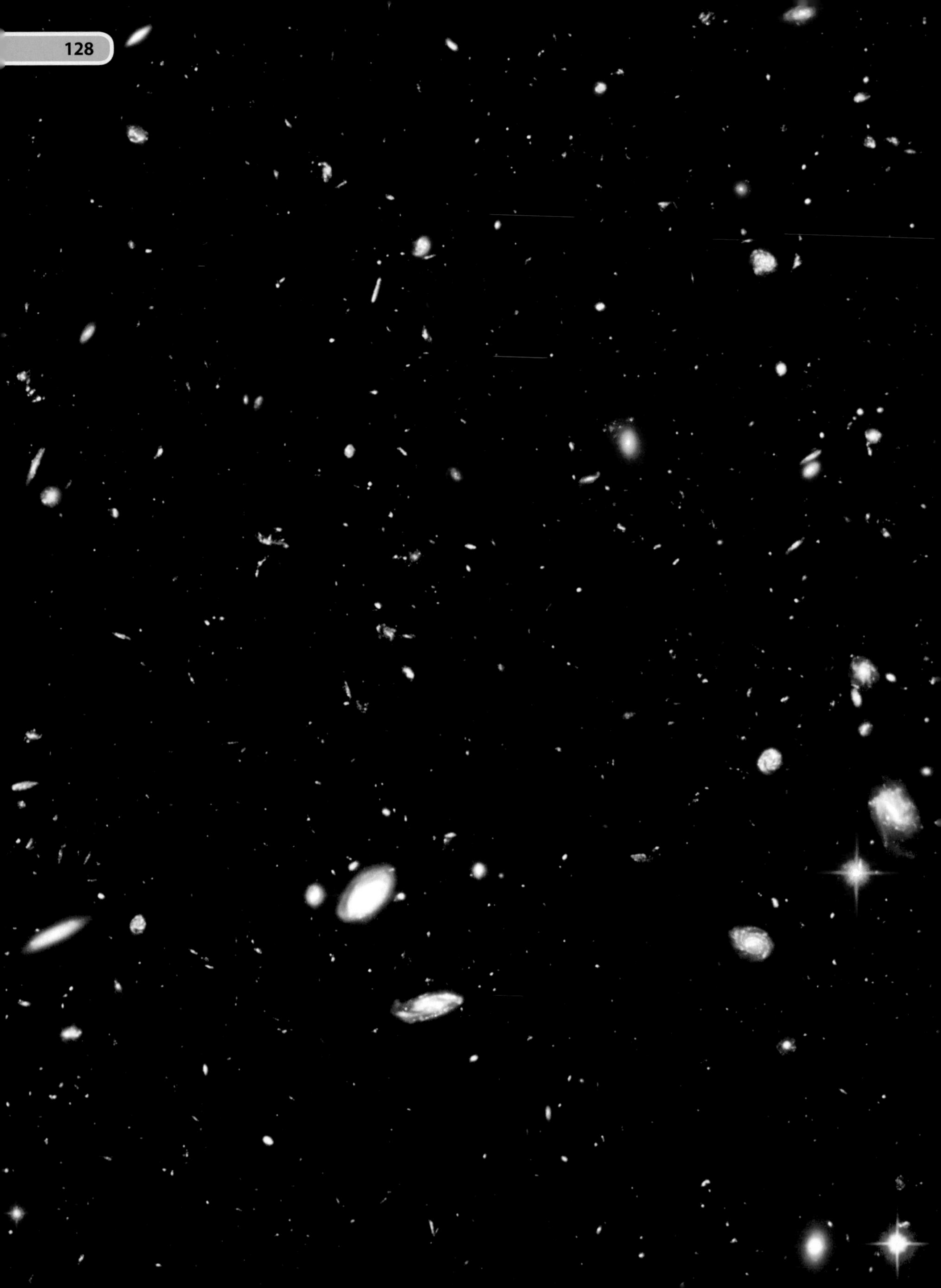

SPACE

THE FIRST GALAXIES
This view is part of an image recorded by the Hubble Space Telescope that shows about 10,000 galaxies. It is the deepest view ever taken of the universe, looking back through time to the very first galaxies.

UNIVERSE

The universe is everything that exists, from the smallest particle on Earth to the vast galaxies of deep space. Every part of it, including space and time, came into existence in the Big Bang—a huge explosion that occurred about 13.7 billion years ago. At that time, the universe looked nothing like it does today, and it has been expanding, cooling, and changing ever since. The hydrogen and helium of the very young universe formed stars, which in turn produced all the other elements in today's universe, including those that make Earth and everything on it, including you.

▼ THE BIG BANG

In the beginning, the universe was unimaginably small, dense, and incredibly hot. Within a trillionth of a second it ballooned from being smaller than an atom to bigger than a galaxy. It was made of tiny particles of energy that turned to particles of matter. Within three minutes, the universe was almost entirely made of the nuclei of hydrogen and helium atoms.

13.7 BILLION YEARS AGO

▼ FORMATION OF GALAXIES

Over millions of years, hydrogen and helium clumped together to form vast clouds. These broke into fragments, which collapsed under gravity and became stars. About one billion years after the Big Bang, a universe of dwarf galaxies had formed. These collided, merged, and changed shape to become spiral and elliptical galaxies.

12 BILLION YEARS AGO

The smallest, reddest galaxies date from about 800 million years after the Big Bang and are the oldest known

Galaxies and stars account for just 4 percent of matter in the universe

10 BILLION YEARS AGO

▶ COSMIC BACKGROUND

By looking at the heat left over from the Big Bang, known as the cosmic microwave background radiation, scientists are able to build up a picture of the early universe. This image is a heat map of the universe 380,000 years after the Big Bang. It shows that matter was not evenly distributed—the hotter areas (red) are more densely packed regions, where galaxies will form.

13.69 BILLION YEARS AGO

Colors denote minute variations in the temperature of the matter—the red areas are the hottest

▶ BIRTH OF THE SOLAR SYSTEM

The solar system formed from a cloud of gas and dust within the disk of the Milky Way galaxy. The spinning cloud, known as the solar nebula, collapsed in on itself under the force of gravity. It first formed a central sphere—the young Sun—and then the unused material surrounding the Sun formed the planets, moons, asteroids, and comets.

4.6 BILLION YEARS AGO

▼ YOUNG MILKY WAY

The Milky Way galaxy, the galaxy where we live, formed at the same time as the other galaxies. Not all of today's Milky Way stars existed at that time. Since its beginning, the galaxy has produced stars that shine brightly for millions or billions of years, but that die eventually. Their remains produce a new generation of stars.

TODAY

▶ HOME PLANET

Earth, the third rock planet from the Sun, is the only place in the universe where life is known to exist. Life started in its oceans about 3.7 billion years ago. Bacterialike cells evolved into sea creatures, then land-based plants, and animals. Humans first walked on Earth about 1 million years ago.

Water—in the oceans, lakes, atmosphere, and ice caps—has been a key factor in the development of life on Earth

4.5 BILLION YEARS AGO

▲ FORMATION OF THE MOON

Earth formed as ever-larger lumps of unused material collided and joined together. Young Earth was hit by a Mars-sized asteroid. Molten rock from the collision splashed into space. This formed a ring of rubble around the Earth, which clumped to form a large sphere—Earth's Moon.

Rock from the Earth's mantle is thrown out as the asteroid hits the planet

GALAXIES

A galaxy is a vast group of stars held together by gravity—it is estimated that there are 100–125 billion in the universe. They are not scattered randomly but exist in clusters, vast distances apart. All the galaxies together take up just two millionths of space.

1 SIZE
Galaxies are huge. The largest are more than a million light-years across (one light-year is the distance that light travels in a year). The smallest, called dwarf galaxies, are a few thousand light-years wide. Andromeda measures 250,000 light-years from side to side.

2 SHAPE
A single galaxy is made of billions or trillions of stars arranged in one of four basic shapes: spiral, barred spiral, elliptical, or irregular. Spirals and barred spirals are disk-shaped with arms of stars. In a spiral, such as Andromeda, the arms wind out from a central bulge, while in a barred spiral, they flow from the ends of a central bar of stars. Elliptical galaxies are ball-shaped. Irregular galaxies have no clear shape.

3 SPIRAL ARMS
Stars exist throughout a spiral galaxy's disk. The arms stand out because they are full of very bright young stars.

4 DUST LANES
Dense clouds and lanes of dust within the galaxy's disk hide stars from view.

5 CORE
The core of a spiral galaxy typically consists of old red and yellow stars, with a supermassive black hole in its center. Andromeda's black hole is as massive as 30 million Suns.

▲ ANDROMEDA GALAXY
Andromeda is one of the closest galaxies to our own, the Milky Way. It is a spiral galaxy 2.9 million light-years away from us—the most distant object that can be seen by the naked eye from Earth.

6 ORBITING STARS

Galaxies do not behave like solid objects. Each star follows its own orbit around the center of the galaxy. Stars in a spiral galaxy typically take a few hundred million years to make an orbit. Those farther away take longer than those closest to the core.

7 DWARF GALAXY

M110 is one of the dwarf elliptical galaxies that orbit Andromeda. It is held in its orbit by Andromeda's gravity.

▼ STAR BIRTH

Stars are formed inside vast clouds of hydrogen gas, such as the Eagle Nebula. A small fragment of cloud collapses under gravity. It becomes increasingly squashed and eventually forms a spinning ball of gas termed a protostar—the first sign of a new star.

Eagle Nebula

Detail of the Eagle Nebula

Trapezium cluster

Sirius, the brightest star in Earth's night sky

Jewel Box cluster

▼ MIDLIFE STARS

Most stars glow steadily for most of their lives. During this stage they are known as main sequence stars—the Sun is one. Planets orbit around some stars; others, such as Fomalhaut, have disks of dusty material that may form planets.

Fomalhaut

Albireo, a double star system

◄ YOUNG STARS

A protostar gets denser and hotter as its gas becomes more squashed. When its core is about 18 billion°F (10 billion°C), nuclear reactions start. Hydrogen is converted to helium, energy is produced, and the star shines. Stars born at the same time and from the same region of cloud exist as a cluster. Some clusters, like the two shown here, remain together for millions of years, but eventually their stars drift apart.

STARS

Stars are huge spinning balls of hot, luminous gas. Each one is unique because stars differ in color, temperature, size, brightness, and mass. Over time, characteristics change and the star evolves from one stage of star life to another. The key to a star's life is its mass—the amount of gas it is made from. Mass determines the star's life span, as well as its other characteristics and how these change.

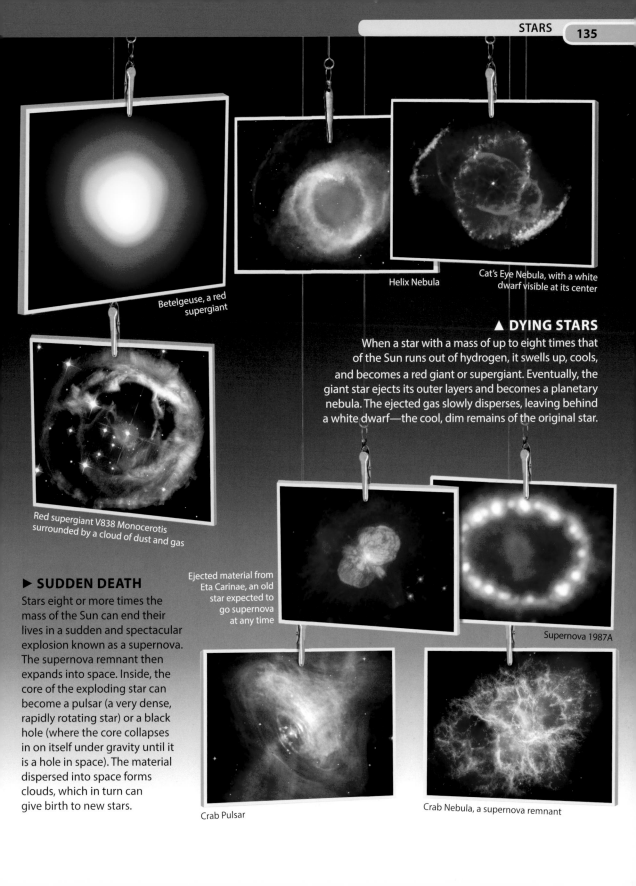

Betelgeuse, a red supergiant

Helix Nebula

Cat's Eye Nebula, with a white dwarf visible at its center

▲ DYING STARS

When a star with a mass of up to eight times that of the Sun runs out of hydrogen, it swells up, cools, and becomes a red giant or supergiant. Eventually, the giant star ejects its outer layers and becomes a planetary nebula. The ejected gas slowly disperses, leaving behind a white dwarf—the cool, dim remains of the original star.

Red supergiant V838 Monocerotis surrounded by a cloud of dust and gas

► SUDDEN DEATH

Stars eight or more times the mass of the Sun can end their lives in a sudden and spectacular explosion known as a supernova. The supernova remnant then expands into space. Inside, the core of the exploding star can become a pulsar (a very dense, rapidly rotating star) or a black hole (where the core collapses in on itself under gravity until it is a hole in space). The material dispersed into space forms clouds, which in turn can give birth to new stars.

Ejected material from Eta Carinae, an old star expected to go supernova at any time

Supernova 1987A

Crab Pulsar

Crab Nebula, a supernova remnant

CONSTELLATIONS

Stargazers have always looked for patterns in the night sky, using imaginary lines to link stars and form the shape of a creature or object. Known as constellations, these patterns help us navigate the sky. The first of them were used about 4,000 years ago. Today, Earth's sky is divided into 88 constellations. Just over half are characters from ancient Greek mythology, such as Orion and Taurus.

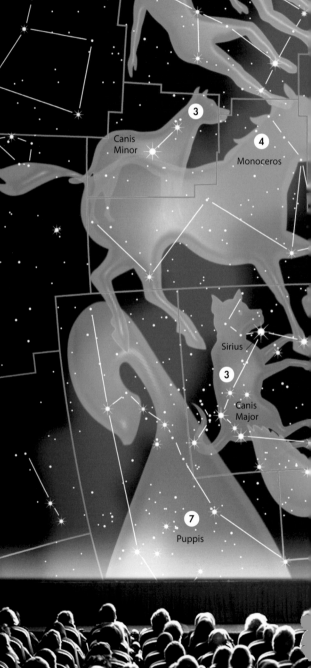

GEMINI
The two brightest stars in Gemini mark the heads of the mythological twins Castor (right) and Pollux (left). Castor's head is in fact six stars, and Pollux's is an orange-colored giant star.

TAURUS
The head of Taurus the bull is drawn around the Hyades, a V-shaped star cluster. Aldebaran, a red giant star, is the brightest of his eyes. The Pleiades star cluster marks his back.

CANIS MINOR AND MAJOR
Orion's dogs are known as Canis Major and Canis Minor. Canis Major, the larger dog, contains Sirius, sometimes called the Dog Star, the brightest star in the night sky.

MONOCEROS
The unicorn Monoceros was introduced in 1613. It lies in the path of the Milky Way—the glowing band of stars that stretches across the sky (here from bottom left to top center).

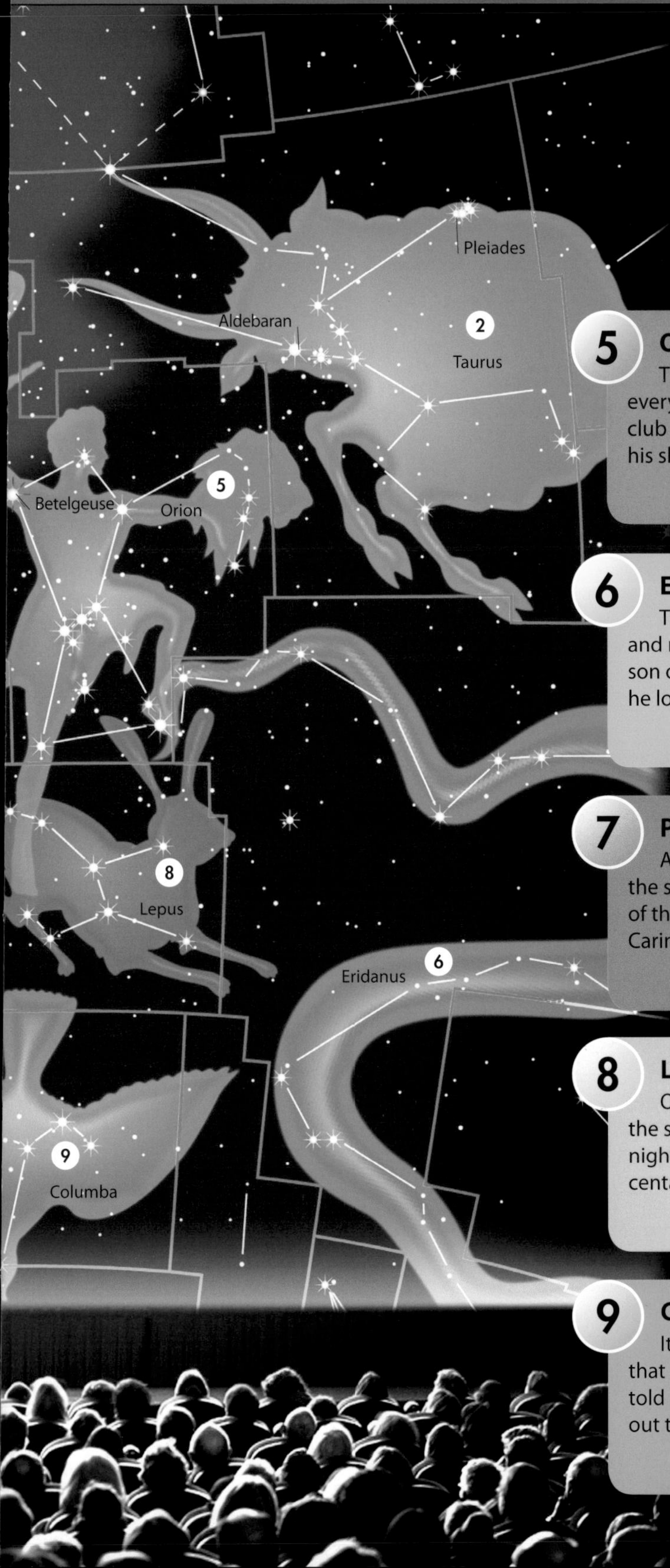

Pleiades

Aldebaran

2

Taurus

Betelgeuse

5

Orion

8

Lepus

6

Eridanus

9

Columba

NIGHT SKY

The region of sky above is centered on the constellation of Orion. Orange lines mark a constellation's boundary, white lines link its bright stars, and the imaginary pattern is shown in light blue.

5 ## ORION

The hunter Orion is visible from nearly everywhere on Earth. His raised arms hold a club and a lion's head. The red star in one of his shoulders is the red supergiant Betelgeuse.

6 ## ERIDANUS

This constellation is the sixth largest in the sky and represents the river into which Phaethon, the son of the Greek Sun god Helios, plunged when he lost control of his father's golden chariot.

7 ## PUPPIS

According to Greek myth, Puppis is the stern of the ship sailed by legendary hero Jason. Other parts of the ship are represented by the constellations Carina (the keel) and Vela (the sails).

8 ## LEPUS

Orion's larger dog chases Lepus the hare across the sky. It is one of more than 40 creatures in the night sky. There are also 13 human figures and two centaurs (half-man, half-horse).

9 ## COLUMBA

It is thought that Columba, the dove, is the bird that was sent from Noah's ark to find dry land, as told in the Bible. It may also represent a dove sent out to guide Jason in ancient Greek myth.

SUN

The Sun is the closest star to the Earth and the center of our solar system. This vast ball consists of hot luminous gas kept together by gravity. About three-quarters is hydrogen and almost all the rest is helium, with small amounts of about 90 other elements. More than half of the gas is squashed in the Sun's core, where nuclear reactions convert hydrogen to helium and in the process produce huge amounts of energy. This energy is released through the Sun's surface, most familiarly as heat and light. The Sun has been producing energy in this way for about 4.6 billion years and will do so for another 5 billion or so. This image shows the Sun not as it appears to the human eye, but in ultraviolet light.

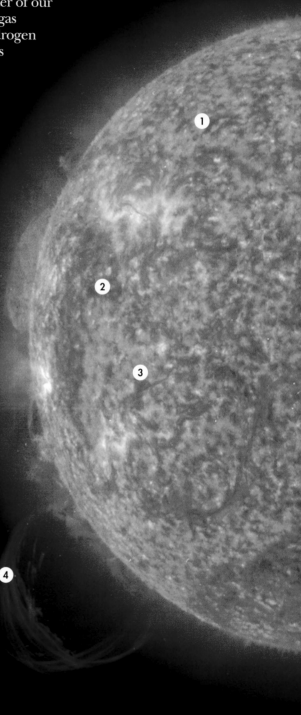

1 SIZE

The Sun is the largest body in the solar system. It measures 870,000 miles (1.4 million km) in diameter, which means that 109 Earths could fit across its face. The Sun is made of 330,000 times more material than the Earth, and 1.3 million Earths would fit inside it.

2 PHOTOSPHERE

Like other stars, the Sun is not solid but has a visible surface called the photosphere—a violent place where jets and flares of gas constantly shoot into space. It is made of 600-mile (1,000-km) wide short-lived granules of rising gas, which together resemble an orange peel.

3 TEMPERATURE

The temperature of the surface is 9,900°F (5,500°C), and it is this that gives the Sun its yellow color. Cooler stars are red, hotter ones are white. Inside is much hotter. The core is 27 million°F (15 million°C) and nuclear reactions here convert 600 million tons of hydrogen to helium every second.

4 PROMINENCE

Giant clouds and sheets of relatively cool gas that loop and arch from the surface are called prominences. This one extends out the equivalent of about 20 Earths. The gas is propelled from the surface by enormous force built up by magnetic fields inside the Sun.

5 SPICULES

Short-lived flamelike jets of gas called spicules continuously leap about 6,000 miles (10,000 km) from the surface.

6 ATMOSPHERE

Directly above the surface is the chromosphere, the inner atmosphere that extends out about 1,550 miles (2,500 km). Beyond is the corona, which extends for millions of miles into space. Only the inner corona is visible here.

7 FACULAE

The hottest areas, which appear almost white, are faculae. They are particularly active regions produced by concentrations in the Sun's magnetic field.

8 SPIN

Unlike Earth, which is solid and spins as a whole, different parts of the Sun spin in different amounts of time. The equator makes one rotation every 25 days; regions near the poles take another five or so days.

9 CORONAL MASS EJECTION

This twisting prominence was associated with a coronal mass ejection—a large bubble of billions of tons of gas that blasted away from the Sun.

PLANETS

Hurtling around the Sun are eight planets. Those closest to the Sun—Mercury, Venus, our home planet Earth, and Mars—are made of rock. The vast outer planets—Jupiter, Saturn, Uranus, and Neptune—are called "gas planets" because all we see of them is their gas. All eight travel in the same direction around the Sun. The time taken to make one circuit, or orbit, increases with distance. Mercury takes just 88 Earth days to orbit, while Neptune's longer journey takes 164.8 Earth years.

Jupiter's visible surface is the top of a deep and thick atmosphere made from bands of swirling gas

JUPITER

The largest and most massive planet, Jupiter is also the fastest spinner, rotating once on its own axis in less than 10 hours. This giant world is made mainly of hydrogen and helium, with a central rocky core. A thin faint ring encircles Jupiter, which also has a large family of moons.

SATURN

Sixth from the Sun, and second largest, is pale-yellow Saturn. Its distinctive feature is its ring system, which is made of billions of pieces of dirty water ice. Saturn is mainly hydrogen and helium with a rocky core. It has a large family of moons.

URANUS

Nineteen times the distance of Earth from the Sun, Uranus is a cold, almost featureless world bounded by a layer of haze. A sparse ring system encircles the planet's equator. Uranus is tilted on its side, so that its rings and moons seem to orbit it from top to bottom.

PLANET SCALES

Jupiter, fifth planet from the Sun, is much larger than all the other planets. It measures 88,846 miles (142,984 km) across and is made of about two and a half times as much material as all the other planets put together. The seven other planets and the three dwarf planets are shown here roughly to scale.

MERCURY

Mercury is a dry ball of rock, covered by millions of impact craters. It is the smallest planet, the closest to the Sun, and has the widest temperature range of any planet. During the day it is baking hot, but at night it is freezing cold.

5 VENUS

Second from the Sun, Venus is the hottest planet. This rock world is permanently covered by thick cloud that traps heat and makes it a gloomy planet.

6 NEPTUNE

Neptune is the most distant, coldest, and windiest of all eight planets. Like Uranus, it is made mainly of water-, methane-, and ammonia ices, with an atmosphere of hydrogen-rich gas. It is encircled by a thin ring system and has a family of moons.

7 MARS

Sometimes called the "red planet," Mars is the most distant rocky planet and a cold, dry world. It has polar ice caps, giant volcanoes, frozen desert, and deep canyons, formed in the distant past. Mars has also two small moons.

8 EARTH

The only place known to have life is Earth, the largest of the rocky planets and the third planet from the Sun. It is also the only planet with liquid water. Movements in the Earth's crust are constantly changing its surface. Earth has one moon.

A thin layer of smoggy haze gives Saturn's banded atmosphere a muted appearance

The ring pieces, which range in size from dust grains to boulders several yards across, reflect sunlight well and make the rings easy to see

The blue coloring of Uranus is due to methane in its atmosphere

9 DWARF PLANETS

The solar system has three known dwarf planets—small, roundish objects that orbit the Sun among other objects. Eris and Pluto orbit beyond Neptune as part of the Kuiper Belt—a belt of rock-and-ice objects. Ceres orbits between Mars and Jupiter within the Main Belt of asteroids.

MOONS

The solar system has more than 160 moons orbiting six of the planets—only Mercury and Venus are moonless. They range in size from Ganymede, a satellite of Jupiter, which is larger than Mercury, to Jupiter's [small]e, only 1.2 miles (2 km) across. All are [m]ade of rock, or rock and ice, and many [h]ave surfaces littered with impact craters, [f]ormed when the moons were bombarded [b]y asteroids in the past. Nineteen solar-[s]ystem moons are more than 250 miles [400 km] wide. These large moons are [r]ound but the more numerous smaller [m]oons are irregular in shape.

1 The Moon

Oceanus Procellarum (Ocean of Storms) is a vast lava-covered plain

2 Io

Dark spots are major active volcanic centers—more than 80 have been identified

3 Europa

4 Ganymede

Callisto's icy surface is covered by impact craters

Callisto

A layer of smoglike haze in the upper atmosphere gives Titan its distinctive orange color

5 Titan

Tethys

Enceladus

Dione

Mimas

Rhea

Iapetus

7

6 Titania

Miranda

Uneven surface may be a result of the moon shattering then reassembling

Umbriel

Oberon

Ariel

Long faults with icy floors formed when Ariel's crust expanded

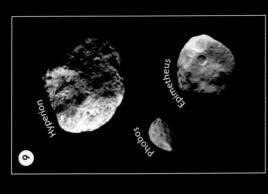

Hyperion

Epimetheus

Phobos

9

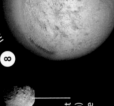

Proteus

Triton

8

Small Proteus, just
273 miles (440 km)
across, orbits Neptune

THE MOON

The Moon is Earth's only natural satellite. It is about a quarter the size of the Earth and the fifth largest of all moons. The surface of this dry ball of rock is covered in impact craters.

IO

Colorful Io is the most volcanic moon in the solar system. Its surface is constantly being renewed as molten rock erupts through its thin silicate-rock crust, and fast-moving columns of cold gas and frost grains shoot up from surface cracks.

EUROPA

This is one of Jupiter's four largest moons, along with Ganymede, Callisto, and Io. These four moons are named the Galileans after Galileo Galilei, one of the first astronomers to see them. Europa's surface has brown grooves that crisscross the blue-gray water ice.

GANYMEDE

At 3,267 miles (5,262 km) across, Ganymede is the largest moon in the solar system and belongs to the largest family of moons—the moons of Jupiter. Astronomers know of 63, but the number is likely to rise as smaller moons are detected. Ganymede is made of rock and ice with an icy crust.

5 TITAN

Titan is the largest of Saturn's 60 moons. On its surface are bright highlands, dark plains, and methane lakes and seas. It is the only moon with a substantial atmosphere, which is rich in nitrogen and extends out for hundreds of miles.

6 TITANIA

Titania is the largest of the 27 moons orbiting Uranus. Titania and the planet's other major moons, Oberon, Umbriel, Ariel, and Miranda, are named after characters in English literature. Impact craters and large cracks are seen on its gray, icy surface.

7 IAPETUS

Iapetus is a moon of contrasts. Most of its crater-covered terrain is bright and icy, but the rest appears to be coated by a dark material. It is one of Saturn's six major moons, along with Rhea, Dione, Tethys, Enceladus, and Mimas.

8 TRITON

Triton is by far the largest of Neptune's 13 moons, a rock-and-ice ball with a young, icy surface. It is nicknamed the cantaloupe because its linear grooves, ridges, and depressions resemble a melon's skin.

9 SMALL MOONS

Most moons are less than 250 miles (400 km) across and irregular in shape, like Saturn's Epimetheus and Hyperion. Many of these smaller moons, like Mars's two moons Phobos and Deimos, started off as asteroids.

► CHANGING COMET

As a comet approaches the Sun it warms up. The snow turns to gas, which, along with loose dust, flows from the nucleus. When the comet passes closer to the Sun than the orbit of Mars, this material forms a head (called a coma) and two tails, one of gas and one of dust.

COMETS

More than a trillion comets surround the planetary region of the solar system. They follow long orbits around the Sun and together make up a vast sphere called the Oort Cloud. Each comet is a lump of dirt and snow, called a nucleus, or "dirty snowball." Comets are so small that they are only visible when they travel close to the Sun and grow large and bright enough to be seen.

Coma A coma has formed around the nucleus of Comet Hale-Bopp as it travels toward the Sun.

Tails The comet's tails increase in length as it nears the Sun. They are pushed away from the Sun and always point away from it.

◄ COMET DISPLAY

More than 2,300 comets have been identified as they passed through the Sun's neighborhood. About 200 make return visits, but most pass by just once. Three or four times a century, a spectacular one, such as Comet McNaught in January 2007, makes a stunning display.

Comet McNaught

This bright dot is the planet Mercury

The comet grows as it approaches the Sun

► PASSING THE SUN

These images from the SOHO spacecraft track the progress of Comet McNaught as it rounds the Sun. Like most comets, it is named after its discoverer, Robert McNaught, who saw it first on August 7, 2006. It was at its biggest and brightest in January 2007, when closest to the Sun.

► COMET STRUCTURE

The nucleus of a comet is a city-sized lump, two-thirds snow and one-third rock dust. Halley's Comet orbits the Sun every 76 years. When it drew close to it in 1986, the *Giotto* spacecraft flew into the comet's coma and captured images of its nucleus.

Tail shapes The gas tail is blue and straight, and the dust tail is white and curved.

Closest to the Sun The tails are longest when closest to the Sun, then shrink as the comet moves away.

Sun's bright disk has to be masked so that the comet can be imaged

Several dozen mini-fragments trail behind the main one

One of more than 30 separate fragments of Comet Schwassmann Wachmann 3

▶ **BREAKING UP**

As a comet passes a massive body, such as the Sun or Jupiter, it may be pulled apart by its gravity. Comet Schwassmann Wachmann 3 orbits the Sun every 5.4 years and astronomers have observed that it is disintegrating.

Jets of dust and gas stream out of the nucleus

The nucleus of Halley's Comet is 9.5 miles (15.3 km) long

METEORITES

Thousands of tons of rocky material enter Earth's atmosphere each year. Most of it originates from asteroids, but some comes from comets, the Moon, and even Mars. As the rocky pieces close in on Earth they are termed meteoroids. Most burn up, but those that survive and land are known as meteorites. There are three main types: stony meteorites, iron meteorites, and stony-iron meteorites—the rarest kind.

▼ ESQUEL

This stony-iron meteorite was collected in Esquel, Argentina, in 1951. Golden-colored crystals of the mineral olivine are embedded in the iron-nickel metal.

► THIEL

The Thiel Mountains stony-iron meteorite was one of the first found in Antarctica, about 40 years ago.

▲ METEOR

Meteoroids burning up in Earth's atmosphere produce bright trails. These short-lived streaks of light are termed meteors, or shooting stars. About a million occur every day.

◄ MURCHISON

Stony meteorites are the most common. This one, the Murchison, fell in Australia in 1969. It is one of the most studied meteorites and contains minerals, water, and complex organic molecules.

► BARWELL

The Barwell meteorite is one of a shower of stones that fell in England in 1965. As it plummeted through Earth's atmosphere, friction caused the outer surface to heat and melt. This later solidified into a black crust.

◀ CANON DIABLO

This sliced and polished iron meteorite is a piece of the asteroid that produced the Barringer Crater (below). The pieces found weigh 30 tons (27 metric tons) in total, yet they are only a small fraction of the original asteroid.

◀ IMPACT CRATER

Meteorites can produce craters when they crash into Earth. The Barringer Crater in the Arizona Desert, shown here under a rare blanket of snow, measures 0.75 mile (1.2 km) across and was formed about 50,000 years ago.

▲ GIBEON

Iron meteorites are the second most common type, after stony meteorites. The Gibeon is mainly iron with a small amount of nickel. It is one of many found in Namibia since the 1830s.

▲ CALCALONG CREEK

More than 50 meteorites found on Earth originated on the Moon, blasted off by asteroid impact. The Calcalong Creek meteorite, found in Australia, is lunar surface soil that was turned to rock by such an impact.

▲ NAKHLA

This stony meteorite is one of more than 30 found on Earth that originated on Mars. It was blasted off the planet and spent many millions of years in space before landing in Egypt on June 28, 1911.

◀ TEKTITES

Small glassy bodies known as tektites can form when a large meteorite hits Earth. The impact shatters and melts surrounding Earth rock, flinging it upward. It cools and hardens, falling back to Earth as glassy pieces.

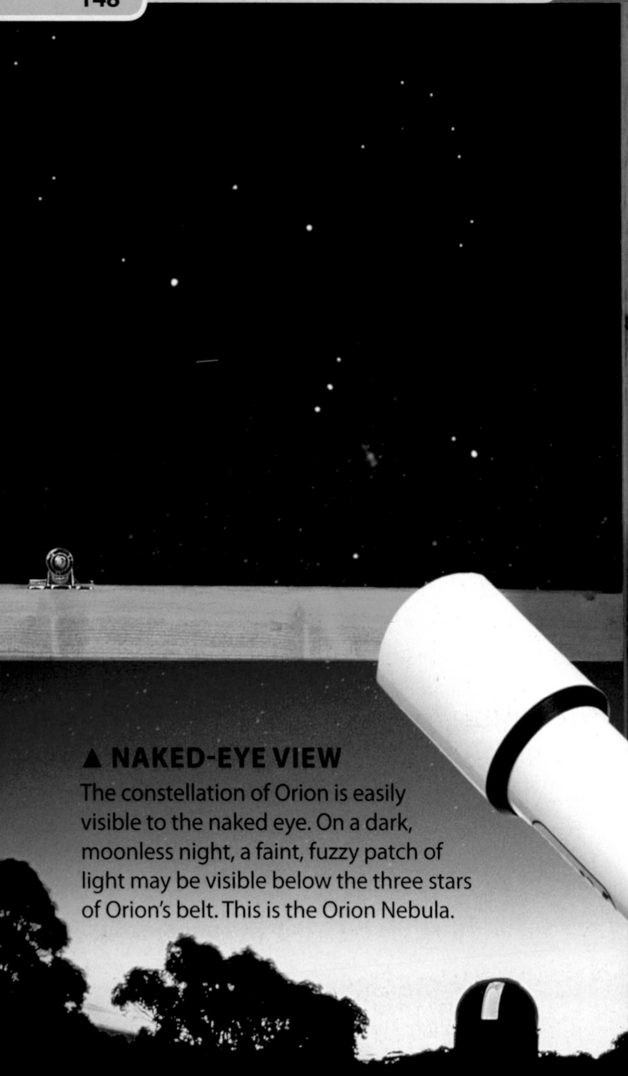

▲ THROUGH BINOCULARS

The Orion Nebula is a massive star-forming cloud of gas and dust. The nebula becomes more obvious when looked at through binoculars— two low-powered telescopes working together. In standard binoculars the two main lenses are about 2 in (5 cm) wide and the image is magnified seven times.

▶ IMPROVED VIEW

A more powerful telescope improves the view of the nebula. Across the world there are about 50 telescopes with mirrors 7–17 ft (2–5 m) across and another 20 with mirrors up to 33 ft (10 m) across. These large telescopes are located on mountaintop sites where the air is clear and still. Computerized controls adjust their position, keeping them tracked on their target as the Earth turns.

▲ NAKED-EYE VIEW

The constellation of Orion is easily visible to the naked eye. On a dark, moonless night, a faint, fuzzy patch of light may be visible below the three stars of Orion's belt. This is the Orion Nebula.

TELESCOPES

A telescope is the astronomer's basic tool. It makes distant objects appear bigger and reveals their detail. Telescopes work by using a lens or mirror to collect light and bring it to a focus, producing an image. Reflectors, which use a mirror, are the most widely used type of telescope—the bigger the mirror, the more powerful the telescope and the better the view.

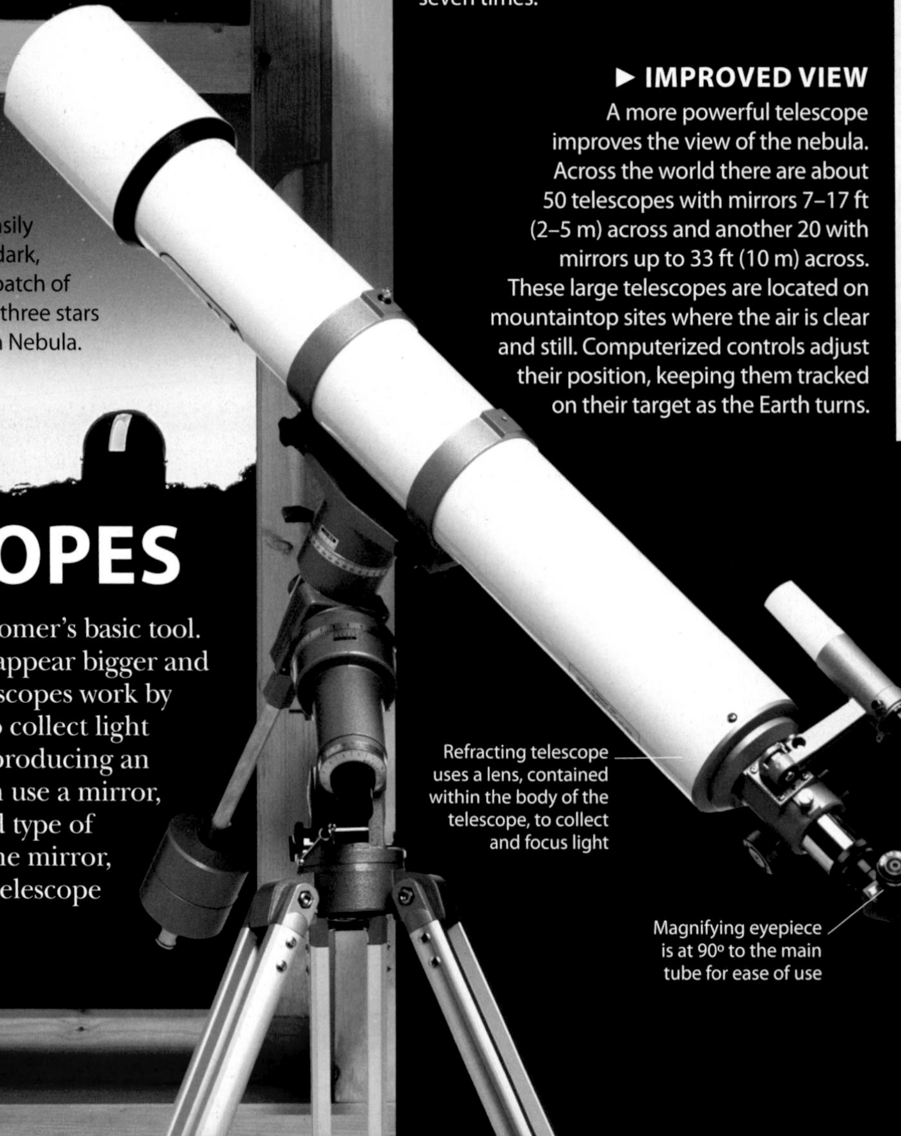

Refracting telescope uses a lens, contained within the body of the telescope, to collect and focus light

Magnifying eyepiece is at 90° to the main tube for ease of use

About 1,000 young stars are visible in this view because of the X-rays they emit

◀ MEDIUM-SIZED TELESCOPE VIEW

The nebula's shape and form become visible through a telescope with a mirror about 8 in (20 cm) across. A camera attached to the telescope collects the light and records the image.

▲ X-RAY AND INFRARED VIEWS

X-rays collected by the Chandra space telescope were used to make this image on the left, which shows the heart of the Orion Nebula. The image on the right shows the same area taken by the Spitzer infrared telescope. Clouds of dust heated by starlight show up in red.

▶ VIEW FROM SPACE

Some telescopes collect forms of energy other than light, such as radio waves, X-rays, and infrared energy. Earth's atmosphere prevents some of these from reaching Earth so they are collected by telescopes in space. This color-enhanced image combines data from two space telescopes—Spitzer, which collects infrared waves, and Hubble, which collects both light and ultraviolet waves.

▶ HEART OF THE NEBULA

Hubble's 8-ft (2.4-m) wide mirror collected the light for this detailed view of the Orion Nebula's bright central area. It includes the Trapezium, a cluster of 10 young, brilliant stars that illuminate the nebula with their ultraviolet energy.

SPACE EXPLORATION

Humans have only been able to send spacecraft to explore space for about 50 years. In that time, more than 100 robotic craft have traveled into the solar system to reveal what its planets, moons, asteroids, and comets are like. They fly by, orbit, or land on these other worlds. Humans have only been to the Moon, but aim to set foot on Mars in the future.

ČESKOSLOVENSKÁ POŠTA

Apollo 15 mis

Apollo 18 wit
three US
astronauts

APOLLO SOY

Dog inside capsule

Russian satellite *Sputnik 1*

Sputnik 2 takes Laika the dog into space

Mercury Atlas 5, with chimpanzee Enos on board

Yuri Gagarin, first human in space

Giotto craft flies into
Halley's Comet

Alexei Leonov makes the first spacewalk

Apollo 8 orbits the Moon

Hubble Space
Telescope launche

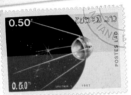

Valentina Tereshkova, first woman in space

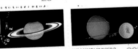

Apollo 11
crew return to
Earth in command
module *Columbia*

Apollo 11 lifts off

In orbit over the Moon

Man walks on the Moon

Reentering Earth's atmosphere

M A

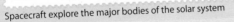

Spacecraft explore the major bodies of the solar system

Lunar Roving Vehicle had a maximum speed of 11.5 mph (18.6 km/h)

Pioneer 10 flies by Jupiter in 1973, followed by its twin, Pioneer 11, in 1974

Pioneer craft investigate Jupiter

Soyuz 19 with two Russian cosmonauts

First international space rendezvous

Viking craft land on Mars

Viking missions to M

Columbia, the first space shuttle, takes off

Mars Pathfinder and its rover, Sojourner, touch down on Mars

TIMELINE OF SPACE EXPLORATION

October 14, 1957
Sputnik 1, the world's first artificial satellite, is launched into Earth's orbit by Russia.

November 3, 1957
Laika, a Russian dog aboard Sputnik 2, becomes the first creature to orbit Earth.

January 2, 1959
Russian spacecraft Luna 1 is the first to escape Earth's gravity.

September 13, 1959
Luna 2 is the first craft to land on the Moon when it crashes onto its surface.

April 12, 1961
Russian Yuri Gagarin is the first person into space. His flight lasts 108 minutes.

June 16, 1963
Russian Valentina Tereshkova is the first woman in space.

March 18, 1965
Russian Alexei Leonov makes the first EVA (extra vehicular activity), or spacewalk.

February 3, 1966
Luna 9 lands successfully on the Moon.

December 24, 1968
US spacecraft Apollo 8 is the first manned mission to leave the Earth's gravity and orbit the Moon.

July 20, 1969
Neil Armstrong and Buzz Aldrin of Apollo 11 are the first humans to walk on the Moon.

April 19, 1971
The first space station, Salyut 1, is launched by the Russians.

December 3, 1973
US craft Pioneer 10 is the first to fly by Jupiter.

March 29, 1974
US craft Mariner 10 is the first to fly by Mercury.

July 17, 1975
US craft Apollo18 and Russian Soyuz 19 make the first international space rendezvous.

October 22, 1975
Russian craft Venera 9 transmits the first images from the surface of Venus.

July 20, 1976
US craft Viking 1 is the first to land successfully on Mars.

September 1, 1979
Pioneer 11 is the first to fly by Saturn.

April 12, 1981
Columbia, the first US space shuttle, is launched.

January 24, 1986
US craft Voyager 2 is the first to fly by Uranus.

February 20, 1986
The first module of Russian space station Mir is launched into orbit.

March 13, 1986
European craft Giotto takes the first close-up look at a comet.

August 24, 1989
Voyager 2 is the first craft to fly by Neptune.

April 24, 1990
The Hubble Space Telescope is launched.

September 15, 1990
US craft Magellan starts a three-year mapping program of Venus.

October 29, 1991
US craft Galileo makes the first flyby of an asteroid as it passes Gaspra.

July 13, 1995
Galileo arrives at Jupiter and releases a probe to enter its atmosphere.

July 4, 1997
US craft Mars Pathfinder and its Sojourner rover touch down on Mars.

November 20, 1998
Zarya, the first module of the International Space Station (ISS), is launched.

November 2, 2000
The first crew arrives to stay aboard the ISS.

February 12, 2001
The NEAR craft lands on asteroid Eros.

August 25, 2003
The Spitzer infrared space telescope is launched into Earth orbit.

December 25, 2003
Europe's first interplanetary craft, Mars Express, orbits Mars.

January 4, 2004
Mars Exploration Rover Spirit lands on Mars, followed by its twin, called Opportunity.

March 2, 2004
European craft Rosetta, carrying lander Philae, starts its 10-year journey to Comet Churyumov-Gerasimenko.

June 30, 2004
US craft Cassini arrives at Saturn to study the planet and its moons. It releases Huygens to land on the moon Titan.

November 20, 2005
Japanese craft Hayabusa lands on asteroid Itokawa.

January 19, 2006
US craft New Horizons is launched on its eight-year journey to Pluto.

August 4, 2007
US craft Phoenix sets off for Mars, arriving in 2008.

January 14, 2008
US craft Messenger makes its first flyby of Mercury. It orbits the planet in 2011.

December 8, 2010
SpaceX is the first private company to launch a spacecraft into orbit and return to Earth.

July 21, 2011
US shuttle Atlantis lands back on Earth, and NASA ends its 30-year space shuttle program.

August 6, 2012
Curiosity is the largest and most advanced Rover to land on Mars.

SPACE TRAVELERS

Since the first manned space mission in 1961, more than 460 people have journeyed into space—26 on missions to the Moon and the rest in orbit around the Earth. To date, only Russia, China, and the United States have sent humans into space. However, humans are not the only space travelers. Animals such as dogs, monkeys, and spiders have all been sent into space to help with research.

ALAN SHEPHERD was the second person, and first American, to journey into space.

YANG LIWEI was the first Chinese astronaut (taikonaut). China's first manned space flight was launched in October 2003.

MICHAEL COLLINS was the third member of the *Apollo 11* mission in 1969. He orbited the Moon, while Armstrong and Aldrin explored its surface.

JIM VOSS and **SUSAN HELMS** set the record for longest spacewalk (8 hours 56 minutes).

HAM was the first chimpanzee to travel in space. In 1961, he was sent to test equipment that would be used in the first US manned space mission.

6 **EILEEN COLLINS** became the first female shuttle pilot in February 1995 and the first female shuttle commander in July 1999.

7 **EUGENE CERNAN** was part of the *Apollo 17* mission in December 1972. He was the last person to walk on the Moon.

8 **LAIKA** was the first animal to orbit the Earth. The Russian dog traveled in *Sputnik 2* in 1957.

9 **SVETLANA SAVITSKAYA** was the second woman in space and the first woman to spacewalk.

10 **DENNIS TITO** was the first space tourist. He paid $20 million for a six-day trip in 2001.

11 **ALBINO RATS** were taken to Spacelab-3 in 1985. There were 24 rats on board.

12 **ALEXI LEONOV** made the first spacewalk in March 1965. He spent 10 minutes in space secured to his *Voskhod 2* craft.

15 **JOHN GLENN** was the first American to orbit the Earth, in 1962. He became the oldest space voyager in 1998, at age 77.

18 **VALERI POLIAKOV** holds the record for the longest time spent in space during one trip. His record stands at 437.7 days.

13 **NEIL ARMSTRONG** was the first person to set foot on the Moon. He spent 2 hours 35 minutes exploring the lunar surface.

16 **YURI GAGARIN** was the first person to fly into space. His trip in April 1961 took him once around the Earth and lasted 108 minutes.

19 **VALENTINA TERESHKOVA** was the first woman to fly into space. She made a three-day journey aboard *Vostok 6* in June 1963.

14 **BAKER,** a squirrel monkey, was launched into space on May 28, 1959. She traveled with a rhesus monkey named Able.

17 **MIKE MELVILL** was the first commercial astronaut. He piloted *SpaceShipOne* in June 2004.

20 **SAM** was a rhesus monkey who was sent into space in 1960 to test equipment that would be used in future manned flights.

21 **ARABELLA,** a spider, was sent to the Skylab space station in 1973. Once space-adapted, she spun perfect webs.

22 **SERGEI KRIKALEV** holds the record for the total time spent in space. In his six trips, he has clocked up 803.4 days in space.

23 **BELKA AND STRELKA** became the first dogs to go into orbit and survive the journey, in 1960.

24 **BUZZ ALDRIN** was the second person to set foot on the Moon.

QUICK QUIZ

What can you remember about Space?
Jot down your answers, then check them on pp.296–97.

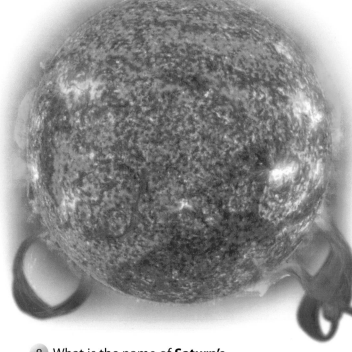

1 What is the **largest moon** in the **solar system** called?

2 Which **galaxy** can you see on the right?

3 How are **stars** formed?
A Inside vast clouds of hydrogen gas
B From a chemical reaction between clouds
C When a child makes a wish
D By a sudden and spectacular explosion

4 Who paid **$20 million** to be the **world's first space tourist** in **2001**?
A Arnold Schwarzenegger
B George W. Bush
C Dennis Tito
D Michael Collins

5 I am an important **member** of our **solar system** and am the source of **heat** and **light**. What am I called?

6 What makes **Uranus** blue?
A There are numerous water bodies on its surface
B There is a thin layer of smoggy haze
C There is methane gas in its atmosphere

7 What is the **constellation** that forms the **shape** of **twins** called?

8 What is the name of **Saturn's largest moon**?
A Ganymede
B Titan
C Lapetus
D Triton

9 What is the name of the **dog** that went to **space** on the *Sputnik 2*?

A Laika
B Enos
C Lucky
D Arabella

10 What is the **brightest star** in the Earth's **night sky** called?

A Eagle Nebula
B Sirius
C The Sun
D Crab Pulsar

11 If you saw this **shoot** across the **sky**, what would you be looking at?

A A comet
B A UFO
C A meteor
D A satellite

12 **Match** the **moons** to their **names:**

1   **2**   **3**   **4**

A Titan   **B** Callisto   **C** Europa   **D** Io

13 What was the **Big Bang**?

A A festival of lights celebrated during ancient times
B A huge explosion in the universe that occurred about 13.7 billion years ago
C A loud noise resulting from an asteroid hitting the Earth
D A test to discover the origin of the universe

16 Humans have only been to the **Moon**, but which **planet** will we try to **set foot** on next?

A Mercury
B Saturn
C Mars
D Jupiter

14 **Match** the **meteorites** to their **names:**

1   **2**

A Thiel   **B** Esquel

15 Which of these is the **coldest, most distant,** and **windiest planet** in the solar system?

A Neptune
B Jupiter
C Mars
D Venus

17 **Yuri Gagarin** was the first man in **space**. But who was the **first woman** in **space**?

A Valentina Tereshkova
B Bella Akhmadulina
C Natalya Gorbanevskaya
D Svetlana Savitskaya

18 How does a **telescope** work?

A It captures the heat from distant objects to create a thermal image
B It moves distant objects and places them close to the observer
C It uses a lens or mirror to collect light and bring it to a focus
D It generates images based on the information available on the internet

FAST FACTS

On a clear, **moonless night**, you can see about **2,500 stars** with the naked eye.

Uranus was discovered in 1781 and **Neptune** in 1846.

The gravity on the **Moon's** surface is just **17 percent** that of Earth. If you can jump 3 ft (1 m) high on Earth, you would be able to jump 19 ft (6 m) on the Moon.

*The **Moon** moves 1¼ in (3 cm) away from the **Earth** each year.*

*The **Moon** appears to be the same size as the **Sun** from Earth because, although the Sun is **400** times wider than the Moon, it is also **400** times farther away.*

The **Sun** contains more than **99 percent** of all the material in the **solar system.**

Space rockets need to reach a speed of **25,000 mph** (40,000 km/h) to escape the gravitational pull of the Earth. This is called the **escape velocity.**

Earth is the densest planet in the solar system, with a density of 3.2 oz/in³ (5.5 g/cm³).

The clouds on Venus are made of sulfuric acid. Its atmosphere is 96.5 percent carbon dioxide.

The Sun viewed from Mars is two-thirds the size of the Sun viewed from Earth.

***Jupiter** is **1,321** times the volume of Earth. **Mercury** is just **0.05** the volume of Earth.*

*In **winter** on **Uranus**, it is **dark** for 21 **Earth years.***

Saturn would **float** in a giant bath, as it is **less dense** than water.

Pluto was classified as a **planet** from its discovery in 1930 until 2006.

More than **22,500 meteorites** that landed on Earth have been **collected** and **cataloged.**

The **same side** of the **Moon** always faces **Earth.** This is because the Moon rotates in the same time as it takes to orbit—27.3 days.

The **dwarf** planet Ceres is the **largest** asteroid, at **596 miles** (960 km) across.

*The largest **volcano** in the **solar system** is **Olympus Mons** on **Mars**. It is 403 miles (648 km) **wide** and 15 miles (24 km) **high.***

The *Great Red Spot* visible on the surface of **Jupiter** is a **storm**, wider than three Earths, that has been observed *raging* for the past **340 years.**

*Jupiter is **rotating** so quickly that it **bulges** in the middle.*

The **black hole** at the center of the Milky Way is as massive as **3 million Suns.**

*There is no wind or rain on the **Moon**, so **footprints** made by astronauts are likely to remain there for **millions of years.***

Neptune is the *windiest* planet. Gusts there can reach *1,340 mph* (2,160 km/h).

At a speed of 60 mph (95 km/h), it would take you 177 years to **drive to the Sun.**

Astronauts are up to **2 in** (5 cm) **taller** in space because their **spines expand** in the **weightlessness.**

*It takes **84 Earth years** for **Uranus to orbit** the Sun.*

The *Sun* is *halfway through its life*. It has been *burning* for *4.6 billion years*, and will run out of fuel in *5 billion years*' time.

Our **Sun** is orbiting the **black hole** at the center of the **Milky Way galaxy** at a speed of **550,000 mph** (900,000 km/h). It takes **225 million years** to complete one orbit.

The universe is expand**ing** in all directions at the speed of light.

*As we look into space we see the **universe** as it was in the **past** because of the **time** it takes for the **light** of distant stars and galaxies to reach us.*

The tail of the **Great Comet**, which passed by Earth in **1843**, was more than **500 million miles** (800 million km) long—about the distance from the Sun to Jupiter.

In 1971, US astronaut Alan Shepard stood on the **Moon** and hit a **golf ball.**

Saturn's rings were first seen by **Galileo** in **1610** using one of the *first ever telescopes.*

The *biggest stars* of all are *500 times larger* than the *Sun* and *100,000 times as bright.*

The **brightest** objects in the Universe are *quasars*—extremely distant galaxies that have incredibly bright centers. The quasars that we can see are so far away that their light has taken *billions* of years to reach Earth.

If you counted the stars in the **Milky Way** at a rate of one a second, it would take you about **5,000 years** to count them all.

The planets of our **solar system** occupy a disk-shaped region extending **2.8 billion miles** (4.5 billion km) from the Sun.

Enke's Comet is the most frequent visitor to Earth, passing by once every **3.3 years.**

There are more than **1 billion asteroids** larger than 1.25 miles (2 km) wide in the Main Belt of asteroids between the orbits of Mars and Jupiter.

About every 50 million years a meteorite more than 6 miles (10 km) in diameter hits Earth.

Two of the world's largest **optical telescopes** are found at the Mauna Kea Observatory in Hawaii. The twin **Keck telescopes** both have mirrors **33 ft** (10 m) in diameter.

*The **largest meteorite** on Earth is the **Hoba West**, which remains where it fell in **Namibia**, southwest Africa. It weighed **66 tons** when it was found in 1920.*

Astronauts on the **International Space Station** have been **growing plants** in space. The techniques they develop will be needed on any future mission to Mars, because the astronauts will need to grow their **own food.**

The *Voyager 1* spacecraft left Earth in 1977 and is now the most distant human-made object in space.

*Light from the Sun takes just over **eight minutes** to reach Earth. The light from the next nearest star, Proxima Centauri, takes **4.3 years** to reach Earth.*

There is *no sound* in space, as sound cannot travel through a *vacuum.*

Mars has **ice caps** at its **poles**, just like Earth.

*The largest canyon system in the solar system is **Valles Marineris on Mars**, which is more than **2,500 miles** (4,000 km) long.*

Volcanoes last erupted on the Moon about 3.2 billion years ago.

The *Orion* vehicle is going to replace the Space Shuttle in **2014**. It will carry astronauts to the **Moon** and, later, on the first stage of a mission to **Mars.**

Yuri Gagarin's **mother** first found out about his **flight into space** when news of the mission broke.

It takes the Space Shuttle *eight minutes* to reach its orbital speed of *17,000 mph* (27,000 km/h).

EARTH

ANTARCTICA
The Transantarctic Mountains
extend across Antarctica, dividing
the continent into east and west.
This region bordering the Ross Sea
is known as Terra Nova and is famous
for its spectacular ice caves.

PLANET EARTH

Earth was created some 4.6 billion years ago from a mass of iron-rich, rocky debris orbiting the Sun. The rocks smashed into the young planet as meteorites and were welded together by heat generated from the energy of impact. The bombardment eventually generated so much heat that the whole planet melted. The heavy iron then sank toward the center to become the Earth's core, while the lighter rocks formed the mantle and crust.

EARTH'S STRUCTURE

The planet is layered like a peach. Earth's rocky crust forms its thin skin, while the hot, mobile rock of the mantle is like the peach's juicy flesh. At the heart of the planet lies its metallic core, like the hard stone at the center of a peach.

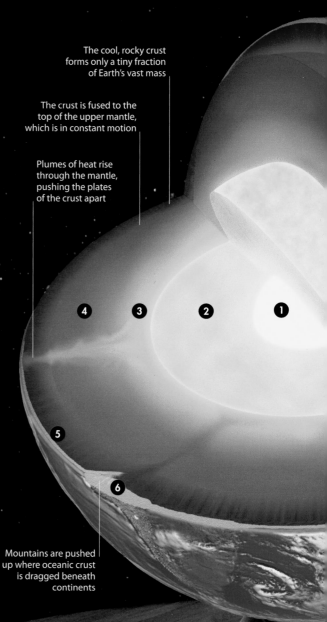

The cool, rocky crust forms only a tiny fraction of Earth's vast mass

The crust is fused to the top of the upper mantle, which is in constant motion

Plumes of heat rise through the mantle, pushing the plates of the crust apart

Mountains are pushed up where oceanic crust is dragged beneath continents

INNER CORE
The inner core is a heavy ball of solid iron and nickel. It is heated by nuclear reactions within the Earth to 8,500°F (4,700°C), but the intense pressure at the core prevents it from melting.

OUTER CORE
The solid inner core is surrounded by a fluid mass of molten iron, nickel, and sulfur. Swirling currents in the molten metal of the outer core generate the Earth's magnetic field.

LOWER MANTLE
The rocky mantle is 1,800 miles (2,900 km) deep, and is heated to 6,300°F (3,500°C) at its base. Intense pressure stops it melting, but rising heat keeps the hot rock moving slowly.

UPPER MANTLE
The upper mantle is heated to almost 1,800°F (1,000°C). Where movement in the mantle cracks the cool, brittle crust, reduced pressure makes the hot mantle rock melt and erupt from volcanoes.

5 OCEANIC CRUST

The crust between the continents is less than 7 miles (11 km) thick. It is made of heavy rock that erupts from the hot mantle at midocean ridges to form the bedrock of the ocean floors.

6 CONTINENTAL CRUST

The lightest of Earth's rocks form vast slabs that "float" on the heavy mantle like huge rocky rafts. Up to 45 miles (70 km) thick, they rise above sea level to form the continents that we live on.

Huge impact craters have filled with dark lava erupted from ancient volcanoes

THE MOON

Soon after Earth formed, it was hit by a planet-sized asteroid that completely disintegrated. Most of its heavy metallic core melted into the Earth, but the lighter rocky fragments drifted into orbit and eventually fused to form the Moon.

The Red Sea is a spreading rift in the Earth's crust that will widen into an ocean

7 LAND SURFACE

Exposed to frost, wind, rain, and hot sunlight, the rocks at the land surface are broken down by weathering and erosion. This releases minerals that are vital to plants and other life.

More than 70 percent of Earth's surface is covered by ocean water

8 OCEANS

The low-lying basins between the continents are filled with water, to an average depth of 2.3 miles (3.7 km). Most of the water erupted from volcanoes as water vapor early in Earth's history.

ON THE SURFACE

Movement in the thick, hot mantle has made the thin, cool crust crack into several huge plates. The boundaries of these plates are marked by earthquake zones dotted with volcanoes, and mountain ridges pushed up where moving plates collide.

9 WEATHER SYSTEMS

The heat of the Sun makes water evaporate from the oceans and rise into the lower atmosphere. The water forms swirling masses of cloud that spill rain onto the continents, allowing life to exist on land.

10 ATMOSPHERE

Earth's mass gives it enough gravity to retain an atmosphere of nitrogen, oxygen, and other gases including carbon dioxide. This keeps the Earth warm at night, and shields it from dangerous radiation.

PLATE TECTONICS

The Earth's crust is the brittle shell of a deep layer of hot rock called the mantle. This is moving very slowly, driven by heat generated deep within the planet. The movement has made the crust crack into separate plates, which are being pulled apart in some places and pushed together in others. As they move, the plates make oceans larger or smaller, and carry continents around the globe.

2 / PLATE BOUNDARIES

At some plate boundaries the plates are pulling apart, while at others they are pushing together. There are also places where one plate is sliding against another. All these movements cause earthquakes, and many boundaries are dotted with volcanoes.

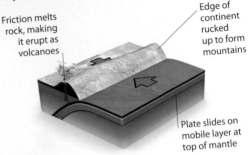

Friction melts rock, making it erupt as volcanoes

Edge of continent rucked up to form mountains

Plate slides on mobile layer at top of mantle

Convergent boundaries
These are found where one plate grinds beneath another. Ocean floors always slide under continents, pushing up mountain ranges.

Erupting lava forms ridges of solid rock

Rift zone dotted with underwater volcanoes

Divergent boundaries
These occur where plates are pulling apart, usually on ocean floors. This allows hot mantle rock to erupt in the rift zone and solidify as new ocean floor.

1 /

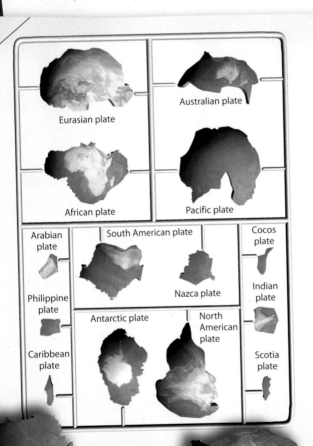

Eurasian plate

Australian plate

African plate

Pacific plate

Arabian plate

South American plate

Cocos plate

Philippine plate

Nazca plate

Indian plate

Caribbean plate

Antarctic plate

North American plate

Scotia plate

◀ KIT OF PARTS

There are 15 large tectonic plates, and almost 40 smaller ones. They form the ocean floors, and some of the largest carry continents. Continental plates are made of thicker, but lighter, rock than the ocean floors. The oceanic parts of the plates are always changing size and shape, but the continents, although moving, do not change so much.

Transform boundaries

These form where two plates are sliding past each other. This causes frequent earthquakes along the fault line, but few volcanoes.

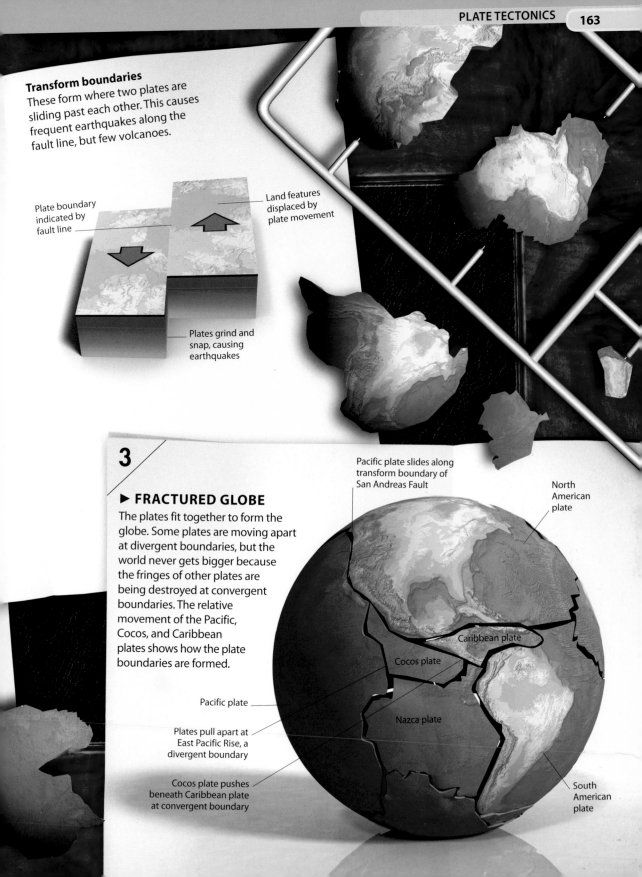

Plate boundary indicated by fault line

Land features displaced by plate movement

Plates grind and snap, causing earthquakes

3

▶ FRACTURED GLOBE

The plates fit together to form the globe. Some plates are moving apart at divergent boundaries, but the world never gets bigger because the fringes of other plates are being destroyed at convergent boundaries. The relative movement of the Pacific, Cocos, and Caribbean plates shows how the plate boundaries are formed.

Pacific plate slides along transform boundary of San Andreas Fault

North American plate

Caribbean plate

Cocos plate

Pacific plate

Nazca plate

Plates pull apart at East Pacific Rise, a divergent boundary

Cocos plate pushes beneath Caribbean plate at convergent boundary

South American plate

VOLCANOES

Volcanoes are the most spectacular and destructive of Earth's geological features. Most volcanoes lie along plate boundaries, where the slabs of rock (plates) that form the Earth's crust meet. Opening rifts and the friction of plates grinding against each other make the hot rock beneath the crust melt and burst up through fissures (cracks). Volcanoes also occur over "hot spots" away from plate boundaries, caused by rising plumes of heat in the mantle beneath the Earth's crust.

Eruptions produce clouds of gas, made mainly of water vapor, carbon dioxide, and sulfur dioxide

Some of the molten rock hurled into the air cools and hits the ground as streamlined "lava bombs"

KILAUEA

The Hawaiian islands are a chain of volcanoes that have erupted from the Pacific Ocean floor as it slips over a hot spot in Earth's mantle. The oldest volcanoes in the north are now extinct, but Kilauea in the south is the most active volcano on Earth.

Lava, cinders, and volcanic ash build up a rocky but fragile ridge around the crater

The erupting lava has a temperature of about 1,830°F (1,000°C), making it glow bright orange

A small cinder cone surrounds Kilauea's most active crater

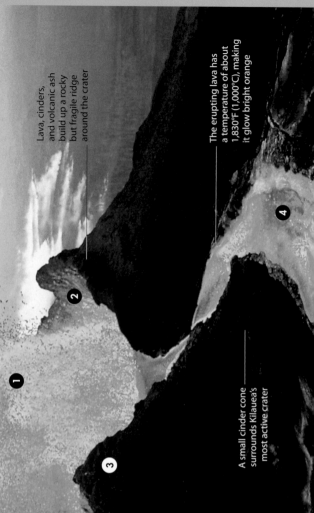

1 ERUPTION

When Kilauea erupts, basalt lava and gas are forced up from deep within the volcano. Basalt lava is very fluid, so a lot of it just spills over the rim of the crater. Erupting gas can also cause explosive "fire fountains" of gas and red-hot lava, like this one.

2 CRATER

Lava boils up through a vent to build up a cone of rocky debris. More eruptions make the inside of the cone collapse or even explode upward to create a roughly circular crater. Its almost sheer walls reveal layers of cinders, ash, and solidified lava.

Lava flows downhill at speeds of up to 60 mph (100 km/h)

The surface of the lava cools to form a wrinkled or rough, fractured skin of solid black rock

The lava that erupts on Hawaii solidifies into black basalt—a heavy, iron-rich rock

5 TYPES OF LAVA

Hawaiian lava is molten basalt rock pushed up from beneath the ocean floor. It is fluid because it contains very little silica (the mineral used to make glass). Other volcanoes erupt lava that is high in silica, which is much stickier and does not flow far.

6 LAVA TUBE

As the lava streams away from the active crater of Kilauea, the surface of the flow cools and hardens. Underneath, however, the hot lava keeps flowing. This creates "lava tubes," which extend to the coast, where the lava spills into the sea in clouds of steam.

3 CONE

This small volcanic cone is just the summit of a huge, dome-shaped shield volcano, which rises all the way from the ocean floor 23,875 ft (7,277 m) below. The dome is built up by the fluid lava that erupts on Hawaii. Volcanoes that erupt stickier, less fluid lava have steeper sides.

4 LAVA FLOW

The lava that erupts from Kilauea is extremely hot, and so fluid that it flows downhill away from the crater like a river of fire. Since 1983 the volcano has been erupting almost constantly, spilling lava over more than 40 sq miles (100 sq km).

EARTHQUAKES

The vast rocky plates of the Earth's crust are always moving. Where the plates meet, the movement causes earthquakes. Frequent slight movement just causes tremors (shaking), but often the rocks on each side of a plate boundary lock together. The strain builds up, distorting the rocks until the locked section gives way. The rock springs back, often shifting several yards, and the shock of this can cause a catastrophic earthquake.

CHILE 1960

The biggest earthquake ever recorded struck Chile in 1960. It reached 9.5 on the Richter Scale, which was devised in 1935 by American scientist Charles Richter as a way of measuring earthquakes using instruments called seismographs.

ALASKA 1964

On March 27, 1964, the Pacific Ocean floor slid 65 ft (20 m) beneath Alaska in a few minutes, causing a colossal earthquake. So few people live in this remote region, however, that only 125 lost their lives.

SAN FRANCISCO 1906

The San Andreas Fault in California marks where the Pacific plate is sliding past North America. San Francisco is built on the fault line, and in 1906 the city was almost destroyed when the fault slipped 20 ft (6 m) and triggered disastrous fires.

MEXICO CITY 1985

Mexico's capital city is built on the dried-out clay bed of an ancient lake. The earthquake that hit the city in 1985 made the clay shake like jelly, making the shock waves six times as destructive. More than 400 multistory buildings in the city were shaken to the ground, and at least 9,000 people died.

KOBE 1995

Japan was created by intense ground movements in the western Pacific, and it has more earthquakes than almost anywhere else. In 1995, an earthquake wrecked the city of Kobe, destroying this elevated highway and killing 6,433 people.

TSUNAMI 2004

The Asian Tsunami that killed more than 283,000 in 2004 was caused by an earthquake on the ocean floor off Sumatra. The shock sent huge waves racing across the Indian Ocean, devastating communities all around its shores.

INDONESIA 2006

In 2006, a serious earthquake struck the Indonesian island of Java, wrecking up to 135,000 houses and killing at least 5,780 people. It also damaged the ancient Hindu temple of Prambanan, a World Heritage Site, but did not destroy it.

Above left: the city of Banda Aceh, Sumatra, Indonesia, as it was in April 2004

Left: the same area pictured in January 2006, after the tsunami had struck

MOUNTAINS

The world's mountains were raised by the titanic forces that keep the plates of the Earth's crust moving. Where the plates grind together, the edges of continents are forced up into high, folded ridges, like the Andes Mountains in South America. Hot rock deep beneath the surface may erupt through cracks in the folded rock to form volcanoes. These also erupt where the crust is being torn apart, and over "hotspots" deep within the Earth. The landscape below has been created from images of the highest peaks on each continent, and one that rises from the depths of the Pacific Ocean.

1 MOUNT EVEREST

The world's highest peak, Everest lies 29,035 ft (8,850 m) above sea level. It is part of the Himalayas, a range of fold mountains created by the collision of India with Asia 50 million years ago. India is still moving north, so the Himalayas are still rising.

2 MOUNT ACONCAGUA

The Pacific Ocean floor is plunging beneath South America, rucking up its western edge to form the rugged, earthquake-prone mountains of the Andes. Mount Aconcagua is the highest peak, at 22,834 ft (6,959 m).

More than 3,000 climbers have reached the summit of Everest
1

The snowy summit of Aconcagua is part of Earth's longest mountain range
2

The Alaskan peak of Mount McKinley is covered with snow throughout the year
3

3 MOUNT MCKINLEY

Rising 20,321 ft (6,194 m) above sea level, Mount McKinley in Alaska is the highest peak of the North American Western Cordillera. Its isolation and bulk make it one of the world's most spectacular mountains.

5 MAUNA KEA

The highest point on Hawaii is the top of a huge volcano that rises 33,000 ft (10,000 m) from the Pacific Ocean floor. So although its peak is only 13,796 ft (4,205 m) above sea level, it is the biggest mountain on Earth.

7 MONT BLANC

The folded ridges of the European Alps have been raised by the northward movement of Africa. Mont Blanc is the highest peak at 15,774 ft (4,808 m), but since its summit is a dome of ice its height varies from year to year.

4 MOUNT KILIMANJARO

The highest mountain in Africa, Kilimanjaro is actually a colossal volcano with three volcanic cones. The highest peak on the tallest cone, Kibo, rises 19,340 ft (5,895 m) above sea level. The other volcanic cones are Mawenzi and Shira.

6 VINSON MASSIF

The most remote mountains on Earth lie on the frozen continent of Antarctica. Overlooking the vast mass of the Ronne Ice Shelf, Vinson Massif in the Ellsworth range is the highest point at 16,067 ft (4,897 m).

8 AORAKI (MOUNT COOK)

The highest peak in New Zealand, Aoraki's name means "cloud piercer" in the native Maori language. The mountain is also known as Mount Cook. Now 12,284 ft (2,744 m) high, Aoraki was 33 ft (10 m) higher before a landslide in 1991.

Mount Kilimanjaro's cone Kibo has a 1.5-mile- (2.4-km-) wide crater on its summit

4

The vast bulk of Mauna Kea is slowly sinking as the ocean floor sags beneath its weight

The frosty crags of Vinson Massif pierce the thick snow and ice shrouding its slopes

6

The icy summit of Mont Blanc can rise 52 ft (16 m) above its highest rocky peak

7

Heavy snowfall feeds two glaciers that flow down Aoraki's flanks

8

5

OCEANS

The oceans cover more than two-thirds of the surface of the Earth, with an average depth of 2.4 miles (3.8 km), but they are not just huge pools of saltwater. The ocean floors are where the great plates of the Earth's crust are splitting apart or grinding together, creating long, high ridges and deep trenches dotted with volcanoes. As a result of this, the oceans are changing their size and shape all the time.

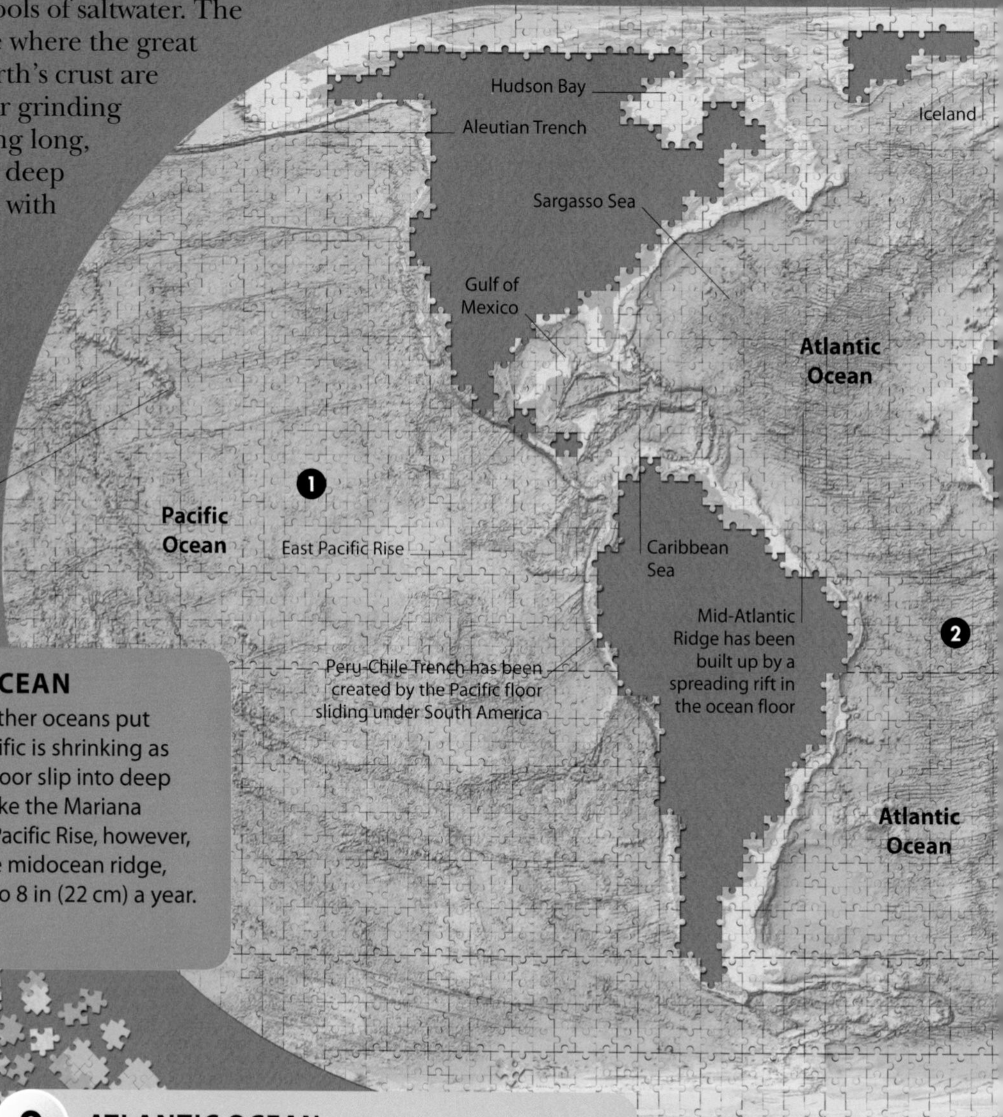

Hudson Bay

Aleutian Trench

Iceland

Sargasso Sea

Gulf of Mexico

Atlantic Ocean

Hawaii is just one of many volcanic islands and seamounts

Pacific Ocean

East Pacific Rise

Caribbean Sea

Mid-Atlantic Ridge has been built up by a spreading rift in the ocean floor

Peru-Chile Trench has been created by the Pacific floor sliding under South America

Atlantic Ocean

1 PACIFIC OCEAN

As big as all other oceans put together, the Pacific is shrinking as the edges of its floor slip into deep ocean trenches like the Mariana Trench. The East Pacific Rise, however, is the most active midocean ridge, spreading at up to 8 in (22 cm) a year.

2 ATLANTIC OCEAN

The Atlantic formed when North and South America split from Europe and Africa and gradually moved west. The ocean is still growing as new ocean floor is created at the Mid-Atlantic Ridge. The ridge breaks the surface in the north to form Iceland, with its volcanoes and geysers.

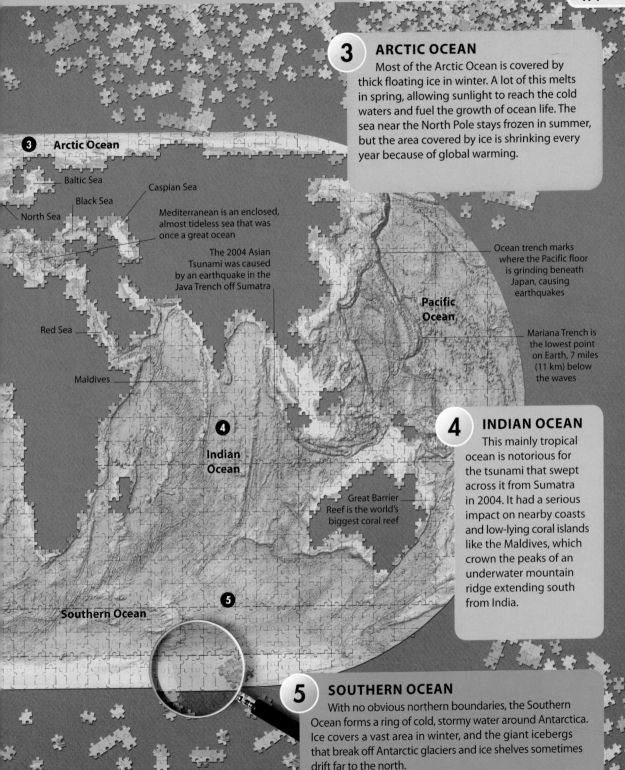

3 ARCTIC OCEAN
Most of the Arctic Ocean is covered by thick floating ice in winter. A lot of this melts in spring, allowing sunlight to reach the cold waters and fuel the growth of ocean life. The sea near the North Pole stays frozen in summer, but the area covered by ice is shrinking every year because of global warming.

3 Arctic Ocean

Baltic Sea

Caspian Sea

Black Sea

North Sea

Mediterranean is an enclosed, almost tideless sea that was once a great ocean

The 2004 Asian Tsunami was caused by an earthquake in the Java Trench off Sumatra

Ocean trench marks where the Pacific floor is grinding beneath Japan, causing earthquakes

Pacific Ocean

Red Sea

Mariana Trench is the lowest point on Earth, 7 miles (11 km) below the waves

Maldives

4 Indian Ocean

4 INDIAN OCEAN
This mainly tropical ocean is notorious for the tsunami that swept across it from Sumatra in 2004. It had a serious impact on nearby coasts and low-lying coral islands like the Maldives, which crown the peaks of an underwater mountain ridge extending south from India.

Great Barrier Reef is the world's biggest coral reef

5 Southern Ocean

5 SOUTHERN OCEAN
With no obvious northern boundaries, the Southern Ocean forms a ring of cold, stormy water around Antarctica. Ice covers a vast area in winter, and the giant icebergs that break off Antarctic glaciers and ice shelves sometimes drift far to the north.

ROCKS AND MINERALS

Rocks are mixtures of natural chemical compounds called minerals that form crystals with distinctive shapes. There are three main types of rock. Igneous rock is formed when molten rock cools and hardens, a metamorphic rock is one that has been changed by heat or pressure, and sedimentary rock is generally made from fragments of rock cemented together.

1 COCKSCOMB BARITE

This whitish mineral is often found in veins running through rocks. Its crystals form clusters that can resemble cockscombs (roosters' head crests).

2 CHALK

A type of limestone, chalk is built up from the remains of tiny marine organisms that sank to the bottom of a tropical sea during the age of dinosaurs.

3 MARBLE

Hard and usually pale, marble is a metamorphic form of limestone. It can be carved and polished into statues, and decorative slabs are used in architecture.

4 CALCITE

The main mineral in limestone and marble, calcite forms the stalactites and stalagmites seen in limestone caves.

5 LIMESTONE

All limestones are made of chalky minerals, particularly calcite. They are easily dissolved by rainwater, creating extensive cave systems.

6 HALITE

Formed by the evaporation of salt lakes, halite is rock salt—the mineral that we use to flavor our food.

7 ECLOGITE

A dense, heavy metamorphic rock formed deep beneath the Earth's surface, eclogite contains bright green pyroxene and glittering red garnet minerals.

8 BERYL

This very hard mineral forms transparent, often greenish crystals that can be cut to create emeralds and aquamarines.

9 GRANITE

One of the main rocks that form continents, granite results from molten rock cooling slowly deep underground to form big quartz, feldspar, and mica crystals.

10 OBSIDIAN

Also known as volcanic glass, this shiny black or dark green rock is formed when molten lava cools too quickly to form crystals.

11 PUMICE

Gas erupting from volcanoes often forms bubbles inside cooling lava. This can then form pumice, which has so many gas bubbles that it floats on water.

12 CORUNDUM

This dull-looking stone is a type of corundum, the hardest mineral after diamond. Its crystals are used to make rubies and sapphires.

13 ALBITE

A pale, sodium-rich form of feldspar, albite is a common ingredient of granite, visible as big, blocky crystals that glint in the sunshine.

14 GRAPHITE

Made of pure carbon—like diamond—graphite is a soft, metallic mineral that leaves a dark streak. It is used to make the "lead" in pencils.

15 SANDSTONE

Sand cemented together by other minerals forms sandstone. This red sandstone was once a desert dune.

16 PYRITE

Known as "fool's gold," this yellow metallic mineral is actually made of iron and sulfur. It often forms big cubic crystals like the ones seen here.

Amethystine spinel is named for its amethyst color.

Mauve spinel is mined in Myanmar (Burma), like most spinels.

Red spinel is often used in place of rubies.

Opal matrix is polished rock with veins of opal.

Green beryl is a paler form of emerald.

Zircon is one of the heaviest gemstones.

Golden sapphire is a golden form of blue sapphire.

Amethystine sapphire is made of hard corundum.

Ruby is the same mineral as sapphire, but red.

Blue zircon is the most desirable form of zircon.

Chrysoprase is prized for its apple color.

Star sapphire has a star pattern on its surface.

Brown tourmaline is one of hundreds of the gem's colors.

Pied tourmaline has two colors in one crystal.

Red tourmaline that looks like ruby is called rubelite.

Tanzanite is named after Tanzania where it is found.

Catseye quartz has a pale, glowing streak or "cat's eye."

Amethyst is a violet form of common quartz.

Chrysoberyl can be honey yellow to mint green.

Yellow beryl is tinted with iron and uranium.

Chrysoberyl is valued as a good luck charm.

Green tourmaline can resemble a fine emerald.

Carbuncle is a polished, domed form of garnet.

Tourmaline has more colors than any other gem.

Green beryl is a pale variety of emerald.

Citrine is a warm yellow type of quartz.

Amethyst is always violet or purple.

Iolite looks different colors from different angles.

Tiger eye is striped with yellow and brown.

Green zircon is more rare than the blue form.

Danburite is colorless, yellow, green, or brown.

Garnet was a favorite with ancient civilizations.

Topaz is said to dispel sadness, fear, and anger.

Green tourmaline is sometimes called verdelite.

Albite is always white.

Brown zircon is one of many color varieties.

Danburite named for th city of Danbur

Andalusite g with green a orange.

Opal has chan colors caused scattered lig

Emerald cats has a pale st

Moonstone magical gem in

Colorless top can be mistak for a diamon

ue spinel, also called cobalt spinel, is rare.

Pink sapphire is the same gem as a pale ruby.

Green tourmaline is tinted with traces of chromium.

Chrysoberyl is often a honey-colored brown.

Morganite is a pink beryl with manganese.

Iolite can look black from some angles.

Sphalerite is a soft stone that sparkles like a diamond.

Sapphire ontaining iron oxide is tinted yellow.

Indicolite is a blue variety of tourmaline.

Chrysoberyl is thought to promote harmony.

Aquamarine is a light blue variety of beryl.

Topaz is meant to protect against sudden death.

Peridot is made from vivid green olivine crystals.

Almandine garnet is bigger than a typical garnet.

een zircon can ter like a green diamond.

Yellow sapphire is rarer than blue but less valuable.

Sapphire frequently shows a starry pattern.

Yellow tourmaline comes from Malawi.

Kunzite often flashes various shades of violet.

Fire opal is a clear opal with red in it.

Topaz is usually yellow but can be colorless.

ink tourmaline catseye has a right highlight.

Jade has been known for at least 7,000 years.

Jade is usually green but can be mauve.

Hematite is a lustrous form of iron ore.

Lapis lazuli was one of the first gems to be worn.

Star garnet glints with a starry pattern.

Opal is often mounted on onyx as a "doublet."

GEMS

The natural minerals that make up rocks can form glassy crystals, which can be cut into glittering gems. Many are extremely hard and contain different impurities that tint gems such as sapphire, tourmaline, and topaz a sparkling array of colors. They can be extremely valuable. The gem collection shown here is worth almost a million dollars.

Jade is often carved, and was once used for tools.

Sinhalite is a rare stone from Sri Lanka.

Rhodolite is a velvety red form of garnet.

Kunzite was unknown until 100 years ago.

Garnet is usually a warm, brownish red.

Turquoise gets its sky blue from copper.

Moonstone is named for its shimmering glow.

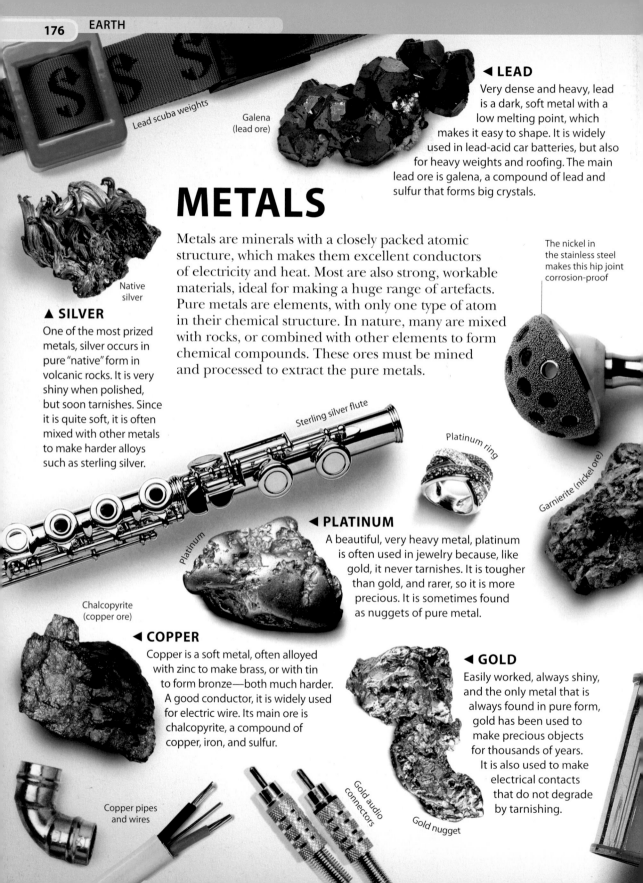

Lead scuba weights

Galena
(lead ore)

◀ LEAD

Very dense and heavy, lead is a dark, soft metal with a low melting point, which makes it easy to shape. It is widely used in lead-acid car batteries, but also for heavy weights and roofing. The main lead ore is galena, a compound of lead and sulfur that forms big crystals.

METALS

Metals are minerals with a closely packed atomic structure, which makes them excellent conductors of electricity and heat. Most are also strong, workable materials, ideal for making a huge range of artefacts. Pure metals are elements, with only one type of atom in their chemical structure. In nature, many are mixed with rocks, or combined with other elements to form chemical compounds. These ores must be mined and processed to extract the pure metals.

The nickel in the stainless steel makes this hip joint corrosion-proof

Native silver

▲ SILVER

One of the most prized metals, silver occurs in pure "native" form in volcanic rocks. It is very shiny when polished, but soon tarnishes. Since it is quite soft, it is often mixed with other metals to make harder alloys such as sterling silver.

Sterling silver flute

Platinum ring

Garnierite (nickel ore)

Platinum

◀ PLATINUM

A beautiful, very heavy metal, platinum is often used in jewelry because, like gold, it never tarnishes. It is tougher than gold, and rarer, so it is more precious. It is sometimes found as nuggets of pure metal.

Chalcopyrite
(copper ore)

◀ COPPER

Copper is a soft metal, often alloyed with zinc to make brass, or with tin to form bronze—both much harder. A good conductor, it is widely used for electric wire. Its main ore is chalcopyrite, a compound of copper, iron, and sulfur.

◀ GOLD

Easily worked, always shiny, and the only metal that is always found in pure form, gold has been used to make precious objects for thousands of years. It is also used to make electrical contacts that do not degrade by tarnishing.

Copper pipes
and wires

Gold audio connectors

Gold nugget

A deep-sea submersible

nautile

nautile

Aluminum baking foil

► ALUMINUM

Abundant and resistant to corrosion, lightweight aluminum is widely used for foil, cans, and in aircraft. Its ore, bauxite, is a rock that contains many aluminum compounds.

Bauxite (aluminum ore)

► TITANIUM

Light yet very strong, titanium is often combined with other metals to make lightweight alloys used in aircraft, spacecraft, and the pressure-proof capsules of deep-sea submersibles. One of its main ores is rutile, a compound of titanium and oxygen.

Rutile (titanium ore)

Steel nuts and bolts

Hematite (iron ore)

► MERCURY

The only metal that is liquid at room temperature is mercury. It is most familiar as the silvery contents of old-style medical thermometers. Its ore, cinnabar, is a compound of mercury and sulfur found near volcanoes.

▲ IRON

The most useful of all metals, iron is strong, abundant, and easy to work with, especially when refined into various types of steel. Its main ore is hematite, an iron oxide—the same thing as rust.

Cinnabar (mercury ore)

Stainless steel hip replacement

◄ NICKEL

Rarely used on its own, nickel is often alloyed with iron to make stainless steel. This is used for all kinds of applications, from knives and forks to replacement hip joints. Nickel is also alloyed with silver to make coins.

Mercury thermometer

▼ ZINC

Zinc is a white metal that is alloyed with copper to make brass. Its main use, however, is plating or "galvanizing" steel to make it rust-proof. Its main ore is sphalerite, a sparkling mineral that is a compound of zinc, iron, and sulfur.

Sphalerite (zinc ore)

Tin can

Cassiterite (tin ore)

▲ TIN

Well known for its use in tin cans—which are actually tin-plated steel—tin is widely used in electronic components because of its high electrical conductivity. It is also alloyed with lead to make the solder used to assemble electronic circuits.

Galvanized chain

PALEOZOIC ERA (ANCIENT LIFE)

Life began in the Precambrian era, more than 3.5 billion years ago, but for most of that time life was restricted to single-celled organisms like bacteria. The beginning of the Paleozoic era 540 million years ago saw an explosion of multicellular life, preserved as the fossils of marine trilobites, fish, insects, green plants, and early reptiles.

Sea lilies were plant-shaped relatives of starfish, attached to the seabed by stalks

Resembling woodlice, trilobites lived on seabeds throughout the Paleozoic era

FOSSILS

The remains, impressions, or traces of organisms (such as plants and animals) that have been preserved in the rocks are known as fossils. The process of fossilization generally takes millions of years, and since special circumstances are needed for fossils to form, only a tiny proportion of Earth's organisms have been fossilized. It is not always easy to date fossils absolutely, so the paleontologists who find, analyze, and identify fossils usually assign them to named eras and periods. These cover the major phases in the long history of life on Earth.

Lobe-finned fish were the ancestors of the first amphibians to live on land

Whole animals such as insects are preserved in amber, or fossilized tree resin

Dinosaur bones like this *Deinonychus* skull are the most spectacular fossils

Finely detailed fossils show the feathers of *Archaeopteryx*, the first known bird

Fossil ammonites (prehistoric sea creatures) were recorded in this book more than 100 years ago

Familar animals, like this dragonfly, were already common 150 million years ago

MESOZOIC ERA (MIDDLE LIFE)

Beginning 252 million years ago, this was the age of the dinosaurs, when giant reptiles stalked the land, pterosaurs swooped through the skies, and marine reptiles such as ichthyosaurs swam alongside squidlike ammonites. Flowering plants and small mammals also appeared on land. The era ended with a mass extinction 65 million years ago.

Fossils from about
10 million years ago
reveal details of
ancient corals

Large collections of
specimens help with
the identification
and dating of fossils

CENOZOIC ERA (RECENT LIFE)

Dinosaur fossils do not appear in rock formed less than 65 million
years ago in the Cenozoic era, showing that they had died out by
that time. Yet mammal fossils become more varied, and include
early relatives of humans, which date back to 3.6 million years
ago. The first true humans appeared about a million years later.

Mammoth tooth
found on the bed
of the North Sea
shows the sea was
once dry land

Hammer and chisel
used to remove rock
from around fossil

Reconstructed
fossil fragments form
this skull of *Homo
habilis*, an ancestor
of modern humans

Geological
hammer

Magnifying
glass

Chisels

PALEONTOLOGY

The word "paleontology" means the study of ancient
bones, preserved as fossils. But paleontologists also study
nonbony life-forms such as mollusks, plants, and even
bacteria. Their work involves carefully removing, cleaning,
and preserving the fossils, as well as identifying them and
recording their features. Special tools ranging from hammers
to medical scanners help them prepare and interpret their finds.

Split rock reveals the
mineralized fossil
of an ammonite,
and a cast of its shell

FOSSILIZATION

Normally only the hard parts of living things, such as shells
and bones, survive as fossils. Over millions of years these
become impregnated with minerals, so they become stony.
Often the original shell or bone dissolves, leaving a mold
later filled by another mineral. Rarely, soft body parts such as
feathers may leave detailed impressions in fine-grained rock.

Opalized
marine
snail

This footprint of a
three-toed predatory
dinosaur is known
as a "trace fossil"

This late Mesozoic clam left a
mold that has become filled
with opal to create a cast fossil

DINOSAURS

Long ago, life on Earth was dominated by the dinosaurs, a group of reptiles that included huge, lumbering plant-eaters and fearsome, agile hunters. They became extinct 65 million years ago (MYA), but their fossilized remains survive in the rocks of ancient continents, allowing scientists to reconstruct what they looked like and how they lived.

1 TYRANOSAURUS

The massive, predatory tyrannosaurs evolved at the end of the dinosaur era, 70–65 million years ago. The biggest, *Tyrannosaurus rex*, grew to 46 ft (14 m) and had razor-sharp teeth up to 6 in (15 cm) long. Its fossilized remains have been found in rocks in North America, notably in Montana and South Dakota.

2 SAUROLOPHUS

A contemporary of *Tyrannosaurus*, this plant-eater had a bony spike on its skull that may have supported an ornamental crest. Fossils from Asia have longer spikes than fossils found in America, showing that there were at least two different species.

3 TRICERATOPS

The bony neck shield and three sharp horns of *Triceratops* enabled it to defend itself from powerful hunters. Judging from fossilized bones found in North America, the animal grew to at least 30 ft (9 m) long.

4 OVIRAPTOR

Similar to the larger *Struthiomimus*, this birdlike dinosaur had short powerful jaws and possibly a beak. Its name means "egg-thief" because the first fossil specimen was found on a nest of dinosaur eggs, and it may have died trying to steal them.

5 STRUTHIOMIMUS

Standing taller than a man, this agile, fast-running dinosaur was more like an ostrich than a typical reptile. It had no teeth in its long jaws, and it is possible that it had a long, horny beak like a bird. It may have hunted small, fast-moving animals.

Prenocephale (80–65 MYA)

Pachycephalosaurus (76–65 MYA)

Muttaburrasaurus (110–100 MYA)

Iguanodon (140–110 MYA)

...osaurus (74–70 MYA)

Stegoceras (76–74 MYA)

105

136

Struthiomimus (76–74 MYA)

Velociraptor (84–80 MYA)

Wuerhosaurus (137–99 MYA)

Kentrosaurus (155–150 MYA)

205F

900R

Stegosaurus (155–144 MYA)

Eustreptospondylus (165–161 MYA)

700

Ceratosaurus (150–144 MYA)

29

Allosaurus (153–135 MYA)

Deinonychus (120–110 MYA)

Diplodocus (155–145 MYA)

8 STEGOSAURUS

Stegosaurus fed on plants in what is now North America, 155–144 million years ago, and could grow to the size of a bus. Scientists have puzzled over the function of the huge bony plates on its back, which are not attached to the backbone. They may have acted as protective armor, but it is more likely that they acted like solar panels to regulate body temperature.

6 IGUANODON

The remains of this big plant-eater were among the first dinosaur fossils to be identified as such. Its teeth were found in England in 1822 by Mary Ann Mantell. Her husband, Dr. Gideon Mantell, saw their similarity to the teeth of living iguanas, and realized that they were the teeth of a giant extinct reptile.

9 VELOCIRAPTOR

Found in Mongolia, the fossil bones of this smallish dinosaur are very like those of the first birds, and recent research shows that it may have had feathers. It was an agile, high-speed hunter that probably hunted in packs, jumping on its prey and slashing with its hooked claws.

7 ALLOSAURUS

Although it probably looked very like *Tyrannosaurus*, the fossils of this massive meat-eater have been found in rocks that are at least 70 million years older. This timespan is longer than the period that separates the last dinosaurs from our own time.

10 DIPLODOCUS

This giant dinosaur lived in what is now North America at the same time as Allosaurus, but used its long neck to browse on leaves at the tops of trees. It was up to 90 ft (27 m) long, with a small head and whiplike tail.

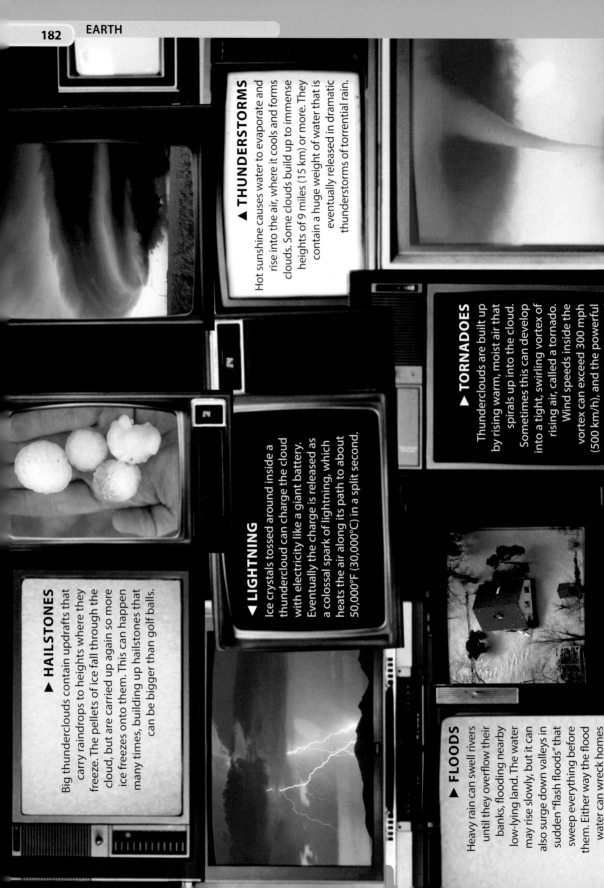

▲ THUNDERSTORMS

Hot sunshine causes water to evaporate and rise into the air, where it cools and forms clouds. Some clouds build up to immense heights of 9 miles (15 km) or more. They contain a huge weight of water that is eventually released in dramatic thunderstorms of torrential rain.

▶ TORNADOES

Thunderclouds are built up by rising warm, moist air that spirals up into the cloud. Sometimes this can develop into a tight, swirling vortex of rising air, called a tornado. Wind speeds inside the vortex can exceed 300 mph (500 km/h), and the powerful updraft can easily rip the roof off a house.

▲ HAILSTONES

Big thunderclouds contain updrafts that carry raindrops to heights where they freeze. The pellets of ice fall through the cloud, but are carried up again so more ice freezes onto them. This can happen many times, building up hailstones that can be bigger than golf balls.

▼ LIGHTNING

Ice crystals tossed around inside a thundercloud can charge the cloud with electricity like a giant battery. Eventually the charge is released as a colossal spark of lightning, which heats the air along its path to about 50,000°F (30,000°C) in a split second.

▲ FLOODS

Heavy rain can swell rivers until they overflow their banks, flooding nearby low-lying land. The water may rise slowly, but it can also surge down valleys in sudden "flash floods" that sweep everything before them. Either way the flood water can wreck homes and even swamp cities.

◄ HURRICANES

The most devastating weather occurs over tropical oceans, where intense heat creates huge storm clouds that revolve around zones of very low air pressure. Winds spiral into the center at 185 mph (300 km/h) or more, heaping ocean water into "storm surges" that can drown coastal cities. Hurricanes that form over the Pacific Ocean are called typhoons.

WEATHER

Driven by the heat of the Sun, circulating currents of air swirl through the lower atmosphere, creating the winds that carry clouds, rain, and snow from the oceans over the land. Without these weather systems the continents would be barren deserts, where life would be impossible. Sometimes, however, the weather can be so violent that it causes destruction on a terrifying scale.

ICE STORMS

Freezing winter weather is normal in many regions, but freak conditions can sometimes cause unusually destructive ice storms. If moist air is swept over a very cold region, falling rain may freeze where it lands to form thick ice. This can bring down power lines, paralyze rail networks, and turn roads into death traps.

► PREDICTING WEATHER

Satellite images like this view of a hurricane in the Gulf of Mexico can help meteorologists predict the weather. Forecasters also gather data on wind, temperature, air pressure, and other variables, and feed them into computers that are programmed with mathematical models of the atmosphere. The computers use the new data to predict how the atmosphere may react, and so produce a weather forecast.

◀ SAND-BLASTING

In deserts, the wind picks up grains of sand and hurls them against bare rock, scouring the surface and widening any cracks. Deep beds of sandstone, like these in North America, may be worn into spectacular wavelike shapes, revealing layers of rock laid down over millions of years.

Wind erosion has turned the Coyote Buttes in Arizona into a natural work of art

The granite walls of El Capitan in California have survived millions of years of erosion

▶ WEATHERED GRANITE

Granite is an extremely hard, crystalline rock, but it can still be broken down by erosion. It is formed deep underground, and when exposed to the air the change of pressure makes the outside layers flake away in a process called exfoliation. It can also be attacked by the acids in rainwater, and scoured by ice.

Horseshoe Bend on the Colorado River formed as the river cut down through uplifted rock

Rock is undercut by the waves so the rock above collapses, leaving a sheer cliff

◀ CLIFFS AND STACKS

Waves crashing against coastal cliffs can cut them away at a dramatic rate. The softer rock gives way first, often leaving headlands and isolated stacks of harder rock. These stacks off the southern coast of Australia near Melbourne are known as the Twelve Apostles.

Moving ice loaded with rock fragments would have once filled this Alpine valley

◄ MESAS AND BUTTES

In arid terrain, occasional flash floods cut down through weak points in the rock to form valleys. These get wider and wider, carrying away the softer rock so the harder layers collapse. Eventually, all that remains are sheer-sided mesas and smaller buttes, each protected by a cap of hard rock.

Rock debris forms steep scree (rubble) slopes below the towering buttes of Monument Valley in Utah

► KARST TERRAIN

Rainwater is slightly acid, and this enables it to dissolve limestone. The result can be a landscape called karst, with heavily weathered bare rock riddled with caves. In tropical areas the rock is often eroded into spectacular pinnacles.

Sharp pinnacles of limestone form the Stone Forest near Kunming, China

◄ RIVER EROSION

Rivers cut V-shaped valleys and steep-sided gorges, especially where fast-flowing water carries a lot of rocky debris. The most dramatic gorges form where the land has been slowly uplifted by titanic ground movements, forcing the river to cut deeper and deeper into the landscape.

EROSION

Landscapes are under constant attack from wind, rain, ice, searing heat, oceanic waves, and flowing water loaded with rock fragments. These forces gnaw away at even the hardest rocks, in the processes known as erosion and weathering. Over time they can flatten the highest mountain ranges, carrying the rocky debris away as gravel, sand, and silt. This is deposited in the lowlands or in the sea—where, eventually, it may form new rocks.

▲ VANISHED GLACIERS

In mountains, and in uplands affected by the last ice age, huge glaciers grinding along the courses of former rivers scoured them out to form deep U-shaped valleys. Where the glaciers have melted, the valleys remain, often with small rivers flowing down them.

► SLOT CANYON

Sandy water pours off high mesas during rare, but torrential desert rainstorms. It funnels through cracks in the rock at the edges of the mesas, eroding them into deep, winding slot canyons. Unlike valleys, these are often broader at the bottom than at the top.

A beam of sunlight gleams through the narrow top of Antelope Canyon, Arizona

RIVERS

Most rivers flow downhill from hills or mountains to the sea. They start as fast-flowing streams, which join together to create small rivers. These often cascade down steep slopes, cutting deep valleys, until they reach flatter ground. Here, regular seasonal flooding creates broad, fertile floodplains. Each river wanders across its floodplain, growing in size but flowing more slowly, until it reaches the estuary or delta where it spills into the sea.

▼ SOURCE

All rivers have a source. It may be a lake, a swamp, or a spring bubbling out of the ground, which feeds the main stream of the young river. In high mountains, the source may be a stream of meltwater pouring from the end of a glacier.

▼ UPPER COURSE

The upland part of a river is known as its upper course. It is usually fast-flowing, with a rocky bed, rapids, and even waterfalls. Here the Churun River cascades over the rim of the flat-topped Auyantepui Mountain in Venezuela, at Angel Falls—the highest waterfall on Earth, at 3,212 ft (979 m).

▼ TRIBUTARIES

The main stream of a river is joined by other streams, called tributaries. They all add to the flow, especially after heavy rain and during the spring thaw, when mountain snow melts. At such times, they turn into torrents, carrying masses of gravel downhill and flowing in "braided" patterns. These braided streams flow down from Aoraki (Mount Cook), New Zealand, to join the Hopkins River.

▼ VALLEYS AND GORGES

As a river flows down from its upper course, the water usually erodes a winding V-shaped valley through the land. Some rivers pass through steep-sided gorges, like Tiger Leaping Gorge on the Yangtze River in China. Gorges are often created by the collapse of limestone cave systems that once concealed underground rivers.

▼ LOWER COURSE

When rivers reach the lowlands they flow more slowly, but carry more water. If they are not controlled they tend to flood each year, spilling over their banks and swamping the landscape. The floodwater leaves layers of fine silt, which build up to form a floodplain of deep, fertile soil. This makes excellent farmland. Here the Willamette River flows across its floodplain in Oregon.

▼ ESTUARIES AND DELTAS

At the coast, fresh river water meets the saltwater that pushes upriver at high tide. As a result, the river drops mud particles, building up the mudflats of an estuary. If the river flow is more powerful than the flow of the tide, the flats extend out from the shore to form a wide flat area with many outlet channels, known as a delta. This view from space shows the delta of the Niger River as it meets the sea in Nigeria.

▼ MEANDERS

As it flows around a bend, river water cuts away the bank on the outside of the bend and drops sand and mud on the inside. This makes the bend more pronounced, so over time its winding course may become a series of exaggerated loops, or meanders. Sometimes a loop is cut off to become an "ox-bow lake," seen here (center left) as the Amazon River flows through rain forest in Peru, South America.

CLIMATE ZONES

Variations in the intensity of sunlight striking different parts of the Earth drive global air movements and weather systems. Between them, these influences create a variety of climate zones, ranging from steamy tropical rain forests to the icy deserts of Antarctica. Most of these climate zones have a distinctive type of vegetation, which is the basis of a whole wildlife community, or biome.

▲ MOUNTAIN

High mountain peaks are very cold, like Arctic tundra, and they have similar tough, low-growing vegetation. Lower mountain slopes are warmer, allowing trees to grow. The upper edge of this zone is called the tree line.

► TROPICAL RAIN FOREST

Intense sunshine near the equator makes moisture evaporate and rise into the air to form huge storm clouds. These spill heavy, warm rain on the land below, fuelling the growth of dense rain forests.

► DESERT

Some regions get so little rain that they are deserts. Many lie in a zone of hot, dry air near the tropics, but others are just too far from oceans. Some plants live in deserts, so they are not quite barren.

► TEMPERATE FOREST

Temperate climates are neither very hot nor very cold. Near oceans, the mild, damp weather allows trees to grow well in summer, but many lose their leaves and stop growing in winter.

▲ POLAR AND TUNDRA

The polar regions get only weak sunlight in summer, and are dark all winter. They stay frozen all year, but in the north this icy region is surrounded by tundra, which thaws in summer allowing some plants to grow.

▲ MEDITERRANEAN

The dry shrublands that lie between the temperate zones and the main desert regions are named after the Mediterranean area where they are most common. The tough-leaved plants that live there can survive drying out in the hot summers.

▼ CLIMATE ZONES

The climate zones of the world form bands, with tropical rain forest near the equator, most deserts in the subtropics, and boreal forest in the far north. Grasslands develop where it is too dry for trees.

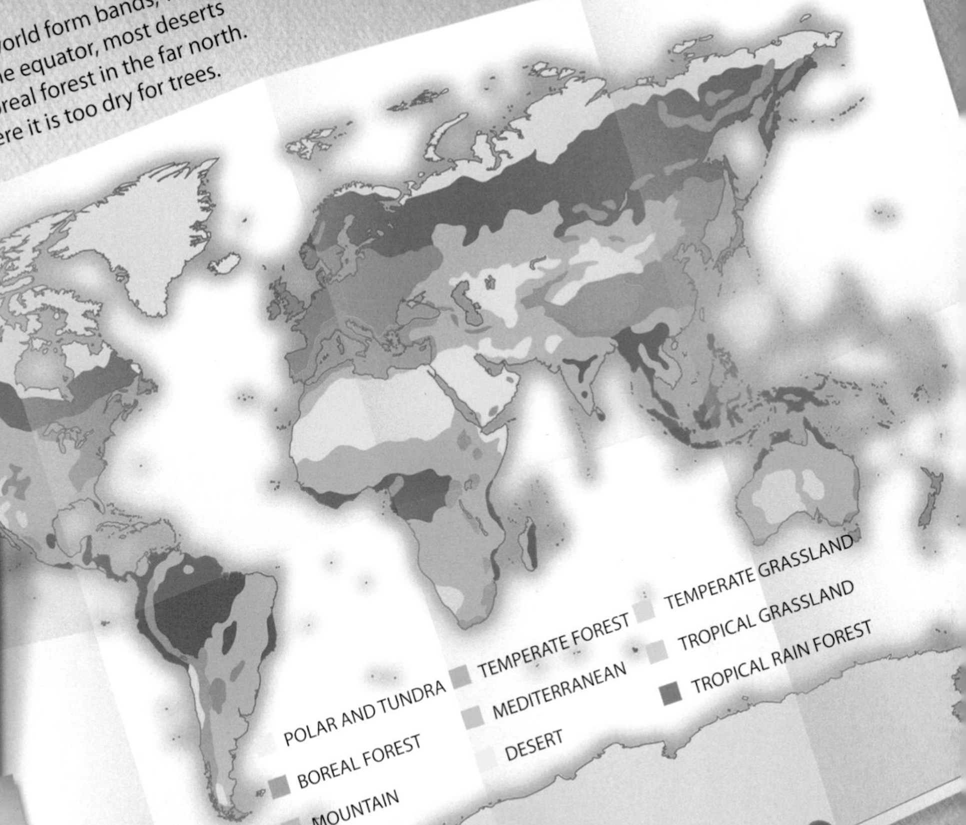

POLAR AND TUNDRA

BOREAL FOREST

MOUNTAIN

TEMPERATE FOREST

MEDITERRANEAN

DESERT

TEMPERATE GRASSLAND

TROPICAL GRASSLAND

TROPICAL RAIN FOREST

▲ TROPICAL GRASSLAND

Tropical regions that are not within the zone of heavy rainfall are too hot and dry to support dense forest. They are seas of grass, often known as savannahs, sometimes dotted with trees that can withstand long droughts.

▲ TEMPERATE GRASSLAND

Some temperate areas get little rainfall, usually because they lie at the hearts of great continents. Too dry for trees, they are naturally grassy steppes and prairies—although many are now farmland.

▲ BOREAL FOREST

To the south of the Arctic tundra, the northern continents support a band of dense forest. Most of the trees are conifers with stiff needlelike leaves that can survive the long, freezing winters.

Corn on
the cob

▲ CORN

The corn grown in the Americas is actually a giant grass that grows well in sunny climates. Its big kernels can be cooked and eaten as they are, or ground into flour to make tortillas and corn chips.

Soybean
pods

Dried
soybeans

Soy flour

▲ SOYBEANS

High in protein and rich in oil, soybeans were once known only in Asia. Now popular with vegetarians, they are grown in warm climates worldwide.

Rice
cakes

Rice seeds

▼ RICE

One of the world's three staple foods—along with corn and wheat—rice is a type of grass that grows in warm climates. It is usually cultivated in flooded "paddy" fields, which cover large areas of the tropics.

Soy sauce

Soya milk

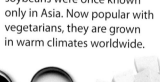

Tofu is a
food made
from soy

Grains
of rice

Cooked rice

Corn tortillas

Corn chips

Fresh
cocoa pod

Dried
cocoa pod

Cocoa beans

◄ COCOA

The main ingredient of chocolate, cocoa beans come from the pods of the cocoa tree, grown mainly in West Africa and tropical America. The beans are first left to ferment in the sun, then dried, roasted, and either ground into powder or made into cocoa butter.

Bar of
chocolate

FARM CROPS

All our plant foods are grown on farms of some kind—from the huge wheat and corn fields of North America, to the banana plantations and coconut groves of the tropics. The crops we harvest today are descended from plants that once grew wild, but which have been bred to give high yields of juicy fruit, edible seeds, or rich vegetable oils.

White potatoes

► POTATOES

The potato is the tuber (storage root) of a plant related to tomatoes. It was brought to Europe from South America in the 16th century, and since then it has become one of the world's main foods.

Red
potatoes

▼ WHEAT

Wheat is the most important grain crop in mild northern climates, where it is cultivated on a vast scale. A member of the grass family, wheat has been bred to have large seeds for grinding into flour.

Vine of red
tomatoes

Fresh
tea leaves

Tea bags

▲ TEA

The leaves used to make tea come from an evergreen bush that grows in tropical and subtropical climates. It is cultivated mainly in China and India, where the leaves are handpicked and quickly dried. Leaf tea can be used as it is, or in paper tea bags.

Bread made
from wheat
flour

► TOMATOES

Closely related to potatoes, and introduced from the same region of South America in the late 1500s, the tomato is now grown almost worldwide.

Bunch of wheat
seedheads

Inside a
yellow tomato

Dried tea leaves

Grapes on the vine

Sunflower oil

► GRAPES

One of the oldest cultivated plants, the grape was grown by Ancient Egyptians 6,000 years ago. Planted in permanent vineyards in warm climates, grapes are harvested for winemaking, eating fresh, and drying as raisins, sultanas, and currants.

Currants and raisins

White grapes

Black grapes

► SUNFLOWERS

The spectacular blooms of sunflowers are made up of hundreds of big seeds. These can be eaten as snacks, but most are processed to produce oil, which is used in cooking. Bees love sunflowers, and they turn the nectar into honey.

Sunflower seeds

Dried sunflower seed head

Sunflower in bloom

Stalk of sugar cane

◄ SUGAR CANE

Grown on plantations in tropical and subtropical regions of the world, sugar cane is the thick stalk of a large grass. More than half the world's sugar comes from sugar cane. It is also made into alcohol used in biofuels (fuels made from renewable organic material, such as plants).

Brown sugar

Molasses is a sticky juice produced when sugar cane is boiled

The coconut grows inside a thick, fibrous husk

Ripe banana

◄ BANANAS

Bananas grow in bunches of up to 200, sprouting from clusters of huge leaves that shoot up from fleshy roots. They are a valuable crop throughout the tropics, and are usually cut while green so they are perfectly yellow and ripe when sold.

Green bananas

Dried coconut

Fresh coconut

Creamed coconut

▲ COCONUTS

The big nuts of the coconut palm are an important crop on many Pacific islands. The fibrous husk is used for matting and rope making. The white "meat" of the nuts is used for food, either fresh, dessicated (dried), as creamed coconut, or as coconut oil.

▼ COFFEE

Coffee is one of the most valuable crops produced in the tropics. It is made from the seeds of a small tree. Each red berry contains two seeds, or beans, which are dried in the sun before being roasted and ground.

Cup of coffee

Roasted coffee beans

Red coffee berries

Inside the coconut is a layer of white "meat"

ENVIRONMENT

As the human population grows and we exploit more of the world's resources, we inflict a lot of damage on our environment. We are doing this partly by destruction of natural habitats, such as forests and wetlands, and partly by pollution of the land, oceans, and atmosphere. Many plants and animals are endangered, and entire ecosystems such as coral reefs and rain forests are under threat.

Coral reefs are dying as oceans become warmer, and many types of coral may soon be extinct

Plastic waste floating in the sea can trap and kill marine animals, as well as pollute beaches

Smog shrouding the Los Angeles skyline

Garbage in Guanabara Bay, Brazil

▲ AIR POLLUTION

Smoke and gases released by industry, power plants, homes, and vehicles have caused visible air pollution, known as "smog," in many cities. Badly polluted air can be dangerous to breathe, but the main threat from this kind of pollution is global warming.

▲ LAND AND SEA POLLUTION

A lot of the things that we throw away end up scattered over the landscape, or dumped in the sea. Most plastic never rots down and is dangerous to wildlife. Raw sewage and other waste is also poisoning enclosed seas such as the Mediterranean.

▲ GLOBAL WARMING

The most serious threat to the environment is global warming. This is caused by pollution of the air by gases that absorb heat and warm up the atmosphere. This may lead to changes in rainfall patterns and rises in sea levels as polar ice caps melt.

▼ ACID RAIN

Smoke and fumes from industry and power plants combine with moisture in the air to form weak sulfuric and nitric acids. When this acid rain falls it can kill trees and turn lakes too acidic to support life. This is a serious problem in Canada, Russia, and China.

The worst effects of acid rain are suffered in areas that are close to industrial regions

▼ DEFORESTATION

All over the world, vast areas of forest are being destroyed each year. Tropical forests in particular are being felled for lumber and to clear land for farming. This is wrecking some of the richest natural habitats on Earth and is one of the main causes of climate change.

Coral reef, Fiji

Forest destroyed by acid rain near the Appalachian Mountains

Rain forest clearance in Chiapas, Mexico

Giant panda in Wolong Nature Preserve, Chengdu, China

◀ LOSS OF BIODIVERSITY

As wild habitats are destroyed, plants and animals have fewer places to live. This makes survival harder for many species. As endangered species die out, it reduces the rich variety of life that is vital to the health of the planet.

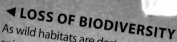

Cycling to work in San Francisco, USA

▶ PROTECTING THE EARTH

Protecting the environment is not just the job of governments. We can all help by altering the way we live. By cycling to work instead of driving, these city workers are reducing the amount of pollution they produce.

QUICK QUIZ

What can you remember about Earth?
Jot down your answers, then check them on pp.296–97.

1 **Aoraki** is the **highest peak** in **New Zealand**, although it **lost some** of its **height** in a landslide in 1991. What does the name Aoraki mean?
- Ⓐ Cloud piercer
- Ⓑ Snow hoarder
- Ⓒ I was once much higher
- Ⓓ Roof of the world

2 This **birdlike dinosaur** is called *Oviraptor*, which means "egg thief." Why was it so named?
- Ⓐ Its criminal records can be found in fossilized police files
- Ⓑ The first fossil specimen of this dinosaur was found on a nest of dinosaur eggs
- Ⓒ Its beaklike mouth was suitable for breaking open delicate egg shells

3 What **soft, metallic mineral** is used to make the "lead" in pencils?
- Ⓐ Lead
- Ⓑ Graphite
- Ⓒ Coal
- Ⓓ Charcoal

4 What is causing many types of **coral reefs** to become extinct?
- Ⓐ Massive tsunamis
- Ⓑ Tourists breaking pieces off
- Ⓒ Oceans becoming warmer
- Ⓓ Fish eating the reefs

5 This is the fossil of the **first known bird**. What is the bird called?
- Ⓐ *Archaeopteryx*
- Ⓑ *Pterodactylus*
- Ⓒ *Quetzalcoatlus*
- Ⓓ *Confuciusornis*

6 This **body of water** is a spreading rift in the **Earth's crust** that will **widen into an ocean**. What is it called?
- Ⓐ The Spreading Sea
- Ⓑ The Red Sea
- Ⓒ The Mediterranean Sea
- Ⓓ The Red Rift

7 What do we call a **sudden flood** that **surges down valleys** sweeping away everything in its path?

8 **Match** the **metal** to its **name:**

- Ⓐ Copper
- Ⓑ Gold
- Ⓒ Platinum
- Ⓓ Silver

9 **Earthquakes** are most frequent along **fault lines**. What causes earthquakes?

Ⓐ New tectonic plates being created
Ⓑ Ocean floor sliding under continents
Ⓒ Tectonic plates pulling apart
Ⓓ Tectonic plates sliding past each other

10 The height of this peak in the **European Alps varies** from year to year, because its summit is a **dome of ice**. What is the peak called?

11 The Earth's crust is **divided into** many large pieces of rock known as **tectonic plates**. These plates **carry continents** and **form the ocean floor**. **Match** the **tectonic plates** to their **names**:

❶

❷

❸

❹

Ⓐ Pacific   Ⓑ Australian   Ⓒ Eurasian   Ⓓ African

12 The **biggest** ever **earthquake** occurred in Chile in 1960. How much did it measure on the **Richter Scale**?

Ⓐ 9.0
Ⓑ 9.5
Ⓒ 10.5
Ⓓ 12.0

13 **Fossils** of early relatives of humans date back to **3.6 million years** ago. Which **ancestor** of **modern humans** did this **skull belong** to?

Ⓐ *Gigantopithecus*
Ⓑ *Australopithecus*
Ⓒ *Homo habilis*
Ⓓ *Homo erectus*

14 Which **gemstone** is said to **dispel sadness, fear,** and **anger?**

15 Which of these is **not** one of the world's three **staple foods**?

Ⓐ Wheat
Ⓑ Legumes
Ⓒ Rice
Ⓓ Corn

16 How was this spectacular **desert landscape** in Arizona formed?

Ⓐ By skateboarders
Ⓑ By a river that has dried up
Ⓒ By wind picking up grains of sand and hurling them against bare rock
Ⓓ By tectonic plate movement

17 The region in **Antarctica** bordering the **Ross Sea** is famous for its spectacular **ice caves**. What is this region called?

FAST FACTS

The rotation of the Earth is slowing down, so days are becoming longer. In the age of the dinosaurs, **60 million years ago**, an **Earth day** was less than **23 hours long**.

At **midnight** on June 21, each year, it is **light** everywhere north of the **Arctic Circle**.

Looking out to **sea** from the **beach**, the **horizon** is about **3 miles** (5 km) away.

*After it was measured using satellites in 1999, the official height of **Mount Everest** was raised from 29,029 ft (8,848 m) to 29,035 ft (8,850 m).*

The **Great Barrier Reef**, at more than **1,200 miles** (2,000 km) long, is the largest living structure on Earth. It is even visible from space.

The pressure at the center of the Earth is *3 million* times greater than that at the surface.

Nine out of 10 volcanoes are under the sea. More than 1,000 of the 1,500 active volcanoes in the world are in the South Pacific Ocean.

In the 20th century, the surface temperature of Earth rose by 33°F (0.6°C).

Coal is made from the compressed remains of plants that died **300 million** years ago.

The world's smallest volcano is *Cuexcomate* in Mexico. It is just *43 ft* (13 m) tall.

Almost 20 percent of Earth's **oxygen** is produced by the **Amazon rain forest**.

*A large thunderstorm cloud, called a **cumulonimbus**, can hold enough water to fill 500,000 baths.*

When the volcanic island of **Krakatoa**, in Indonesia, erupted in **1883**, it could be heard a quarter of the way around the world.

There are about **750** different species of **tree** in *2.5 acres* (one hectare) of the **Amazon rain forest**.

Over half the planet is covered by water more than 1 mile (1.6 km) deep.

It would take a heavy object more than an hour to sink from the surface to the seabed at **Challenger Deep** in the Pacific Ocean, which is **36,201 ft** (11,034 m) deep.

Six million tons of **gold** is dissolved in the water of the world's oceans.

The volume of water in the Pacific Ocean is the same size as the Moon.

*In 1811, an earthquake sent water in the **Mississippi River** flowing temporarily in the **wrong direction**.*

Lightning strikes Earth 100 times every second.

China's Yellow River is the world's *muddiest* river. Two billion tons of mud wash down it every year.

Fresh snow is more than *90 percent* trapped air.

The biggest **desert** in the world, the **Sahara**, covers a **third** of the area of **Africa**.

Sand dunes move like waves across deserts at a speed of about 3 ft (1 m) per year.

*The lowest temperature ever recorded is -128.5°F (-89.2°C) at **Vostok, Antarctica**, on July 21, 1983.*

The strongest gust of wind ever recorded blew at **231 mph** (372 km/h) on **Mount Washington**, in 1934.

The highest temperature ever recorded was **134°F** (56.7°C) at **Furnace Creek Ranch, California,** on July 10, 1913.

*The **driest** place in the world is the **Atacama Desert** in **Chile**. When it rained there in **1971**, it ended a **drought** that had lasted for **400 years**.*

The driest continent is *Antarctica* because it receives so little rain.

There is enough **electricity** in a single fork of **lightning** to **light** a town for a year.

Seawater freezes at **28°F** (-2°C) because the salt in it lowers its freezing point.

The surface of the **Dead Sea** in the Jordan Valley is 1,368 ft (417 m) below sea level and is shrinking rapidly. Its water is so **salty** that nothing can live in it except simple organisms, such as algae.

*The world's **shortest river** is the **North Fork Roe River**, in Montana; it is just 59 ft (18 m) long.*

In **1873**, *frogs* rained down from the sky in Kansas City. In **1948**, a group of golfers in Bournemouth, England, was showered with *herring*. The animals had been swept up into the clouds by strong winds.

*The **hardness of rocks** is measured using the **Mohs scale**, with **soft talc** at 1 and **hard diamond** at 10.*

The largest meteor crater is **Vredefort in South Africa, which is 186 miles (300 km) wide. It was created when a meteor about 6 miles (10 km) wide collided with Earth 2 billion years ago.**

As **deserts** grow larger, the amount of **land available** to grow **crops** is **shrinking** at a rate of **40,000 sq miles** (100,000 sq km) every year.

*Enough water to fill **2 million bathtubs** flows out of the **Amazon River** into the Atlantic Ocean in one second. This is **five times** as much water as the second-largest flow, from the **Ganges River**.*

On average, there are just **five days** a year when it doesn't **rain** on Mt. Waialeale in Hawaii.

On the afternoon of May 31, 1985, **41 tornadoes** were reported around the states of Pennsylvania and Ohio in the US. **Seventy-five** people were killed.

The eruption of **Mount St. Helens** in the US on May 18, 1980, set off an **avalanche** traveling at 250 mph (400 km/h).

The **oldest rocks** in the **Grand Canyon** were formed **2 billion** years ago.

The Holderness coastline in east England is being eroded away by the North Sea at a rate of 5 ft (1.5 m) per year.

No two *snowflakes* have the same shape, but they all have **six sides**.

More than **30 percent** of New Zealand's greenhouse gas comes from methane in the **burps** and **farts** of the country's 30 million **sheep** and 10 million **cows**.

Greenland is the **largest island** in the world, with an area of **836,109 sq miles** (2,133,086 sq km). **Australia** is **larger**, but is considered to be a **continent** rather than an island.

*The **largest diamond mine** in the world is at Mirna in Siberia. The hole in the ground is **4,000 ft** (1,200 m) across—so big that **helicopters** are **sucked into it** if they fly too close.*

There are **14 mountains more than 26,000 ft (8,000 m) high, all of them in the Himalayas.**

Clouds contain tiny droplets of water floating in air. A raindrop contains up to **2 million** cloud **droplets**.

Earth's atmosphere is **430 miles** (700 km) thick.

A delay of **three seconds** between seeing **lightning** and hearing **thunder** means that the lightning is **half a mile** (1 km) away.

There are **15,000 bush fires** in Australia every year, as trees and shrubs burst into flames in the extreme heat. Many plants rely on these fires to release their seeds.

Over the last 10,000 years, **80 percent** of the world's **forests** have been **cut down** by humans.

Seven percent of the world's **oceans** are covered in **ice**.

PEOPLE AND PLACES

PAINTED BRIDE
At a traditional wedding in the Balkan village of Donje Ljubinje, the bride's face is painted to ward off bad luck. The custom is unique, as is the villagers' language—a mixture of Serbian, Macedonian, and Turkish.

AFRICA

The recent discovery of fossilized remains in Africa has led experts to agree that the world's first humans originated from this continent millions of years ago. Today, the population stands at over one billion, with many people living in rural regions of the 53 countries. Africa's diversity is seen in its varied cultures, long-standing customs, striking scenery and wildlife. This captivating mix attracts a steady stream of visitors.

INDUSTRY

Nigeria, Algeria, and Libya are major sources of oil and natural gas, while South Africa have made gold and diamonds. Minerals and copper are mined in prosperous. Congo and Zambia. Namibia. tin are exported from

FOOD

Africa's staple foods are crops such as corn, yams, cassava, and plantains; but are Africa's, cassava, and main dish including Morocco added and lentils. Fish and meat are rarely other ingredients all over Morocco beans and Tunisia, people sell their homegrown produce at local markets.

MUSIC

Celebrations in Africa are usually accompanied by music, with percussion instruments the most popular. Many types of drums are used to create traditional beats, with different sounds. and shells blown to make different sounds. Stringed instruments, such as the kora, and double bells, such as the kuge, are also played.

Nigeria is one of the world's main oil producers

The Masai "jump-dance" to music, as a show of strength

Sahara desert

Mount Kilimanjaro lies on the Tanzania/ Kenya border and rises 19,340 ft (5,895 m)

Johannesburg has some of the deepest and richest gold mines in the world

Injera is an African flat bread, served here with beef stew and vegetables

Moroccan spices

Drum

Kuge

Kora

Stunning views over Cape Town and Table Mountain in South Africa

Mediterranean Sea

Gulf of Sirte

TUNISIA

LIBYA

EGYPT

ALGERIA

MOROCCO

Tropic of Cancer

LANDSCAPE

North Africa boasts the world's largest desert, the Sahara, where emperatures can top 122°F (50°C). Africa's centre is mainly rain forest and rivers, a contrast to the grassy plains down south. Natural landmarks include Kilimanjaro (Africa's highest mountain), the Nile (the longest river), and Lake Victoria (the largest lake).

WILDLIFE

Game reserves in Kenya and Tanzania have been established to protect Africa's wildlife. Today, elephants, giraffes, zebras, and big cats roam freely without fear of human hunters. The continent's three-quarters rich with wildlife. Three-quarters of Madagascar's animals are found nowhere else.

Ring-tailed lemurs are native to the island of Madagascar.

Zebra

Endangered mountain gorillas live in Rwanda's Volcanoes National Park

Cocoa pod

Dates

TOURISM

Visitors to Africa go on safari to see the wildlife at close range. The economy is also boosted by tourists soaking up the sun on the beaches of Tunisia, Morocco, and South Africa, as well as the islands of the Seychelles. Africa's most visited historic site is the ancient pyramids of Giza in Egypt, built some 4,500 years ago.

The Sphinx and Great Pyramids attract tourists to Egypt all year round

FARMING

Many Africans in rural villages grow root vegetables and corn to sell at markets. Northern Africa has the best climate for cultivating dates, olives, and citrus fruits. Kenya's rainfall yields high tea production, while the Ivory Coast produces half the world's cocoa. Cotton is grown for export.

Fibers from the cotton boll plant are used to weave cloth

Head of corn

GULF OF ADEN

DJIBOUTI

SOMALILAND (not internationally recognized)

SOMALIA

ETHIOPIA

ERITREA

SUDAN

SOUTH SUDAN

UGANDA

KENYA

RWANDA

BURUNDI

TANZANIA

SEYCHELLES

COMOROS

MAURITIUS

MADAGASCAR

INDIAN OCEAN

Equator

MALAWI

MOZAMBIQUE

Mozambique Channel

ZAMBIA

ZIMBABWE

SWAZILAND

LESOTHO

SOUTH AFRICA

BOTSWANA

NAMIBIA

ANGOLA

DEM. REP. CONGO

CONGO

GABON

CENTRAL AFRICAN REPUBLIC

CAMEROON

EQUATORIAL GUINEA

SAO TOME & PRINCIPE

Tropic of Capricorn

CHAD

NIGER

NIGERIA

BENIN

TOGO

GHANA

BURKINA

IVORY COAST

LIBERIA

SIERRA LEONE

GUINEA

GUINEA BISSAU

SENEGAL

GAMBIA

MALI

Freshwater crocodile

Tiger

"Bollywood" films take their name from of the "B"of Bombay, now called Mumbai

WILDLIFE

Some of the world's most endangered mammals are found in Asia, including the snow leopard, red panda, and Asiatic black bear. The forests of Malaysia, Indonesia, and Borneo shelter elephants, tigers, and orangutans from the heat. Off the coast of Southeast Asia is where sharks, turtles, and manta rays live among the reefs.

The *Sasakia charonda* butterfly, nicknamed Japanese emperor, is Japan's national butterfly

South Korea is the fifth-largest car manufacturing nation in the world

INDUSTRY

By exporting resources of oil and natural gas, Asian nations such as Saudi Arabia, Iraq, and Kuwait have become wealthy. Japan, too, has seen rapid economic growth. India, China, and other Asian countries have benefited from mass-producing cars, clothes, and electronics for export.

The stock exchange in Tokyo is the third largest in the world

Judo

SPORT

There is a long tradition of martial arts in Asia, which includes judo, karate, and sumo wrestling in Japan and kung fu in China. Mongolians and Tibetans were once expert horseback riders, and racing remains a common pursuit. India, Pakistan, and Sri Lanka excel at cricket, while table tennis is also popular.

Table tennis, along with soccer, is China's most popular sport

India is one of the world's main tea growers. The plants are grown in the cooler hill regions of the north

Rice is Asia's staple food and has been cultivated for more than 9,500 years

NEW GUINEA

INDONESIA

BRUNEI

SINGAPORE

MALAYSIA

PHILIPPINES

JAPAN

NORTH KOREA

SOUTH KOREA

VIETNAM

LAOS

THAILAND

CAMBODIA

MYANMAR BURMA

CHINA

MONGOLIA

RUSSIAN FEDERATION

BANGLADESH

BHUTAN

NEPAL

INDIA

SRI LANKA

KAZAKHSTAN

UZBEKISTAN

KYRGYZSTAN

TAJIKISTAN

TURKMENISTAN

AFGHANISTAN

PAKISTAN

IRAN

OMAN

YEMEN

SAUDI ARABIA

QATAR

UAE

KUWAIT

IRAQ

JORDAN

ISRAEL

LEBANON SYRIA

CYPRUS

TURKEY

GEORGIA

ARMENIA AZERB.

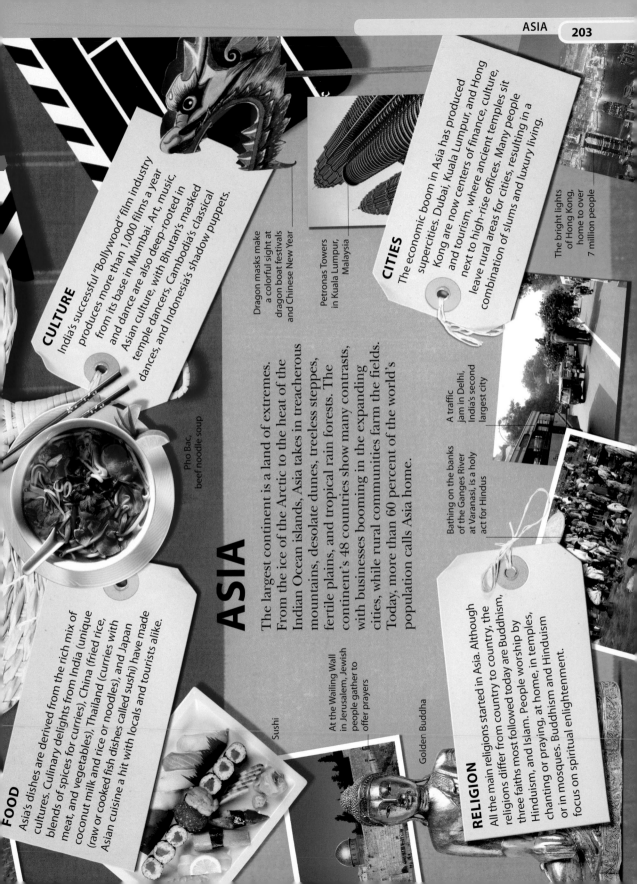

ASIA

The largest continent is a land of extremes. From the ice of the Arctic to the heat of the Indian Ocean islands, Asia takes in treacherous mountains, desolate dunes, treeless steppes, fertile plains, and tropical rain forests. The continent's 48 countries show many contrasts, with businesses booming in the expanding cities, while rural communities farm the fields. Today, more than 60 percent of the world's population calls Asia home.

CULTURE

India's successful "Bollywood" film industry produces more than 1,000 films a year from its base in Mumbai. Art, music, and dance are also deep-rooted in Asian culture, with Bhutan's masked temple dancers, Cambodia's classical dances, and Indonesia's shadow puppets.

Dragon masks make a colorful sight at dragon boat festivals and Chinese New Year

Petronas Towers in Kuala Lumpur, Malaysia

CITIES

The economic boom in Asia has produced supercities. Dubai, Kuala Lumpur, and Hong Kong are now centers of finance, culture, and tourism, where ancient temples sit next to high-rise offices. Many people leave rural areas for cities, resulting in a combination of slums and luxury living.

The bright lights of Hong Kong, home to over 7 million people

A traffic jam in Delhi, India's second largest city

Bathing on the banks of the Ganges River at Varanasi, is a holy act for Hindus

Pho Bac, beef noodle soup

FOOD

Asia's dishes are derived from the rich mix of cultures. Culinary delights from India (unique blends of spices for curries), China (fried rice, meat, and vegetables), Thailand (curries with coconut milk and rice or noodles), and Japan (raw or cooked fish dishes called sushi) have made Asian cuisine a hit with locals and tourists alike.

Sushi

At the Wailing Wall in Jerusalem, Jewish people gather to offer prayers

Golden Buddha

RELIGION

All the main religions started in Asia. Although religions differ from country to country, the three faiths most followed today are Buddhism, Hinduism, and Islam. People worship by chanting or praying, at home, in temples, or in mosques. Buddhism and Hinduism focus on spiritual enlightenment.

FOOD

The US is famous for its fast food, especially hamburgers, hot dogs, and soft drinks. These foods can be prepared and served quickly. A wealth of fresh fruit and vegetables grown in California and Florida provide a healthy option. In Mexico, the preference is for spicy foods with chiles.

Most of the peanuts grown in the US are made into peanut butter

CULTURE

American movies and TV shows are popu around the world. Many famous music sty such as rock 'n' roll, jazz, blues, country, an soul, have their roots in the US. Canada's annual Calgary Stampede celebrates its cattle-trading roots, while Mexico has parades and feasts on saints' days.

Elvis Presley became the ultimate icon of US rock 'n' roll music

Canada's maple trees produce 75 percent of all maple syrup—a favorite on pancakes

The US grows a quarter of the world's oranges

Baseball glove and ball

SPORTS

The highlight of the football calendar is a championship game called the Super Bowl. This is the most watched television event in the US. Baseball and basketball are also long-standing favorites. The colder climate of Canada has made skiing, ice-skating, and ice hockey the main winter pursuits.

Statue of Liberty

LANDMARKS

New York's Statue of Liberty welcomed immigrants arriving by boat, while the Empire State Building is the city's tallest skyscraper. Another US landmark is Mount Rushmore, in South Dakota, where the faces of four US presidents are carved into the rock. The ruins of the Aztec and Mayan civilizations, found in Central America, are far older landmarks.

Mount Rushmore

The blade on the ice-hockey skate enables the player to glide across the ice

PACIFIC OCEAN

UNITED STATES OF AMERICA

Gulf of Alaska

CANAD

UNITED STATES OF AMERICA

MEXICO

Gulf of Mexico

BAHAM

GUATEMALA
EL SALVADOR
BELIZE
HONDURAS
NICARAGU
COSTA RICA
PANAMA

JAMAICA
CU

Oscars are statues given to movie industry winners at Hollywood's Academy Awards

Mexico's guitar groups play and sing their traditional mariachi music

LANDSCAPE
One-third of Canada lies inside the Arctic Circle and stays frozen most of the year. North America contains mountainous regions, including the snowy Rocky Mountains and the forested Appalachians. In the Midwest are grassy plains, known as prairies. US topography is varied, with a mix of plains, deserts, mountains, and temperate and tropical forests. Farther south are the beaches of Mexico and the Caribbean.

The Rocky Mountains stretch from Alaska in the north to the US border in the south

NORTH AMERICA

Before the arrival of Europeans in the 16th century, tribes of native peoples were the only inhabitants of North America. Since then, there have been waves of immigration to both Canada and the US, both of which quickly became pioneers of financial growth and contemporary culture. The mainly Spanish-speaking countries of Central America have lush, mountainous landscapes and are rich in tradition and culture.

The Grand Canyon was formed by water and ice over millions of years

Bison

Canada's harp seal pups are born with fluffy white fur for extra warmth

Gray-banded kingsnake

Football helmet

INDUSTRY
The US grew wealthy by producing vast quantities of wheat, iron, steel, electronics, cars, and aircraft. Fishing is an important industry along the Pacific Coast, with salmon canned for export. Canada is the largest exporter of forest products, mainly softwood used in construction, while Mexico sells its natural gas and oil reserves.

WILDLIFE
Northern parts of Canada are home to more animals than people. Bears, elk, and moose live in the Rocky Mountains. Across the US, national parks such as Yosemite and Yellowstone protect bison, antelope, and deer. Florida's Everglades is a unique wetland area, with many rare animals such as the Florida panther and manatee. Snakes and scorpions can survive the heat of Mexico's Sonoran Desert.

Computer chips from California, the center for microelectronics

Combine harvesters farm wheat on the American prairies

Cadillac

GREENLAND (TO DENMARK)

Coffee beans

CROPS

Brazil produces a quarter of the world's coffee, while Ecuador's climate is ideal for growing tomatoes and bananas. Steep hillsides are terraced for farming in Chile and Peru, where potatoes are planted on the higher slopes of the Andes, and corn is sown lower down.

The tango dance evolved in Argentina's slums during the late 19th century

In 2002 Brazil won soccer's World Cup for a record-breaking fifth time

Sap is collected from rubber trees in the Amazon rain forest to produce rubber

Banana

CULTURE

Music and dance form the heart of South American culture. The rhythmic dance of Rio de Janeiro's famous five-day carnival, samba is a notable highlight of the carnival, which features spectacular parades and parties in Brazil's capital. It is also common to see soccer games played on the streets and beaches.

Brazil nuts

WILDLIFE

The Amazon is the world's largest rain forest and home to more than 15,000 animal species. Jaguars, sloths, and tapirs live under the tree canopy, while the forest floor teems with snakes, lizards, and insects. Colorful toucans, macaws, and kingfishers swoop over the Amazon River, where dolphins and turtles swim.

In the rainy season, the Amazon River floods, covering large parts of the rain forest in water

Angel Falls in Venezuela drops 3,212 ft (979 m) and is the highest uninterrupted waterfall in the world

Red-eyed tree frogs are active at night, searching for insects to eat

The toucan's large beak enables it to pick fruit from trees

PHYSICAL FEATURES

Three contrasting landscapes dominate South America. From the west rise the towering peaks of the Andes Mountains, leading half of the dense Pacific Ocean. In the northeast spreads across into Amazon rain forest, which means vast, grassy plains called Brazil. To the south are the pampas (which means "flat" in Spanish).

The Patagonia region at the southern tip of the continent is known for its dramatic glaciers

Sharp-teethed, meat-eating piranhas swim in South American rivers

A T L A N T I C   O C E A N

VENEZUELA

COLOMBIA

ECUADOR

Equator

Gulf of Darién

Gulf of Panama

PANAMA

C A R I B B E A N   S E A

TRINIDAD & TOBAGO

GUYANA

SURINAM

FRENCH GUIANA (TO FRANCE)

Equator

BRAZIL

Beef is a key component of Argentine cuisine

INCAS

The Incas were the last great civilization to emerge in South America. During the 12th century, expert architects created their capital at Cuzco. By the 15th century, their empire had spread from Ecuador through Peru to Chile. Hearing of great riches, the Spanish arrived in 1532 to set up colonies and ended the Inca reign.

This ear ornament was made by the Chimu; a people who were eventually conquered by the Incas

Peruvian dolls were handmade from llama or alpaca wool

Yerba mate leaves are used to make a popular tea, drunk from a hollow gourd (shell)

SOUTH AMERICA

Rich in history, language, and culture, South America is a vibrant place. Nature has made its mark in the trees of the Amazon rain forest, while ancient civilizations have left theirs in the city of Machu Picchu in the Andes Mountains. The influence of Spanish and Portugese colonization remains in the languages, while samba sounds and traditional tangos resonate at the festivals.

TREES AND PLANTS

About 60 percent of the continent is pampas (grassy plain), which is one of the richest grazing areas in the world. Variety comes from the Amazon rain forest, where more than 6,000 species of plants flourish. Unique plants grow in Venezuela's sandstone hills and Chile's Atacama Desert, where species have adapted to survive the lack of water.

Hippeastrum is a colorful plant that thrives in Peru and Chile; it produces flowers up to 10 in (25 cm) across

Cardon cactus

FOOD

Corn is a staple food used in bread and cakes stuffed with meat or cheese. Potatoes, squash, rice, and different types of beans are also mealtime favorites. Peruvians love spicy foods, so hot chile peppers are often on the menu.

Roger Federer celebrates winning a Wimbledon title at the famous tennis competition in London

SPORTS

The British, Spanish, and Italian soccer leagues are considered the best in the world. Soccer and rugby are played throughout the year, tennis and cricket are summer sports, and mountain ski resorts have busy winter seasons.

The Tour de France was first held in 1903 and is now the world's biggest cycling race

This famous clock tower is part of Britain's Houses of Parliament

Formula 1 car racing is a popular sport in Europe

Portugal has some of the best deep-sea fishing in Europe

Germany is one of the world's leading car producers

The steel industry is thriving in eastern Europe

INDUSTRY

Germany is the continent's industrial leader, with its car production and high-tech goods industries. Forestry flourishes in Finland and Sweden, while cod-fishing is big business in Norway and Iceland.

Flower farming, especially tulips, is an important industry in Holland

About 60 percent of farmland in Greece is used to grow olives

Map labels

PARIS

BIG BEN

SHETLAND ISLANDS

Outer Hebrides

Orkney Islands

SCOTLAND

NORTHERN IRELAND

NORTH SEA

IRELAND

UNITED

DENMARK

Isle of Man (to UK)

WALES   KINGDOM

ENGLAND   NETHERLANDS

Channel Islands (to UK)

English Channel

BELGIUM

LUXEMBOURG

GERMANY   POLAND

CZECH REPUBLIC

BAY OF BISCAY

FRANCE

SLOVAKIA

SWITZERLAND   AUSTRIA

LIECHTENSTEIN   SLOVENIA   HUNGARY

CROATIA   ROMANIA

MONACO

PORTUGAL   BOSNIA & HERZEGOVINA

SAN MARINO

Corsica   MONTENEGRO   SERBIA

SPAIN   ANDORRA   ITALY   BULGARI

MALLORCA   MENORCA   ALBANIA   MACEDONIA

IBIZA

Gibraltar (to UK)   Sardinia   Aegean Sea

Ceuta (to Spain)   Balearic Islands   GREECE

Melilla (to Spain)   MEDITERRANEAN   Tyrrhenian Sea

Sicily   Ionian Sea

SEA   Malta

NORWAY   SWEDEN   FINLAN

Gulf of Bothnia

ESTONIA

GOTLAND   LATVIA

LITHUANIA

RUSS. FED. (KALININGRAD)

BELARU

BALTIC SEA

MOL

CITIES

Many European cities feature castles and cathedrals. The center of the eastern European city of Prague is a World Heritage Site. Paris and Milan are fashion leaders, while the financial centers of London and Geneva are among the world's richest cities.

Norway's spectacular fjords are one of Europe's most photographed landscapes

LANDSCAPES

Across the continent, landscapes differ dramatically. Iceland's glaciers and Norway's fjords contrast with the mountain ranges of the Alps and Pyrenees. Around the Mediterranean are fertile fields and sandy beaches.

The active volcano of Mount Vesuvius in Italy stands 4,200 ft (1,280 m) tall

EUROPE

For a small continent, Europe has made a big impact. In centuries past, its inhabitants spread across the globe, building empires. Those days are gone, but the continent's influence remains clear in the European languages, architecture, and entertainment still evident around the world. Thanks to industrial growth and big business, many of the 44 countries are wealthy, with people enjoying a high standard of living.

RUSSIAN
FEDERATION

Bronze statue crafted by celebrated 20th-century British sculptor Henry Moore

Russia is famous for its ballet companies, such as the Bolshoi Ballet of Moscow and the Kirov Ballet of St. Petersburg

KAZAKHSTAN

Painted in 1888, *Sunflowers* by the Dutch painter Vincent Van Gogh is one of the world's best-known works of art

CULTURE

Europe has a rich heritage of literature, art, music, opera, and ballet, with many pioneering writers, artists, composers, and dancers capturing the public imagination. Museums, theaters, opera houses, and art exhibitions draw crowds in the major cities.

UKRAINE

Sea of
Azov

Paella is a rice-based dish containing meat and seafood

BLACK SEA

GEORGIA

AZERBAIJAN

TURKEY

FOOD

Pizza and pasta are Italian favorites, while France is synonymous with strong cheese, crêpes, and mussels. Germans serve smoked sausages, Spaniards prepare their specialty paella, and sweet-toothed Belgians are known for their luxurious chocolates.

Crêpe is a type of thin pancake

Mussels are a popular dish in Belgium and France

Aboriginal art depicts patterns or scenes from the natural world

Religious and mythical symbols were carved into the wood of Polynesian dolls

CULTURE

The beliefs, culture, and art of the continent's original inhabitants form a rich heritage. Aboriginal Australians have a deep-rooted respect for the natural world. The Maori of New Zealand practice a traditional dance called the haka. The Polynesians of the Pacific Islands enjoy a family-centered culture.

Maori tools were blessed by their creators to ensure they worked well

SPORTS

The climate allows Australasians to make the most of the great outdoors. Cricket, rugby, and golf are popular pastimes, while sailing and surfing are coastal favorites. Preferred spectactor sports are tennis, cricket, and rugby, with Australia's cricket team and New Zealand's rugby union team enjoying huge success.

WILDLIFE

Australasia's best-known native creatures are marsupials (mammals that hold their young in a pouch), such as kangaroos, koalas, and wombats. Many birds are also unique to the continent, including kookaburras and emus. Some of the world's deadliest snakes and spiders live there as well.

Funnel-web spiders live in eastern Australia; they can kill a person with a single venomous bite

MICR

PALAU

PAPUA NEW G

New Guinea

Koala

Australia's thorny devil is a spiny lizard that blends in with its desert surroundings

The trunk of the baobab tree stores water to survive periods of drought

Kangaroo

AUSTRALI

Kangar
Islan

TREES AND PLANTS

Australasia has many trees and plants that don't grow anywhere else. About 80 percent of New Zealand's plants are unique, while nearly all the world's eucalyptus trees originated in Australia. The country's center is hot and barren, but trees, plants, and fungi thrive in the humid rain forests.

INDUSTRY

Sheep and cattle farming has made lush New Zealand a major exporter of wool, meat, and dairy products. Rich in natural resources such as iron ore, gold, nickel, silver, and diamonds, Australia is a leading exporter of coal. Minerals such as copper and gold are Papua New Guinea's main exports.

Eucalyptus leaves

Gabiny fruit

PHYSICAL FEATURES

From New Zealand's geysers and glaciers to Australia's coral reefs and coastlines and the many volcanic islands of the Pacific, the region is a kaleidoscope of dramatic panoramas. The ancient rock of Uluru and the steaming vents of New Zealand are two of the region's most famous features.

Australia's cricket team

New Zealand's All Blacks rugby team

MARSHALL ISLANDS

KIRIBATI

KIRIBATI

NAURU

TUVALU

Tokelau (to NZ)

Cook Islands (to NZ)

SAMOA

French Polynesia (to France)

SOLOMON ISLANDS

TONGA

Niue (to NZ)

VANUATU

FIJI

New Caledonia (to France)

The huge sandstone rock of Uluru is an ancient site sacred to Aboriginal people

Gushing springs of hot water, called geysers, erupt regularly on New Zealand's North Island

Australia's Sunshine Coast is a popular stretch of beaches and bays

AUSTRALASIA

This southern-hemisphere region includes Australia, New Zealand, Papua New Guinea, and neighboring Pacific islands. Because all 14 countries are islands, much of the wildlife is unique and the landscapes are largely unspoiled. Settlers from Southeast Asia first arrived in Australia thousands of years ago. By the 18th century, European immigrants had reached the region, which is now home to 30 million people.

Diamonds

NEW ZEALAND

Tasmania

Sydney Opera House

Gold nugget

The Three Sisters is a distinctive rock formation in the Blue Mountains, Australia

There are about 30 million sheep in New Zealand, some sheared for their wool

TOURISM

Australia and New Zealand are popular tourist destinations all year round, thanks to the stunning scenery. Bustling harbor cities, such as Sydney and Auckland, offer a mix of beach life and culture. Famous buildings include the Sydney Opera House and Sydney Harbour Bridge.

Telescopes at Concordia research base provide astronomers with exceptional views of the clear skies above Antarctica

RESEARCH

About 40 permanent and 100 temporary research stations have been set up in Antarctica. Scientists analyze Antarctica's weather, climate, wildlife, and geology. Projects include monitoring ice samples to detect changes in the atmosphere, and tracking penguins.

Tourists stay on board the cruise ships overnight because there are no resorts

The Amundsen-Scott research base is named after the two famous expedition leaders who raced to reach the South Pole in 1911

TOURISM

Since the 1950s, cruise ships have brought tourists to Antarctica, and today about 10,000 people visit each summer. They arrive either by ship or take sightseeing trips by plane over the South Pole, the southernmost point on the planet. Insulated clothing and goggles are essential at all times.

ANTARCTICA

In the coldest continent on Earth, the temperature can drop to -112°F (-80°C) and human skin can freeze in seconds. Yet, thanks to scientists who are specially equipped to brave this harsh habitat, research on some of the world's most remote landscapes and wildlife is underway. Only discovered in 1820, Antarctica covers 5.5 million sq miles (14 million sq km) and, incredibly, 97 percent of it is covered with ice.

The largest penguin of all, the emperor penguin huddles in groups to keep warm during blizzards

Despite their name, crabeater seals eat krill (tiny marine creatures)

WILDLIFE

Animals face a struggle for survival in Antarctica, but fish, seals, and whales can thrive in the sea. The Antarctic Peninsula has the mildest climate of the continent, making it a hub for wildlife. In summer, millions of seals and birds breed on the peninsula and nearby islands.

Humpback whales are sociable mammals, preferring to eat and travel in groups, which are called pods

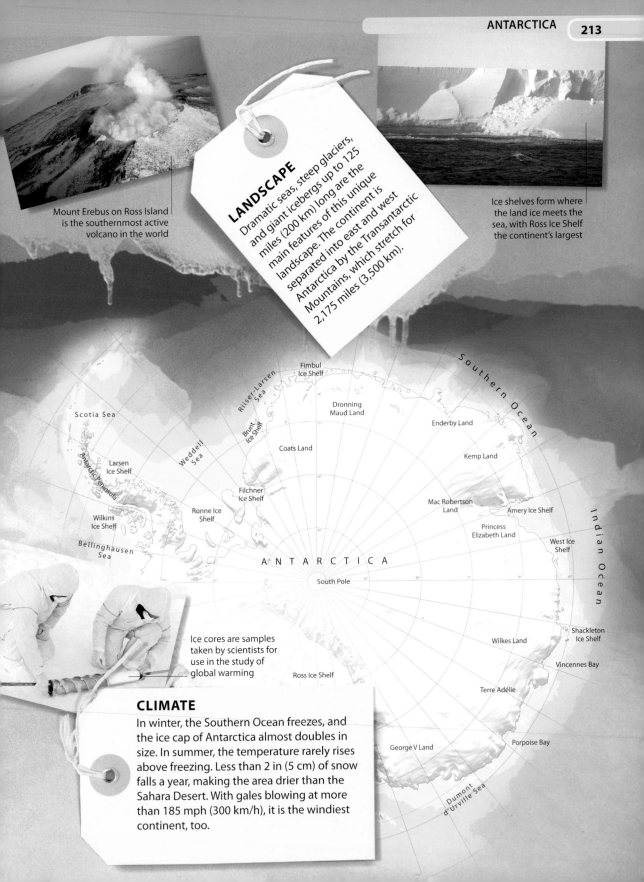

Mount Erebus on Ross Island is the southernmost active volcano in the world

LANDSCAPE

Dramatic seas, steep glaciers, and giant icebergs up to 125 miles (200 km) long are the main features of this unique landscape. The continent is separated into east and west Antarctica by the Transantarctic Mountains, which stretch for 2,175 miles (3,500 km).

Ice shelves form where the land ice meets the sea, with Ross Ice Shelf the continent's largest

Ice cores are samples taken by scientists for use in the study of global warming

CLIMATE

In winter, the Southern Ocean freezes, and the ice cap of Antarctica almost doubles in size. In summer, the temperature rarely rises above freezing. Less than 2 in (5 cm) of snow falls a year, making the area drier than the Sahara Desert. With gales blowing at more than 185 mph (300 km/h), it is the windiest continent, too.

Fimbul Ice Shelf
Riiser-Larsen Sea
Scotia Sea
Southern Ocean
Dronning Maud Land
Enderby Land
Brunt Ice Shelf
Coats Land
Kemp Land
Weddell Sea
Larsen Ice Shelf
Antarctic Peninsula
Filchner Ice Shelf
Mac Robertson Land
Amery Ice Shelf
Ronne Ice Shelf
Princess Elizabeth Land
Wilkins Ice Shelf
West Ice Shelf
Bellinghausen Sea
ANTARCTICA
Indian Ocean
South Pole
Shackleton Ice Shelf
Wilkes Land
Vincennes Bay
Ross Ice Shelf
Terre Adélie
George V Land
Porpoise Bay
Dumont d'Urville Sea

FLAGS

Historically, army leaders carried flags into battle as rallying points for the soldiers. Today, flags are used to decorate buildings, mark public events, start races, honor the dead, or to spell out messages or warnings from one ship to another. But by far the most recognizable ones are national flags—vibrant in color and unique in symbolism. Organizations and citizens fly the flag for their countries, building up a strong sense of identity, pride, and unity.

1 AUSTRALIA
The flag features a combination of Britain's flag, the Commonwealth Star (with its points symbolizing the original states of Australia), and the Southern Cross constellation (only visible in the Southern Hemisphere).

2 SOUTH KOREA
A red and blue Yin Yang symbol on the South Korean flag represents the Chinese philosophy that everything in the universe has an opposite. The four surrounding trigrams (groups of three lines) represent the ideals of balance, circulation, harmony, and symmetry.

6 MEXICO

Traditionally, these colors had religious and military connotations, but the new meanings are defined as hope (green), unity (white), and the blood of heroes (red). The central image is a symbol from an earlier Aztec heritage.

7 IRELAND

This has been the flag of Ireland since 1919. The orange stands for Protestants, the green for Catholics, and the white for the peace between them.

8 GERMANY

During the Napoleonic wars of the 19th century, German soldiers wore black uniforms with red braid and gold buttons. These became the country's official colors, appearing on the national flag. Public buildings often fly the flag vertically.

3 INDIA

At the center of the tricolor (three colors) is the *ashoka chakra*, meaning "wheel of law." This symbolizes the hope that the country will continue to move forward peacefully.

9 SPAIN

This young flag was created in 1981. On the left-hand side where the flag gets hoisted, is the Spanish coat-of-arms, which includes the royal seal.

4 UNITED STATES

This flag is nicknamed the "Stars and Stripes." The 50 stars represent the states of the union, while the red and white stripes represent the 13 original colonies that declared independence from British rule.

10 JAMAICA

The flag of this Caribbean country shows a yellow diagonal cross, which embodies the shining Sun; green, for the fertile land; and black, which represents strength and creativity.

5 KENYA

Since 1963, Kenya's flag has been dominated by a shield and spears, used by the country's Masai people. This symbol shows how the nation is determined to defend its freedom.

United Kingdom

MAPS

Maps provide visual representations of the world, revealing the layout of our planet in a variety of ways. Some depict Earth's geographical features, or the borders and boundaries between nations. Other maps detail road routes and street names, or aid navigation on urban transportation networks. Scales on maps can be used to figure out real distances, and keys explain map symbols.

SATELLITE IMAGE

Space satellites are used to photograph Earth, capturing its surface in great detail. Orbiting thousands of miles above the planet, satellites track changes in the land, the ocean, and the atmosphere.

TRANSPORTATION MAP

Simplicity is the key when designing maps of transportation networks. Although distances are not specified, the direction and order of stops must be conveyed accurately. This allows travelers to check their best route quickly.

STREET MAP

Useful tools for navigating cities and towns, street maps include road names and notable landmarks such as railroad stations, hospitals, churches, and parks. Street maps are available online and via most cell phones.

BUILDING PLAN

When planning a new structure, engineers first map out the building. Details such as layout, walls, and entrances are marked to assist workers during the construction. Precise measurements are added to give the true size of the project.

GEOLOGICAL MAP

Different rock types are coded by color on geological maps. Geologists study these maps to determine the location of minerals and oils, while structural engineers ensure rock types suit their construction plans before laying foundations.

SAILING CHART

Nautical maps of coastal or ocean areas are called charts. They include information about tides, currents, depths, potential hazards, and features of the seabed. Sailors carry these charts on board their ships to help with marine navigation.

POLITICAL MAP

National and state borders are shown on political maps. Contrasting colors highlight different countries, so the legal boundaries stand out more clearly. To aid understanding, major cities, rivers, seas, and oceans are also labeled.

PHYSICAL MAP

Permanent natural features are depicted on physical maps. Deserts, mountains, lakes, rivers, and oceans are identified, as well as the contrast between high and low land. Some physical maps go into more detail, pointing out land use and soil type.

ROAD MAP

Covering a much larger area than a street map, road maps use different colors and lines to represent highways, main roads, and country roads. Electronic satellite navigation systems are often used by drivers today.

ECONOMY

Since ancient times, farmers have taken goods to markets, where customers bargained over prices and sales were agreed upon. Today, the range of goods is massive, but the principles remain the same. Societies function by people working together to grow, build, manufacture, and distribute products for consumers who want them. Such a system, for the production, distribution, and consumption of goods, is called an economy.

These umbrellas for toes might seem useless, but if there is a demand, then a supply will follow

▶ SUPPLY AND DEMAND

An economy works because there are people supplying goods and services to people who will pay for them. When there is a big demand, the price of these goods and services goes up, but if there is a huge supply, the prices drop to encourage the demand.

▶ PRODUCTION

Every country uses its raw materials and its people to make all kinds of products to sell. The best ways to maximize profit are to reduce production costs, pay the workforce less, and use the speediest manufacturing tools. As production increases, so the economy grows.

▶ TRADITIONAL ECONOMY

In less wealthy countries, a traditional economy is more common. People produce a few goods for themselves and sell what is left. Rural farmers may grow produce such as fruit and vegetables to feed their families, and then sell the rest at local markets.

◀ DOMESTIC WORK

Any unpaid work done at home is not counted as part of the economy. Housework, for example, only contributes to the market economy if a cleaner is paid for the job.

◀ COMMAND VERSUS MIXED

The government takes control in a command economy, and it is in charge of the country's economic activity. However, in a mixed economy, some industries, such as health and transportation, are publicly owned and run by the government, but the rest are privately owned.

▶ RAW MATERIALS

Some goods are used to create a different product. These are usually raw materials or partly finished items, such as steel, coal, wood, and paper. These goods are often unrecognizable in the final product.

▶ CONSUMER GOODS

Producers must recognize what people want in order to create consumer goods that will prove popular, sell well, and increase profit. A wide range of goods, such as cars, clothing, toys, and food, are offered by many different producers to ensure that individual consumer needs are satisfied.

German flag

French flag

▲ CITIZENSHIP

People born into a country or state are called its citizens. This gives them the right to protection by the government as well as the right to vote. Along with rights come responsibilities, and citizens are expected to abide by the laws of the land. Immigrants and refugees can sometimes become citizens of another country. Each country or state is identified by its national flag.

▼ PROTEST

If the citizens of a state or nation do not agree with the actions or policies of the ruling government, they sometimes rally together to stage a public protest. Often marching to the government's headquarters, people voice their concerns in an attempt to bring about change.

Protesters demonstrate outside the Philippine presidential palace in 2007

In times of war, governments can call upon citizens to fight for their country

A passport is an official government document that allows each citizen to travel abroad

THE STATE

Throughout history, countries have been run by a variety of leaders and governments. At one time, heads of state were royalty, ruling with absolute authority. In many countries, power has now passed to the people, as democratic elections have replaced royal rule. Many citizens have the right to vote for their political leaders and to protest against them when necessary. Having won a place at the forefront of government, prime ministers and presidents run many world states.

Megaphones are often used by protesters to make their voices heard

Ceremonial mace is kept in the UK's House of Commons

▶ LEGISLATURE

States have elected representatives who are responsible for making laws, known as legislating. Government members debate new policies or changes to existing laws. Once the laws have been agreed upon, they are officially drafted by the legislatures. These laws must then be followed by all citizens.

In the House of Commons, ministers debate changes to law and government policy

United States Congress where new laws are passed

Colored rosettes are sometimes worn by members of political parties to show their allegiance in the run-up to an election

Wigs are worn by judges in some countries as part of legal tradition

A ballot box is a locked container into which citizens place their confidential votes

◄ LAW AND ORDER

A country's judges, collectively called the judiciary, make rulings on criminal allegations or civil disputes in courts of law. They interpret and uphold laws passed by the government before delivering their verdicts to the citizens involved. The law in most countries is upheld by a police force.

German police cap

▲ DEMOCRACY

In democratic societies, citizens have the opportunity to vote for their preferred candidate from a range of political parties. On election day, people cast their vote and the party with the majority is established as the new government.

A gavel and block used by a judge to maintain silence in court

United States presidential seal

Presidents in South America, such as Chile's leader, Sebastián Piñera, wear sashes as symbols of office

◄ MONARCHY

In the past, most countries were ruled by a king or a queen and, as head of state, the monarch's word was considered law. Although some countries still maintain a monarchy, their role is mainly ceremonial. It is the elected government that generally takes responsibility for how the country is run.

▲ REPUBLICS

Countries that have a president as their head of state instead of a king or queen are called republics. Presidents can be elected by the citizens or appointed by the legislature, and usually act as head of the nation's government.

This imperial seal of China shows a dragon guarding a pearl, which represents wisdom

Crafted with priceless gems in 1838, the State Crown was first worn by Britain's Queen Victoria

► ABRAHAM LINCOLN

A passionate opponent of slavery, Lincoln led the Union States to victory in the Civil War of 1860–65. His speech at Gettysburg, on the principles of human equality, is one of the greatest in American history.

▼ JAMES GARFIELD

The 20th US president was James Garfield, an army general. In 1881, he was assassinated after less than four months in office.

◄ BENJAMIN HARRISON

Electricity was first installed in the White House during the Harrison presidency (1889–93)—his wife would not touch the switches, fearing electrocution.

US PRESIDENTS

The United States is a superpower, dominating global affairs. The nation's head of state, the president, is regarded as one of the most powerful people in the world. Presidential elections are followed closely by other countries, since political decisions made by the US president can impact the rest of the world. The president serves a term of four years, and today can hold office for a maximum of two terms.

► GROVER CLEVELAND

Grover Cleveland is the only president to have served two nonconsecutive terms in office, 1885–89 and 1893–97. His second term was plagued by industrial strikes.

◄ HARRY TRUMAN

Truman saw the US through a difficult postwar period. The Cold War (period of tension with communist USSR) began, and the country entered the Korean Conflict (1950–53).

◄ HERBERT HOOVER

The Hoover presidency saw the Great Depression of 1929 and public opposition to Prohibition (the banning of alcohol). He did not win a second term.

▲ FRANKLIN D. ROOSEVELT

"FDR" served a record four terms in office from 1933–1945. He brought an end to the Depression with a "New Deal" to bring relief to the unemployed, and took the US into World War II.

▲ GERALD FORD

Called to office after Nixon's resignation in 1974, Gerald Ford is the only president not to have been elected either president or vice president.

▲ JIMMY CARTER

During Carter's term of office, the US was beset by crises. At home, there was recession. Abroad, US citizens were taken hostage in Iran.

◄ RONALD REAGAN

Shortly after taking office in 1981, former Hollywood actor Ronald Reagan survived an assassination attempt. He went on to cut taxes, increase national defense, and improve relations with the Soviet Union.

▲ GEORGE BUSH

George Bush became president in 1989. From 1990–91, he led an alliance of troops in the Gulf War, in response to Iraq's invasion of Kuwait.

▶ THEODORE ROOSEVELT

A reformer, Roosevelt promised a "Square Deal" for all. The teddy bear takes its name from him, after he was given a stuffed toy in 1903.

◀ CALVIN COOLIDGE

Coolidge believed the government should not control too many aspects of people's lives. A man of few words, he was nicknamed "Silent Cal."

▶ WILLIAM MCKINLEY

The first to campaign using advertising techniques, McKinley won the 1896 election promising to tax foreign goods.

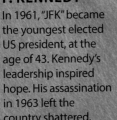

▲ DWIGHT EISENHOWER

Known as "Ike," Eisenhower launched the race between the US and the Soviet Union to explore outer space.

▶ JOHN F. KENNEDY

In 1961, "JFK" became the youngest elected US president, at the age of 43. Kennedy's leadership inspired hope. His assassination in 1963 left the country shattered.

▲ RICHARD NIXON

In 1974, Nixon became the only president to resign, because of his involvement in the Watergate scandal (illegal spying in the Democratic Party's headquarters).

▼ GEORGE W. BUSH

George W. Bush sent troops into Afghanistan and Iraq as part of his "War on Terror," in response to the attacks on the US on September 11, 2001.

▲ BARACK OBAMA

Obama is the first African-American to become US president. He won a second term in 2012 with a platform of making healthcare and social reforms for Americans.

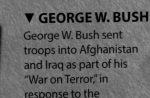

▲ BILL CLINTON

A long period of economic growth meant that, despite allegations of scandals, Bill Clinton always remained popular.

George Washington	1789–97
John Adams	1797–1801
Thomas Jefferson	1801–09
James Madison	1809–17
James Monroe	1817–25
John Quincy Adams	1825–29
Andrew Jackson	1829–37
Martin Van Buren	1837–41
William Harrison	1841
John Tyler	1841–45
James Knox Polk	1845–49
Zachary Taylor	1849–50
Millard Fillmore	1850–53
Franklin Pierce	1853–57
James Buchanan	1857–61
Abraham Lincoln	1861–65
Andrew Johnson	1865–69
Ulysses S. Grant	1869–77
Rutherford Hayes	1877–81
James Garfield	1881
Chester Arthur	1881–85
Grover Cleveland	1885–89
Benjamin Harrison	1889–93
Grover Cleveland	1893–97
William McKinley	1897–1901
Theodore Roosevelt	1901–09
William Taft	1909–13
Woodrow Wilson	1913–21
Warren Harding	1921–23
Calvin Coolidge	1923–29
Herbert Hoover	1929–33
Franklin D. Roosevelt	1933–45
Harry Truman	1945–53
Dwight Eisenhower	1953–61
John F. Kennedy	1961–63
Lyndon B. Johnson	1963–69
Richard Nixon	1969–74
Gerald Ford	1974–77
James Carter	1977–81
Ronald Reagan	1981–89
George Bush	1989–93
William Clinton	1993–2001
George W. Bush	2001–09
Barack Obama	2009–

Bishop's miter This miter (hat) is worn by a bishop in the Roman Catholic Church, the largest Christian body.

Saint Antony People who have led especially holy lives are named as saints by the Church.

CHRISTIANITY

Christianity is based on the belief that Jesus Christ is God's son. The Bible, Christianity's sacred book, contains the story of Jesus' life and how he was put to death. Christians believe his sacrifice means that followers will have an eternal life with God.

Cross Because Jesus died on a cross, it is a powerful symbol of the Christian faith.

Icon of Christ Paintings remind Christians that God lived as a human through Jesus.

Chalice In the ritual of Holy Communion, bread and wine represent the body and blood of Jesus. The wine is often served in a chalice.

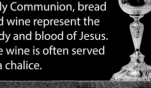

Buddha The founder of Buddhism, Siddhartha Gautama, was born in what is now Nepal in 563 BCE.

Statues of Buddha are often made of gold to show his importance

Merit sharing Buddhists believe that if they live caring lives, they will build up merit (good will) and have a better next life. They can pass on merit to others in a merit-sharing ceremony.

In the temple, water is poured from one vessel to pass along merit to others

BUDDHISM

Unlike most religions, Buddhism is not based on worshipping a god or gods. Instead, it is based on the teachings of the Buddha, who showed his followers how to live a good life and avoid suffering by controlling their desires. Buddhists hope to achieve true wisdom, known as enlightenment.

Chanukiah This nine-branched candlestick is used to celebrate Hanukkah, the Jewish festival of light. The central branch holds the candle used to light the others.

Prayer wheel and prayer As this Buddhist prayer wheel turns, a mantra (a blessing or prayer) written on a scroll inside "repeats" itself over and over again.

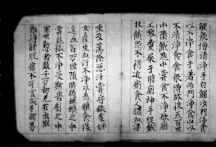

JUDAISM

This is the religion of the Jews, also called Hebrews. Judaism was the first successful religion based on the idea that there is only one God, and it formed the basis for both Christianity and Islam. Central to Jewish belief is that God chose the Jews as a special holy nation, and gave them a set of laws to follow. The story of the first Jewish people is told in the Hebrew Bible (the Christian Old Testament).

Kippas Some Jewish men wear skullcaps, known as kippas, when they pray as a sign of respect to God.

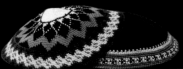

Water shaker In one Hindu ritual, priests sprinkle water over the worshipers.

HINDUISM

One of the oldest religions, Hinduism began 5,000 years ago in India. Hindus believe in a supreme spirit, Brahman, who reveals himself through hundreds of gods and goddesses. Hindus practice their faith in different ways, but share a belief in reincarnation—the idea that a person's soul has lived before and will live on after death in another form.

Ganesh Hindus pray to Ganesh, the elephant god of wisdom and help, when facing a new challenge.

Om This is an image of the sacred sound, Om, spoken after Hindu prayer.

Krishna This popular Hindu god is thought to bring great happiness to believers.

Krishna is usually shown as a smiling youth with sky-blue skin

Islamic scribe Because the Qur'an is believed to contain God's exact words, great care is taken when Muslim scribes recreate them.

ISLAM

Muslims believe that God revealed his words through an angel to the prophet Muhammad, who collected them in the Qur'an, the holy book. The faithful try to live by the rules in this book. The most important duties are the Five Pillars: prayer, helping the needy, fasting for one month a year, making a pilgrimage to Mecca, and showing faith in God.

Prayer beads God, or Allah, is thought to have 99 names. This string of 99 prayer beads can be used to remind Muslims of the many names of the one God.

Islamic tile The sacred words of the Qur'an appear on many decorative objects, such as this tile.

Quiblah Muslims must face the holy city of Mecca when they pray, five times a day. This instrument helps them to find its location.

Torah scroll The most important book in the Jewish faith, the Torah contains a list of instructions for everyday life.

RELIGION

A religion is a set of beliefs that helps explain life's mysteries. People seek guidance from their religion on how they should live their lives. Most people with religious faith believe in either one God or many gods. They express their faith through rituals, such as gathering together with others to worship, and by studying sacred books. There are many different religions, but those included here have the most followers around the world.

FESTIVALS

Across the world, people celebrate festivals for a range of reasons. Although many form part of religious worship, others were created to mark a change in seasons, to focus on cultural traditions, or to celebrate an important milestone in history. Some festivals take place on the same day every year, others are based on ancient calendars or a new Moon, so the dates change. Special food is almost always a part of each festival.

3 THANKSGIVING
This North American festival is held on the fourth Thursday of November in the US and the second Monday in October in Canada. Families get together to give thanks for the first good harvest of the European settlers more than 400 years ago.

1 CHRISTMAS
This Christian festival celebrates the birth of Jesus Christ and is celebrated in most countries on December 25. Traditions include decorating fir trees, exchanging gifts, attending church, and waiting for a visit from Santa Claus.

2 DAY OF THE DEAD
During this Mexican festival, held on November 1, families believe that the souls of dead relatives are able to return to the land of the living for one night. They decorate altars in homes and cemeteries with candles and flowers.

4 DRAGON BOAT FESTIVAL
This festival is celebrated in east Asia. According to legend, when a Chinese official named Qu Yuan drowned in a river, people rowed out on boats with dragon-head prows and dropped parcels of rice wrapped in bamboo (zongi) into the water to divert the hungry fish away from his body.

Family and friends gather for a Christmas meal, with treats such as this stollen, a spicy fruit cake

Pumpkins, a type of squash, are made into pies at Thanksgiving

Sticky rice, with sweet or savory filling, is wrapped in triangular packages

Skulls made from sugar and water may be decorated with the names of the dead

A mooncake is cut into wedges and served with tea

5 MIDFALL FESTIVAL

This east Asian celebration, which dates back more than 3,000 years, falls near the traditional harvest, when the Moon is at its lightest and brightest. Family and friends gather in the evening to eat mooncakes, rich rounds of pastry with lotus-seed fillings.

7 FEAST OF ST. LUCIA

Each year, on December 13, people in Sweden and Norway celebrate the feast of Saint Lucia (a Christian girl who died for her faith). Early in the morning, a young girl dressed in white (often the youngest daughter in the house) takes a tray of hot saffron buns to her family.

9 PASSOVER

In March or April, Jews celebrate Passover to remember when Moses led the Israelites from slavery in Egypt. Passover lasts for seven or eight days and includes a special meal called a seder. Each part of the meal has a symbolic meaning.

6 EID AL-FITR

This Muslim festival marks the end of Ramadan, a month-long fast. The celebration lasts for three days, starting with the sighting of the new moon. People dress in their best clothes and go to the mosque.

8 DIWALI

Also known as the Festival of Lights, Diwali celebrates the victory of good over evil. Hindu families light oil lamps and put them on ledges and balconies. They also send cards with wishes for a good year.

10 EASTER

The Christian festival of Easter recognizes the resurrection of Jesus on the third day after his death. It falls between late March and April each year. People attend church and exchange Easter eggs.

During Eid, children enjoy sweets made with pastry, nuts, and honey

Matzoh, a flat, crackerlike bread, is eaten to remember how Jews left Egypt in haste, not waiting for their bread dough to rise

Horseradish represents the bitterness of slavery

A roasted egg reminds Jews of sacrifices made in the temple in Jerusalem in Biblical times

Shank bone is a reminder of lamb sacrifices made in the temple

Parsley is dipped in saltwater to remember the tears of the slaves

Apple and nut mix represents the mortar that held Egyptian buildings together

Green vegetable, often lettuce, represents new life

Chocolate or painted eggs are given as Easter gifts

During Diwali, people take gifts of sweets to the houses of their friends

CITIES

Cities have existed since ancient times, when they functioned as trading hubs, often at the heart of sprawling empires. By the early 20th century, one in 10 people lived in a city. Industrialization has led to massive urbanization, and more than half the world's population are now city-dwellers. Modern cities are centers of commerce, culture, and government.

▶ HIGH-RISE

The first high-rise buildings, now known as "skyscrapers," were constructed in the 1880s. With limited space in city centers, building upward became the solution. Today, more than 7,000 skyscrapers tower above the city of Hong Kong.

▼ CITY-STATE

In ancient Greece, it was common for cities to establish themselves as independent states with their own political systems. By the 5th century BCE, there were hundreds of city-states, and Athens was one of the most important. Today, Athens is the Greek capital.

Modern Athens was built around the ruins of the ancient city-state.

▲ RELIGIOUS CENTER

Some cities are important religious sites. Mecca, in Saudi Arabia, is sacred to Muslims as the birthplace of the prophet Muhammad. All Muslims should make a pilgrimage to Mecca once in their lifetime.

▶ RIVER LIVING

Towns and cities were often built next to rivers, to take advantage of the trading opportunities and transportation links they offered. Founded by the Romans, the city of London now spreads far and wide on both sides of the Thames River.

The Palace of Westminster is home to the British parliament

▶ CONURBATION

When a city expands to merge with neighboring towns, it becomes one huge urban area called a conurbation. The world's largest conurbation is Tokyo, Japan, with more than 34 million inhabitants.

▼ POPULATION GROWTH

Until recently, the majority of the world's population lived in rural areas. Today, most people live in cities, where they have migrated in search of work and opportunity. In many cities, such as Mumbai in India, this has lead to overcrowding as temporary shelters spring up on the outskirts.

▶ WORLD HERITAGE

The United Nations Educational, Scientific, and Cultural Organization (UNESCO) has listed sites of outstanding cultural or natural importance in order to preserve them. Called World Heritage Sites, these include cities such as Djenné in Mali, with its large mud-brick mosque.

◀ DESERT CITY

At night, the lights of Las Vegas shine out across the Nevada Desert. Las Vegas means "the meadows," because the vast city was once just a place where travelers stopped for water as they crossed the United States.

▲ SPECIALLY BUILT

Until 1960, the capital of Brazil was Rio de Janeiro on the east coast. However, the government wanted to encourage growth and development in the center of the country, and so a brand new capital was built in the interior—the modern capital of Brasília.

▶ CITY WITHIN A CITY

Few city-states remain today, but one exception is the Vatican City in Rome, Italy, home of the Pope and the center of the Roman Catholic Church. The Vatican remains a city-state with its own flag, coins, national anthem, and postage stamps.

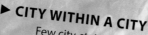

EXTREME LIVING

Humans have found a way of living in some of the most inhospitable environments on Earth—including the scorching deserts, the icy Arctic, and the steamy rain forests. Desert dwellers have to cope with the daily problem of finding water. In the Arctic, the challenges are keeping warm and finding food to eat. The rain forests are full of life, but many of the animals are dangerous, and some of the plants are poisonous.

Tuareg headscarf Wound around the head and neck, this headscarf protects the Tuareg people from the blistering sun and sandstorms.

Sun hat Worn by the Fulani of West Africa, this hat shades the face.

Boomerang This throwing stick, was used by Australian aborigines for hunting wild animals.

Snowmobile This motorized sled has skis for gliding over the snow.

ARCTIC

The frozen Arctic is one of the toughest places on the Earth to survive. There are no plant foods, so Arctic people came to rely on hunting seals, walruses, whales, birds, and fish. Without lumber, they used skins and bones to build shelters, sleds, and boats. Modern inventions, such as the snowmobile, have made life in this frozen wilderness easier.

Icebreaker A sharp pick is used to break thick, solid ice.

Fishing rod Arctic dwellers fish through holes in the ice.

Lapp stick This stick with a shovel-like blade is used by the Arctic Lapp people for probing and digging.

Hammock The hammock allows people in the rain forest to sleep in midair, away from snakes and insects.

RAIN FOREST

Unlike the Arctic and the desert, the South American rain forest has a wide variety of animals and plants. The problem is that many of the animals and birds suitable for eating live high up in the canopy. Hunters scan the trees above for prey, such as monkeys, and then shoot them down using blowpipes firing poison darts.

Poison dart frog This frog produces deadly poison, used to tip blowpipe darts.

Mosquito net Protection from insect bites is crucial when sleeping, since diseases like malaria are spread in this way.

DESERT

The extremes of temperature faced in the desert—extremely hot during the day, and very cold at night—is the main problem desert dwellers face. They are constantly on the move, searching for freshwater supplies, sometimes using the flight of birds and insects as their guide. Having found water, they must make sure that not a drop is wasted.

Ostrich egg The San people of the Kalahari desert, in southern Africa, fill ostrich eggs with water and bury them for using later.

Camels Bedouins travel using camels, which can go without water for long periods thanks to the fat stored on their backs.

Goatskin bag The Arabian Bedouin draw water from deep wells and transport it in goatskin bags.

Skin shoes The Sami of Northern Scandinavia wear shoes made of reindeer skin.

Traditional parka The Inuit of the Canadian Arctic wear thick, warm clothing made from caribou skins.

Modern Arctic clothes These are just as warm as the traditional wear, but are lighter and more flexible.

House on stilts People who live in the rain forest build these as protection from flooding and insects.

Blowpipe Crafted from wood, blowpipes are used to hunt birds and monkeys.

QUICK QUIZ

What can you remember about People and Places?
Jot down your answers, then check them on pp.296–97.

1 What is **Pho Bac**?
A Chinese for "come back"
B A Vietnamese beef noodle soup
C A battle cry during a karate move
D Korean New Year

2 This is the **Wailing Wall** in Jerusalem. Why is it important for the Jewish people?
A They gather here to offer their prayers
B They share their sorrows around this wall
C The wall wails to warn them of impending danger
D The wall was erected to celebrate the Jewish festival of Sabbath

3 Match the **US presidents** to their **names**:

A George W. Bush
B Ronald Reagan
C John F. Kennedy
D Jimmy Carter

4 The **Grand Canyon** is a steep-sided canyon in Arizona. How was it formed?
A By water and ice over millions of years
B By a violent movement of tectonic plates
C By an asteroid strike in the Triassic Age

5 What do we call a country that has a **president** as its head of state?
A Democracy
B Republic
C Monarchy
D Presidency

6 What is a **bishop's miter**?
A A staff a bishop carries at all times
B A chess move in which a bishop can leap over other pieces
C A hat worn by a bishop in the Roman Catholic Church
D A robe worn by a bishop

7 What is the name of the **traditional Spanish dish** made of rice, meat, and seafood?

8 This distinctive **rock formation** in the **Blue Mountains**, Australia, is a **spectacular** sight. What is it called?

9 The **original inhabitants** of **New Zealand** practice a **traditional dance** called the *haka*. What are these inhabitants known as?
A Aborigines
B Kiwis
C Maori
D Polynesians

10 About **10,000 tourists** visit **Antarctica** each summer. Where do they stay?

A In igloos

B On board the cruise ships they travel in, because there are no resorts

C Beside the Transantarctic Mountains, sheltered from the fierce winds

11 This **city-state** in **Italy** has its own **flag**, **coins**, **national anthem**, and **postage stamps**. What is its name?

12 **Match** the **flags** to the **country** names:

 1

 2

 3

 4

A Germany

B Spain

C Kenya

D Jamaica

13 On November 1, **Mexican families decorate altars** in homes and **cemeteries** with candles and flowers. Which **festival** are they celebrating?

A Mexican New Year

B Passover

C Day of the Dead

D Thanksgiving

14 Which **country** is home to the **funnel-web spider**, which can **kill a person** with a single **venomous bite**?

A India

B Mexico

C Kenya

D Australia

15 The **San people** of the Kalahari Desert store **water** and **bury it for later** use. But what do they store it in?

A Goatskin bags

B Ostrich eggs

C Earthen pots

D Skulls

16 Cocoa is the **key ingredient** in chocolate. Which **African country** produces **half the world's** cocoa?

17 Which **country** in Europe uses about **60 percent** of its **farmland** to **grow olives**?

18 The faces of **four US presidents** are carved into this rock. What is this **famous landmark** called?

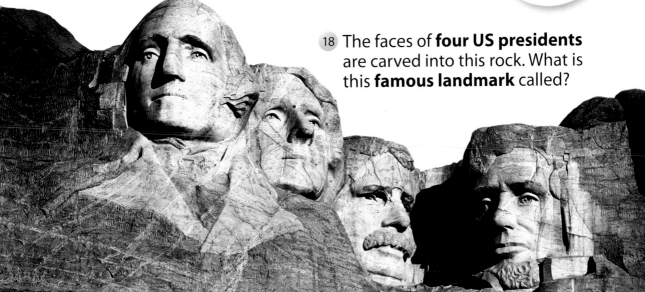

FAST FACTS

Vatican City isn't actually a city. It is a **country**, although it is only the **size** of **50 football fields** and its **population** is around **800 people**.

Nigeria is the most densely populated country in Africa, with more than **100 million people**, but **Sudan** is the largest country geographically, with a total area of **967,490 square miles** (2,505,800 sq km).

Uganda has the youngest population in the world. More than half its inhabitants are aged 14 or under.

Singapore is both a city and a state. It is the only member of the UN with a completely urban population.

China and India both have more than **1 billion inhabitants. The next biggest country by population, the US, has fewer than 315 million.**

Istanbul in Turkey is the only city to straddle two continents—Europe and Asia.

Damascus in Syria is the world's **oldest city**. People have lived there for more than 10,000 years.

*Before humans arrived in **New Zealand** around 1,000 years ago, there were **no mammals** there except bats. **Flightless birds**, such as the **kiwi**, walked the land instead.*

The bricks of the traditional **rondavel** houses of Rwanda are stuck together using **COW dung**.

The city of **Troy** was thought to be **mythical** until its **ruins** were found in Turkey in the 1870s.

The **tallest building** in the world is the **Burj Dubai Tower** in Dubai, and it is getting taller. It will be more than **2,500 ft** (800 m) high when it is finished, the tallest structure ever built by humans.

There are **194 countries** in the **world**.

*There is **enough stone** in the **Great Pyramid** in Egypt to build **a wall** 3 ft (1 m) high around France.*

The flag of **Nepal** is the only national flag that is not rectangular. It looks like one **triangle** on top of another.

The soccer **World Cup** has only ever been won by countries from **Europe** or **South America**.

It is estimated that **3.9 billion** people watched the **2004 Athens Olympic Games** on TV.

*Mongolia is the most **sparsely populated** country in the world. There are only 4.4 people per sq mile (1.7 per sq km).*

With more than **40 million** registered players (mostly in China), **table tennis** is the most popular competitive **sport** in the world.

WalMart, a US company with a chain of stores, is the largest company in the world, with **1.9 million** employees.

France is the world's most **popular** vacation destination, with more than **80 million** tourists each year.

Between 1800 and 2000, the population of the world grew from **1 billion** to **6 billion**.

In 27 CE, **Rome** became the **first** city to have **1 million** inhabitants.

*In 2008, for the first time in history, more than **half** the people of **the world** lived in cities and towns rather than rural communities.*

There are **50 states** in the US. The most recent to join was *Hawaii*, on August 20, 1959.

Tokyo is the *largest city* in the world. If you include all its suburbs, its population is *35 million*.

English is an official language in

58

countries.

There are about **110,000 Inuit people**, almost equally distributed among **Alaska, Canada,** and **Greenland.**

About 6,000 different languages are used around the world, of which half are spoken by fewer than 10,000 people.

The first map to name the newly discovered continent **America** was drawn by German cartographer Martin Waldseemüller in 1507.

Fewer than 100 people still speak **Votic**, a language of northern Russia.

583 different languages are spoken in Indonesia.

Argentinians eat more *meat* than anyone else.

Two million people converge on the holy city of **Mecca**, in Saudi Arabia, each year during the week of the Muslim pilgrimage called the **hajj.**

The **oldest known map** was drawn around *2,500* BCE on a clay tablet in *Babylonia*, in *modern-day Iraq*, showing the area around the *Euphrates River*.

Iceland's **Althing** is the oldest parliament in the world. Its first meeting was held in 930 CE.

*In 1978, Argentinian **Emilio Marcos Palma** became the first person to be born in **Antarctica**.*

About 4,000 people, mainly **scientists**, live in **Antarctica** in the **summer**. This number drops to 1,000 in the winter.

About *1 billion* people do *not* have enough to *eat*.

Absolute monarchies are states that are ruled directly by a hereditary leader. **Saudi Arabia, Brunei, Oman,** and **Swaziland** are the only absolute monarchies that survive today.

*The **Trans-Siberian railroad** runs from **St. Petersburg** in the west to **Vladivostok** in the east. It is **5,772 miles** (9,288 km) **long** and goes through **eight different time zones**, without ever leaving **Russia**.*

There are more than **20** megacities with more than **10 million** inhabitants in the world.

The widest avenue in the world is **Avenida 9 de Julio** in **Buenos Aires**, Argentina. It has **12 lanes of traffic**.

The first country to give women the vote was New Zealand in 1893.

At any given time of day, around **60,000** people are in the **air** somewhere over the US.

*There are **1 billion bicycles** in the world, **400 million** of them in **China**.*

The United Nations was formed by **51** countries in **1945**. It now has **192** members since **Montenegro** joined in **2006.**

There are **55** different **ethnic groups** in **China** besides the Chinese.

Three million people make their living working on *fishing boats*.

Experts predict that India will overtake China as the most populous nation on Earth by 2030.

The first cell phone network was launched in Sweden in 1956.

The world's **busiest airport** is **Atlanta** in the US. More than **88 million people** pass through its doors each year.

Russia, the largest country by area, is almost twice the size of the second largest, Canada.

About *half* the world's people regularly eat *insects*. About *1,500* different species appear on the menu.

*The **Rio de Janeiro Carnival** in Brazil is the world's biggest street party, with more than 2 million people packing the streets. London's **Notting Hill Carnival** in England is the second largest.*

80 percent of the world's **toys** are made in **China.**

HISTORY

BYZANTINE MOSAIC
This detail from a mosaic of colored tiles shows Theodora, wife of Emperor Justinian (527–565), with court officials. The Byzantine Empire, based in the eastern Mediterranean, was an offshoot of the Roman Empire.

PREHISTORY

Our distant past, before writing was invented, is called prehistory. Without written records, we rely on the objects that prehistoric people left behind them, such as tools, to find out how they lived. The first tools, made around 2.5 million years ago, were of stone, bone, and wood. Later, prehistoric people learned to use metals—first copper, then bronze, and finally iron.

Sickle A long flint, mounted in a wooden handle, forms a farmer's sickle, used to harvest grain.

Polished ax This ax, with its polished flint blade, was used by farmers to clear land to create fields.

Flint blade

Chopper This chopper was made 2.5 million years ago, by chipping a pebble to make a cutting edge. It would have been used to smash bones to get to the marrow inside.

Handax Invented 1.5 million years ago, the handax was the first stone tool made to a design. The pointed end was used for cutting meat or digging up edible roots.

Adze This adze, with its flint blade set in a wooden sleeve, was used to shape wood.

Iron pyrite

Flint

Scraper The best stone tools were made from flint, which forms sharp edges. This tool would have been used for scraping animal skins clean.

Antler hammer A toolmaker used an antler hammer to strike flakes from a flint to shape it.

Making fire Prehistoric people learned to make fire by striking flints against lumps of iron pyrite.

Mammoth-shaped hook held the spear in a long, straight handle, which launched the spear with greater force and speed

Spear thrower From 30,000 BCE, people made carvings of the animals they hunted. This spear thrower is in the shape of a mammoth.

▲ THE AGE OF FARMING

Between 10,000–9,000 BCE, people in the Middle East invented a new way of life—farming. They learned to store and sow the seeds of plants, and to breed animals, such as sheep and goats. By controlling their food supplies, farming people were able to settle down in permanent villages. As the supply of food became more regular, populations rose and the farming way of life spread.

▲ HUNTER-GATHERERS

For most of prehistory, people lived by hunting animals and gathering wild plant foods. Hunter-gatherers lived in small bands, which were often on the move, following herds of animals and looking for fresh sources of food. The first humans lived in Africa, but gradually spread across the globe, settling first Asia and then Europe. Humans reached Australia by 50,000 BCE, and the Americas between 30,000–14,000 BCE.

Antler pick European farming people mined for flints, digging with picks made from deer antlers.

Arrowheads Farming people continued to hunt wild animals, using bows and arrows with skillfully shaped flint heads.

▼ COPPER AND BRONZE

The next discovery was how to make tools from metals. Around 5,000 BCE, people in Europe and Asia learned how to extract copper by heating certain rocks. They used the bright metal to make tools and jewelry. Around 3,500 BCE, they discovered that adding a small amount of tin to copper made a harder metal, called bronze.

Sickle Iron was used for everyday tools, such as the blade of this sickle, set in an antler handle. A sickle was used for cutting hay or crops.

Neck ring This bronze neck ring was worn by a British Iron Age warrior as a protective charm.

Bronze sword The discovery of tougher bronze led to the invention of a new weapon—the sword. This one has been cleaned to show its golden color.

Royal dagger This bronze dagger, decorated with sea creatures in gold and silver, belonged to a ruler of Mycenae in Greece.

Iron dagger The scabbard of this iron dagger is decorated with bronze strips. It was found in the Thames River, England, and dates from c. 550-450 BCE.

Belt boss This decoration, which would have hung from a belt, was made by flattening a piece of bronze and hammering patterns into it.

Spearhead This is the head of a huge spear, which would have been thrust rather than thrown. Together with its wooden shaft, it measured more than 7 ft (2 m).

Iron Age sword Iron made stronger swords than bronze. This fine iron sword, which is 2 ft 4 in (70 cm) long, was discovered in 1987 in an Iron Age grave. It is a rare find because iron objects are usually destroyed by rust.

Bronze pin Bronze, with its gleaming golden color, was popular for jewelry among the rich. These pins were used to fasten clothes.

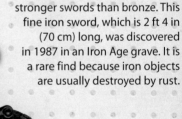

Mirror This is the back of an intricately decorated bronze mirror. The other side was highly polished to give a reflection.

Ax head Bronze tools, such as this ax head, were made by pouring the molten metal into molds.

Short sword This Ancient Egyptian weapon has a smooth handle so that it could be gripped tightly. The blade is ridged for extra strength.

▲ THE IRON AGE

Although iron is the most common metal on Earth, it was the last to be used to make tools. Unlike copper and tin, iron does not melt when heated in a fire. People did not learn how to shape iron, by heating and beating it with a hammer, until around 1,550 BCE. While bronze was a metal for the rich, everyone could afford iron.

1 KING
Sumerians believed that kingship was handed down from the gods. This king wears no crown, but his importance is shown by his kilt and the fact that he is larger than everyone else.

2 SERVANTS
Two men move between the king and his guests, bringing food and drink. Their low status is shown by their smaller size. They would have lived in the palace or in mud-brick homes.

3 NOBLES
These men may have been priests, relatives of the king, or wealthy landowners. They are shown sitting on chairs with delicately carved legs, evidence of luxury at the palace.

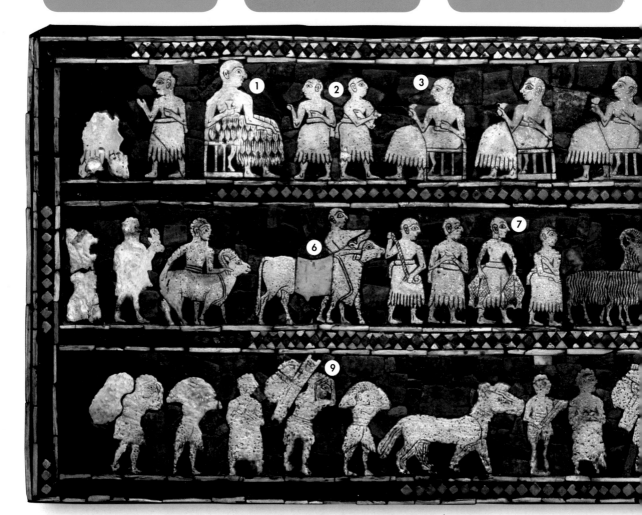

FIRST CIVILIZATIONS

More than 5,000 years ago, farming peoples in the river valleys of Mesopotamia (modern-day Iraq), Egypt, and India, created the world's first civilizations. In Sumer, southern Mesopotamia, people known as Sumerians built the first cities. Each city was ruled by a king, who governed on behalf of the local god. This scene shows the king of the city of Ur receiving goods from his people.

4 MUSICIANS

This man is shown playing a lyre, which has a wooden sound box decorated with the head of a bull. Other instruments from the time included harps, lutes, reed pipes, and drums.

5 SINGER

The only woman in the scene is singing with the lyre player to entertain the guests. Music and dancing played a key role in religious rituals, such as giving thanks for a good harvest.

6 FARMERS

Although the area was hot and dry, silt from the rivers kept the soil fertile. Farmers also dug canals to divert water to their crops, which included barley, turnips, onions, and dates.

7 FISHERMEN

Rivers offered a plentiful supply of fish for all early civilizations. From the Indus in India, the Nile in Egypt, and the Euphrates and Tigris in Sumer, fish were caught with nets or spears.

8 ANIMALS

Sheep, goats, cattle, and pigs were vital to the first civilizations. They provided meat, milk, leather, and wool. Oxen were used to pull plows and donkeys for transportation.

9 WORKERS

This man carries a bundle on his back, the heavy load strapped to his head. It was thanks to the toil of workers like this that massive temples for the gods could be built.

10 CLOTHING

Made from either wool or flax, both men and women wore tufted kilts, designed to resemble sheepskins. Wealthy men and women also owned elaborate gold jewelry.

▲ **THE STANDARD OF UR**

This mosaic of blue lapis lazuli, red sandstone, and white shell was made in the city of Ur in about 2,500 BCE. It decorates one side of a small wooden box found in a royal grave. The purpose of the box is not known. This side shows a peaceful banquet, while the other side depicts scenes of war.

CLASSICAL WORLD

The civilizations of ancient Greece and Rome are collectively known as the "classical world." The word "classical," in this instance, refers to culture of the highest quality. The Greeks were pioneers in science and the arts. They influenced the Romans, who spread this style of art, architecture, and literature across their own empire. Men in both societies were eager to find fame, often through military might.

Although little is known about Homer's life, it is generally thought that he was blind

Socrates was described as having a round face and a snub nose

Lionskin headdress of legendary hero Heracles, renowned for his superhuman strength

HOMER

During the 8th century BCE, Homer wrote two great epic poems about the legendary Greek war against the city of Troy. The *Iliad* recounts the story of the Greek warrior Achilles. The *Odyssey* describes the adventures of another hero, Odysseus, as he journeys home after the war. Homer's writing is so powerful that it is said to have influenced writers through the ages. He was so important to the Greeks that they simply called him "the poet." Homer's poems were originally sung or chanted, to the accompaniment of a lyre.

PYTHAGORAS

A philosopher, astronomer, and mathematician, Pythagoras lived in the 6th century BCE. He is remembered today for his work in geometry—particularly his theorem about triangles—but he was also a religious teacher. Pythagoras wanted to unlock the secrets of the universe and saw mathematics as the key to everything. He believed that numbers were the ultimate reality.

SOCRATES

Socrates (469–399 BCE) was an Athenian thinker whose influence on philosophy was so great that all earlier philosophers are referred to as "pre-Socratic" (before Socrates). However, unlike previous thinkers, such as Pythagoras, Socrates did not try to understand the universe. He believed that it was more important to find the best way to live. Accused by his enemies of being a bad influence, he was put on trial and sentenced to death by drinking poison.

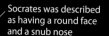

ALEXANDER THE GREAT

One of the world's greatest generals and bravest of soldiers, Alexander (356–323 BCE) was king of Macedon, to the north of Greece. After forcing the Greeks to unite under his leadership, he conquered a vast empire, stretching from Egypt to northwest India. By the time of his death at the age of just 32, he had won lasting fame and was forever known as Alexander the Great.

PERICLES

A statesman and general, Pericles (c. 495–429 BCE) was a leading figure in Athens when the state was a democracy (meaning "power by the people"). He filled Athens with temples, such as the Parthenon, which was dedicated to Athena, goddess of the city. Pericles also promoted the arts, and made Athens the cultural center of Greece.

Julius Caesar was known to be balding and combed his hair forward to try and disguise the fact

Like Augustus, Trajan wears the oak wreath, called the civic crown

Oak wreath was an award given to Augustus for saving Roman lives

Trajan's goatskin cloak is worn for godly protection and displays the image of the snake-haired Medusa

Although Augustus lived to be 76, his statues always showed him as a handsome young man

JULIUS CAESAR

Politician, general, and writer, Julius Caesar (c. 100–44 BCE) is famous for his conquest of Gaul (modern-day France), which he described in his book *The Gallic Wars*. He also fought and won a civil war against a rival Roman general, Pompey. Caesar marched on Rome and was declared dictator for life. He was later murdered for acting like a king, which went against the principles of the Roman republic.

EMPEROR AUGUSTUS

Augustus (the revered one) was the title given to Julius Caesar's adopted heir, Octavian, when he became Rome's first emperor. Augustus (ruled 27 BCE–14 CE) took power after defeating his rival, Mark Antony, in battle. He ruled Rome for more than 40 years, and brought peace and stability to the empire after years of civil war.

SULLA

As a Roman general, Sulla (138–78 BCE) was a ruthless and ambitious man. His quarrels with a rival general, Marius, led to the first in a series of bloody civil wars in which Romans fought against each other. Sulla was the first general to march on Rome as the head of an army and seize power. Julius Caesar later followed his example.

TRAJAN

A Spaniard by birth, Emperor Trajan (ruled 98–117 CE) was the first Roman ruler to be born outside Italy. He was a successful general, and his conquests in the Balkans and what is now Iraq brought the Roman Empire to its largest size. In Rome, a famous column was built in his honor decorated with scenes of his campaigns.

AGRIPPINA

The wife of Emperor Claudius, Agrippina (15–59 CE) was a powerful and ambitious woman. She persuaded her husband to adopt Nero, her son from a previous marriage. She is thought to have then poisoned Claudius so that the 16-year-old Nero could come to the throne. At first, Nero was dominated by his mother, but he eventually grew tired of her interference and had her murdered.

Castles were the stately homes of France's richest nobles

Wheat was cut using a curved blade called a sickle

Women covered their hair with a linen headdress called a wimple

The falconer was a well-paid professional huntsman

HUNTING

The Duke of Berry was a very powerful man and had many castles and lands. This painting shows his castle at Etampes, where a group of richly dressed nobles take birds of prey to hunt partridges, swans, ducks, pigeons, and other birds. Throughout the Middle Ages, hunting was the favorite sport of the rich.

The castle was a fortress and a garrison for soldiers

Vineyards surrounded by walls

A peasant sows seeds—like most farm work, this had to be done by hand

Peasants had few rights— they could not marry or leave the village without the lord's permission

FEUDAL SOCIETY

Medieval society was organized into a "feudal system," based on giving land in exchange for service. At the top was the king, who granted land to his nobles. In return, the nobles supplied the king with soldiers. At the bottom were the peasants, who worked the land in exchange for a piece of land to farm for themselves.

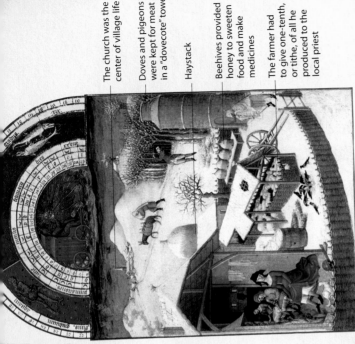

The church was the center of village life

Doves and pigeons were kept for meat in a "dovecote" tower

Haystack

Beehives provided honey to sweeten food and make medicines

The farmer had to give one-tenth, or tithe, of all he produced to the local priest

FARMHOUSE

This painting shows life on a farm in winter. Farmhouses were usually simple buildings with just one or two rooms where everyone would eat, sleep, and live together. The windows were small and did not have glass, which was very expensive.

BOOK OF HOURS

These paintings are taken from a prayer book called a "Book of Hours." It was made for the French Duke of Berry around 1410 and details prayers to say at different times of the day and year. In the Middle Ages books were rare and precious objects, handwritten and illustrated by monks, and most were religious texts.

The castle was designed both to show off the lord's power and wealth and to repel enemy armies

Drawbridge

The low wall at the tournament ground separated the knights as they charged each other on horseback armed with lances

Peasant life was harsh and many children did not live beyond the age of 10

CASTLE BUILDING

In September, the grapes were harvested, as seen here in the grounds of the castle of Saumur. Many magnificent castles and cathedrals were constructed during the Middle Ages, using only simple tools and the great skill of the masons who cut and carved the stone.

MEDIEVAL LIFE

Medieval means "middle age," and is the name given to the period of European history between the fall of the Roman Empire, in the 5th century, and the beginning of modern history around 1500. During the Middle Ages, 90 percent of the population lived in the countryside as peasants, poor laborers who worked for wealthy nobles

AMERICAN CIVILIZATIONS

Until the arrival of European invaders in the 16th century, complex and powerful civilizations flourished in the Americas. From 250 to 900 CE, the Mayan kingdoms of Central America built cities with huge stone temples and developed systems of mathematics and astronomy. From the 14th century, the mighty Aztec empire built pyramid temples and made sacrifices to their Sun god. In the 15th century, the Inca empire stretched for more than 2,000 miles (3,200 km) along the Pacific coast of South America, with a network of roads and fortress cities high in the Andes Mountains.

2 EVERYDAY LIFE

The Aztec, Inca, and Mayan civilizations were all based on farming. The most important food crop was maize (or corn), used to make pancakes, called tortillas, and beer. In addition to farming the land, people had to serve their rulers as soldiers, builders, or laborers.

1 POTTERY

Native peoples in the Americas made pots by rolling clay into long strips, which they coiled to make the walls of their vessels. Pottery served both a practical purpose, such as carrying liquids and boiling food, and a decorative one.

Pipes of different lengths make different notes

An Inca walks behind a Spanish invader

Flint blade with serrated edge

Knife There were no metal tools, so knives were made of stone.

Music The Incas made music by blowing across the top of cane pipes.

Drink The Incas drank "chicha" (maize beer) from painted wooden beakers.

Inca pots The Incas used these pots to carry and store beer. People carried them on their backs, using a rope passed between the handles.

Conical base for standing the pot in a hollow on the ground

Inca designs were influenced by basketry weaving patterns

A blue hummingbird perches on the rim, ready to take a sip

Mixtec cup This cup was made by the Mixtecs, the Aztecs' southern neighbors.

The hunters, disguised as deer, creep on all fours

Plate Paintings on pots often reveal details of daily life. This Mayan plate shows how people hunted deer using blowpipes.

3 GODS

The Aztecs and Mayans worshiped many gods and goddesses, whose statues they kept in pyramid temples. They believed that the gods made the Sun rise in the morning, the rain fall, and the crops grow. For the Incas, the Sun, the Moon, and the Earth were themselves gods. Inti, the Sun god, was the most important of them.

4 KEEPING RECORDS

These civilizations had various ways of keeping records. The Aztecs used a picture writing system, with pictures standing for words and ideas. The Maya had a more complex system, with signs standing for sounds. The Incas did not write, but kept records using lengths of knotted string, called quipus.

5 RITUALS

People believed that the gods needed to be given offerings to ensure their continued goodwill. The most precious offering was human life, and the Aztecs, Maya, and Incas all practiced human sacrifice. The Aztecs and Maya went to war to capture prisoners, whose hearts were offered to the gods.

Rain god Chac, the Mayan rain god, had a long nose and fangs.

3

Chac carries a ball of incense, which was burned at religious ceremonies

Offering Gold figurines were left by the Incas as offerings to the Sun and the Earth.

Gold was the "sweat of the Sun" to the Incas

Calendar This book is a calendar, used by Aztec priests to predict the future.

Aztec signs for different days

4

Mayan records Mayan books were painted on paper made from fig tree bark, which folded up like an accordion.

Quipu The color, size, number, and position of the knots all had a significance to the Incas.

Knots were used for counting

Shield Aztec warriors wore colorful costumes and carried shields decorated with feathers.

Jaguar skin decorated with feathers

5

Tezcatlipoca, an Aztec god of war and strife

Funerary urn Burned bones of Aztec warriors who died in battle were buried in urns.

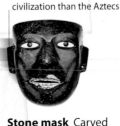

This mask is from Teotihuacán—an earlier civilization than the Aztecs

Stone mask Carved stone masks were placed as offerings in Mexican temples.

Eye shapes were often part of the knife's decoration

Sacrificial knife Aztec priests used stone knives to cut out the hearts of prisoners of war.

SEAFARERS

Seagoing craft have been built for at least 50,000 years. The first boats were probably log rafts or hollowed out tree trunks. At some point, people came up with the idea of catching the wind by raising a piece of cloth—the first sail. As ship building methods improved, sailors set off on longer voyages, using their ships to explore, to trade, and to raid.

Taut rope running from each end of the ship prevents it from sagging

▲ EGYPTIAN SHIP

This Egyptian seagoing merchant ship is constructed from planks tied together with rope, and dates from 2,450 BCE. Its collapsible mast carried a single square sail. Traveling against the wind, the crew lowered the mast and used oars.

Oars were used to power the ship when the wind dropped

The size of the sail could be adjusted with ropes

◄ VIKING LONGSHIP

From the 8th to 11th centuries, Vikings built ships strong enough to sail the stormy Atlantic Ocean, and light and slim enough to travel up shallow rivers.

► CARAVEL

The caravel was a ship for exploration, invented by the Portuguese in the 15th century. It had lateen (triangular) sails, which are much better at sailing into the wind than square sails. In ships like this, explorers found the sea route to India.

Sails are painted with Christian crosses

A lookout sat in the crow's nest on the mast

◄ GALLEON

This 16th-century English galleon warship was also used in trading and exploration. It had several decks, with many openings in the sides of the hull from which guns were fired. European navies used the galleon until the 18th century.

The stern post was carved into the shape of a swan's neck for luck

▶ ROMAN MERCHANT SHIP

The Romans built merchant ships with big, round bellies that could store large amounts of cargo. This shape made them stable, but very slow. They were usually safe from attack, because the Romans had rid the Mediterranean Sea of pirates.

◀ ARAB DHOW

Since the 8th century, Arab merchants and fishermen have crossed the Indian Ocean in dhows. They sail with the monsoon winds, trading goods between India and North Africa.

A pair of lateen (triangular) sails could catch side winds

Sail made from fiber matting

▶ CHINESE JUNK

The stern-mounted rudder, easier to control than a steering oar, was invented by the Chinese, 2,000 years ago. Chinese ships, called junks, could have up to nine masts, and were the largest wooden sailing ships in history.

Clippers had dozens of sails, making them very fast

▶ CLIPPER

The clipper was a 19th-century trading ship with a long, slim hull and multiple sails. The name "clipper" was originally a nickname for a fast horse. British and US clippers sailed all around the world on trading journeys.

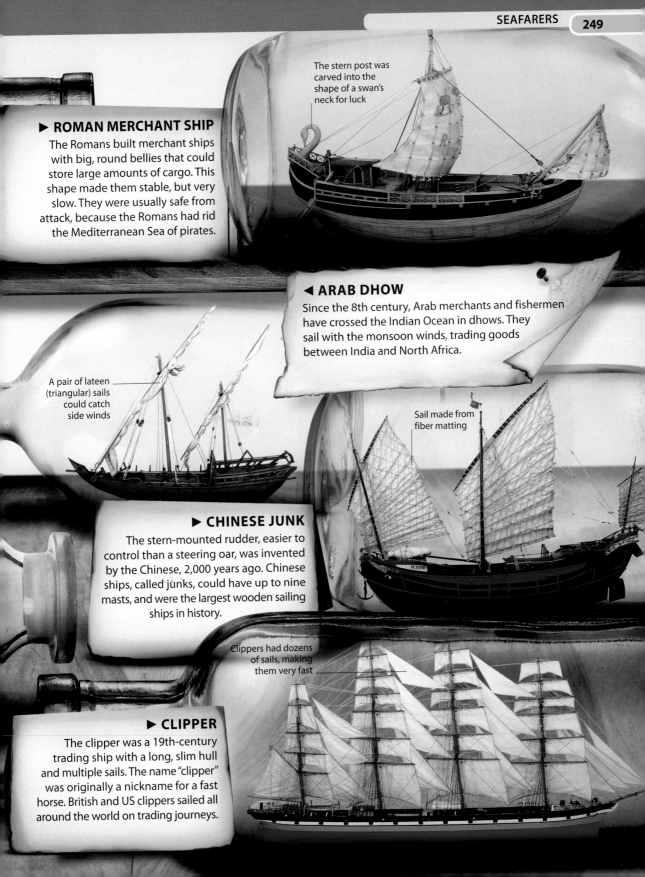

WAR

Throughout history, wars have broken out between tribes or nations over land, resources, and status. Methods of fighting changed over time, as people invented new, deadly weapons to fight with and improved ways of protecting soldiers from injury in battle.

1 **BOW AND ARROW**

The bow and arrow, invented more than 12,000 years ago, is one of the oldest weapons used in war. There are various types. The longbow was often used by foot soldiers, while this short Mongol bow is designed to be used from horseback.

2 **ARMOR**

The earliest soldiers wore armor made from wood, leather, and bone. After people discovered how to work metals, soldiers could wear armor made of mail (interlocking metal rings) or metal plates.

Mace (heavy club) was used to strike down enemies fleeing on foot

Iron mace

Leather helmet

Armor made of hardened leather plates sewn together

Bow

1

Quiver

Red leather quiver could hold up to 60 arrows

Dagger and ornamental scabbard (holder)

▲ **Mongol archer** In the 13th century, Mongol warriors from east Asia conquered the largest land empire in history. They fought on horses, using bows and arrows.

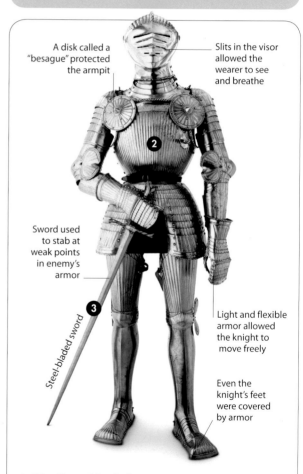

A disk called a "besague" protected the armpit

Slits in the visor allowed the wearer to see and breathe

2

Sword used to stab at weak points in enemy's armor

3

Steel-bladed sword

Light and flexible armor allowed the knight to move freely

Even the knight's feet were covered by armor

▲ **Medieval knight** European knights saw warfare as a way to win honor. Knights wore expensive suits of armor to protect themselves and as a display of wealth.

3 SWORD

Swords are weapons for close combat (hand-to-hand fighting). They have a point for stabbing and one or two sharp edges for slashing. A crossguard above the hilt (handle) prevents the user's hand from sliding down onto the blade and protects it from an enemy's sword.

5 FIREARMS

Invented in China in the 14th century, firearms (portable guns) increased a soldier's ability to kill his enemy from a distance. These weapons ended the age of the knight, whose expensive armor could offer little protection.

4 UNIFORM

In the confusion of battle, soldiers need to be able to tell friend from foe. Uniforms mark out which side a soldier belongs to and encourage discipline—soldiers wearing identical uniforms are more likely to act together as a group.

6 CAMOUFLAGE

In the 20th century, brightly colored uniforms were replaced by clothes that helped soldiers blend in with their surroundings. Colors and patterns like the green and black stripes on this uniform are known as camouflage, from the French *camoufler* (to disguise).

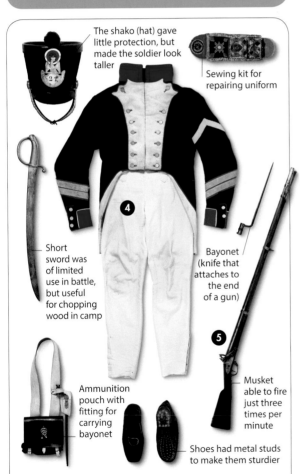

The shako (hat) gave little protection, but made the soldier look taller

Sewing kit for repairing uniform

Short sword was of limited use in battle, but useful for chopping wood in camp

Bayonet (knife that attaches to the end of a gun)

Ammunition pouch with fitting for carrying bayonet

Musket able to fire just three times per minute

Shoes had metal studs to make them sturdier

▲ **French infantryman** In the Napoleonic wars (1803–15), soldiers marched in ranks to the beat of a drum. At a signal, one line all fired their muskets.

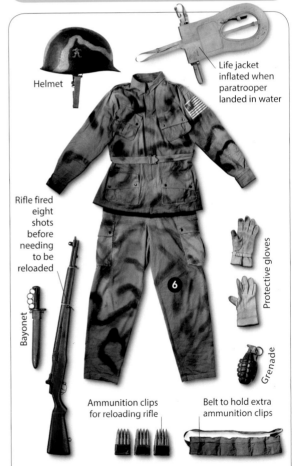

Helmet

Life jacket inflated when paratrooper landed in water

Rifle fired eight shots before needing to be reloaded

Protective gloves

Bayonet

Grenade

Ammunition clips for reloading rifle

Belt to hold extra ammunition clips

▲ **US paratrooper** In World War II, some soldiers attacked the enemy from the air. They leaped from airplanes wearing parachutes, landing behind enemy lines.

INDUSTRIAL REVOLUTION

From the late 18th century, the invention of machines that could do things faster than ever before brought dramatic changes in the way people lived and worked. Known as the Industrial Revolution, these changes took root in Britain and quickly spread to Europe and the US. It began in the textile industry, with new machines powered first by water and later by steam. This led to a huge demand for coal, to fuel the engines, and iron, to make the machines. New towns sprang up as farm laborers moved from the countryside to work in the factories.

Factory workers endured hot, humid conditions and air thick with cotton dust

▲ FACTORIES

Huge buildings, called factories, were constructed to house the new machines, row upon row. Machines, such as these looms for weaving cotton into cloth, were powered by a steam engine and the noise they made would have been deafening.

Woolen shawl

Woolen shirt

► FACTORY WEAR

Factory owners preferred to hire women and children rather than men, because they were cheaper and easier to discipline. Women in the factories wore heavy, durable clothes, which were products themselves of the Industrial Revolution's textile boom.

Skirt made from thick, coarse cotton fabric called muslin

Leather boots studded with hobnails for durability

► RAILROADS

In 1804, British inventor Richard Trevithick built the first steam-powered locomotive. Early locomotives carried coal from mines. From 1825, passenger trains were built, and armies of workers lay down railroad tracks.

"Puffing Billy," built in 1813–14, is the world's oldest surviving steam locomotive

▲ NEW TOWNS

In the factory areas, villages grew into huge towns almost overnight. Workers' houses were built as cheaply as possible, and they were often crammed closely together. The industrial towns were dark places, where the air was filled with smoke from the factory chimneys.

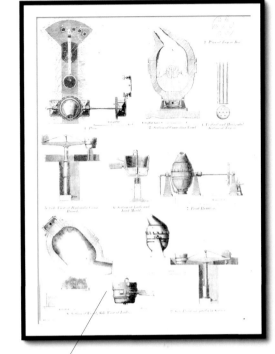

Plans for a new method of converting iron into steel, invented by Henry Bessemer in 1855

▲ INVENTIONS

The driving force of the Industrial Revolution was the rapid development of new ideas, methods, and machinery. Newly invented steam engines were used to power innovative new machines that transformed the mining, textiles, and metalworking industries.

▼ DISEASE

People lived crowded together in the new factory towns. They had no proper sewers, garbage collection, or clean drinking water. Diseases like cholera, typhus, and typhoid often swept through the towns, killing thousands.

Medicine box used to treat cholera

DISEASE

Wherever people have lived together in large numbers, diseases have spread. As ships traveled around the world, diseases like bubonic plague, the flu, and cholera spread from country to country. In the past, treatment was often ineffective since people did not understand the true causes of these diseases. We now know that they are caused by microscopic bacteria and viruses.

Some doctors wore birdlike masks stuffed with herbs believed to ward off the plague

◀ BUBONIC PLAGUE

In the 1340s, bubonic plague killed around half the population of Europe, and millions more in Asia and Africa. People believed that they could catch the plague by breathing bad air. The true cause was bacteria, passed on by flea bites.

◀ CHOLERA

These bones in the Paris catacombs are from victims of cholera, a disease that originated in India and was brought to Europe by merchant ships in 1829. It is caused by drinking water polluted with sewage, which carries the cholera bacteria. Victims die a painful death, after hours of vomiting and diarrhea.

Smallpox caused painful raised blisters, which left scars behind after they healed

▶ FLU PANDEMIC

A widespread outbreak of disease is called a pandemic. The worst case in history took place in 1918–20, when a deadly strain of flu spread around the globe, killing 50–100 million people. Face masks were widely worn, for it was correctly understood that flu is spread by coughs and sneezes.

▲ SMALLPOX

Smallpox was a disease that could scar, blind, and even kill its victims. Like the flu or the common cold, it was caused by a virus, a minute agent that can only grow or reproduce inside the cells of living things. Smallpox is one disease that has been wiped out by modern medicine.

JEYES' DISINFECTANTS

Fluid'
Powder
hold
oap.

Toilet Soap
Soft Soap
Prize Medal
Awarded

◀ **HYGIENE**

Until the 1860s, people did not understand the importance of hygiene in preventing infections. Surgeons did not even wash their hands before operating. In 1865, an English surgeon named Joseph Lister began to clean the wounds of his patients with carbolic acid. This killed the bacteria that infected the wounds.

A nurse washes her hands in disinfectant in a 19th-century advertisement

▶ **BACTERIA**

Bacteria are microscopic single-celled organisms that infect wounds and cause diseases. In 1928, Scottish scientist Alexander Fleming discovered that a mold growing in his laboratory killed harmful bacteria. He used this discovery to create a new type of antibacterial medicine, called an antibiotic.

Fleming grew bacteria in a petri dish

A new sewer is built in London in 1845

▲ **SANITATION**

The 19th century saw several cholera pandemics in Europe. These were eventually ended by building proper sewers, which stopped bacteria from polluting drinking water. The last European pandemic took place in Russia in 1923. Cholera is still a problem in Asia, with an outbreak in Iraq in 2007.

◀ **VACCINATION**

A vaccine is a weak form of a disease that helps the body fight a more serious disease. English doctor Edward Jenner realized that people who caught cowpox (a mild form of smallpox), did not get the deadlier disease. In 1796, he injected eight-year old James Phipps with pus from a cowpox blister. When he later tried to infect the boy with smallpox, James did not catch the disease and the first vaccine had been created.

MONEY

Before money existed, people traded by bartering, or swapping different goods. The problem with bartering was that each trader had to want what the other trader was selling. Money was invented as a medium of exchange—something with a recognized value that could be used to buy other goods. Money is usually made of rare materials, such as precious metals or colorful feathers. The first written records of money date back to Mesopotamia (now in southern Iraq) where weighed silver was used about 4,500 years ago.

Gold doubloons made by the Spanish invaders of Central America

1 EGYPTIAN HOARD

In ancient Egypt, payments were made with various metals and their value was based on weight, not shape. This resulted in a wide array of bars, rings, and pieces of gold, silver, and copper.

2 BURMESE WEIGHTS

During the 18th century, silver weights called "flower silvers" were used as money in Burma (now Myanmar). Liquid silver was poured into a mold and a floral pattern was added.

3 TRADER'S MANUAL

Coins were regularly shipped overseas in the 16th century. To identify the different coins and their value, Dutch merchants used handbooks detailing foreign currency.

4 FEATHER MONEY

The Pacific Islanders of Santa Cruz used long coils made of feathers to buy canoes. The brightest and boldest feathers had the highest value.

5 BANK NOTE

Paper money has its origins in 10th-century China. Handwritten receipts provided by merchants gained such importance that the government started printing paper receipts for specific amounts.

6 CHINESE COINS

In 500 BCE, bronze coins in China were made to resemble tools or the cowrie shells of an earlier currency. The shapes were so awkward they were replaced by circular coins with square holes.

7 WAMPUM

Native Americans created belts known as wampum from white and purple clam shells. These belts represented money and were used to seal deals.

8 STONE MONEY

Heavy currency was used by the islanders of Yap in the Pacific Ocean. The huge stone disks they used to pay for items were often too weighty to lift, some measuring 12 ft (4 m) across.

9 CHECK

An alternative to cash is a check—a form that details how much money should be transferred from one bank account to another. In medieval times, the Knights Templar issued checks to pilgrims so they could travel across Europe without carrying money.

10 CREDIT CARDS

First used in 1920s America to buy gas, plastic credit cards are now a part of everyday life. Issued by banks and businesses, cards are a convenient alternative to cash.

Tobacco leaves were the currency for the British settlers in North America in the 17th and 18th centuries

At different times in history, cowrie shells have been used as payment in China, India, and Africa

Shells stored in wicker container

Red feathers were woven into rolls

4

5

BANCO DI S. SPIRITO DI ROMA

This bank note from Rome was issued in 1786

6

Japanese ingot coins in the 17th century were hammered gold or silver bars

7

8

Embedded microchip acts as a computer

10

9

Up until the 17th century, silver rings were the method of payment in Thailand

20TH CENTURY

The 20th century saw more changes in the way people lived their lives than any other century. Among the century's many new inventions were television, computers, the internet, and nuclear power. The century began with the first airplane flight, lasting just 12 seconds, in 1903. By 1969, US astronauts had flown to the Moon and walked on its surface.

Protests
The 1960s saw many people march in antiwar protests.

CONFLICTS

World War I (1914–18) left 20 million dead, mostly young soldiers. Military air power during World War II (1939–45) made cities vulnerable to attack. Around 60 million people died, many of them civilians. This was followed by the Cold War, a long standoff between the US and communist USSR.

Gas masks These were issued to soldiers in World War I, and to both soldiers and civilians in World War II.

UN The United Nations (UN) is an international organization that was set up in 1945 to help prevent wars.

Cold War emblem The hammer and sickle was the emblem of communist Soviet Union, the US's Cold War rival.

The hammer and sickle signifies the unity of peasants and workers

Refrigerator
Mass production of home refrigerators began after World War II.

World's Most Convenient R
Hotpoi
Special Cold Zones Provide For Every Refrigeration Need

LOOK TO HOTPOINT FOR T

ENTERTAINMENT

Radios were invented at the beginning of the century, and the 1920s saw the arrival of radio broadcasts. In the 1930s and 1940s, going to the movies was the most popular leisure activity. In the 1950s and 1960s, the popularity of movie theaters waned, as people stayed at home to watch the new invention, television.

Walkman In the 1980s, the personal cassette player let people listen to music on the move.

Television Early televisions were small and showed only grainy black-and-white pictures.

Radio In the early part of the century, the whole family would sit around listening to the radio.

Gramophone The first record players were powered by turning a handle at the side.

AIDS From the 1980s onward, a terrible new disease called AIDS claimed the lives of millions of people around the world.

Famine Many countries faced humanitarian crises.

Movies People flocked to movie theaters to watch their Hollywood idols.

DOMESTIC LIFE

Many new labor-saving devices were invented for the home, including refrigerators, freezers, washing machines, dishwashers, and vacuum cleaners. The ability to stop food from decaying by freezing it enabled food to be transported greater distances and allowed people to buy and store it in bulk. Shortly after, precooked frozen meals emerged, changing mealtimes forever.

TV dinner Prepackaged meals could be heated, then eaten while watching television.

TRAVEL

The developments in transportation in this century allowed people greater freedom to travel. Millions of families bought cars and new highways were built to make journeys faster. The air travel industry really took off from the 1930s. Journeys, which before the airplane would have taken days by rail or sea, could now be completed in a matter of hours.

Globe Faster transportation opened up the world to more people.

Bikini A week in the sun on a foreign beach became a regular vacation event for many.

Air travel Cheaper air travel allowed many families to travel overseas for foreign vacations.

Souvenirs As overseas travel increased, many countries came to rely on tourism for income.

Apartheid

Nelson Mandela led the successful struggle to win equal rights for black South Africans.

ISSUES

The world's population rose from 1.65 to 6 billion people during the century, with a widening gap between rich and poor nations. There was inequality between men and women and people of different races.

Votes This medal was given to a female hunger striker in the UK campaigning for the vote for women.

WORK

The role of women in the workplace greatly changed during the century. Women had limited career options in the early decades, but gained more employment rights and opportunities as the century progressed. The workplace was also transformed by new methods of communication, including the computer and internet. New technologies led to automated factories, reducing the need for manual labor.

Computer technology From the late 1970s, personal computers began to revolutionize the workplace.

Women in the workplace In the 1970s, women fought for the right to the same work opportunities and pay as men.

Typewriter For much of the century, office workers used typewriters to write documents.

Telephone Improved communication technology enabled businesses to go global.

QUICK QUIZ

What can you remember about History?
Jot down your answers, then check them on pp.296–97.

1 Which of these was **not** used by **prehistoric people** to make **tools**?

A Bone
B Stainless steel
C Stone
D Iron

2 The first civilizations were created more than **5,000 years ago**. What are the people who built the first cities in **southern Mesopotamia** called?

A The Mixtecs
B The Mayans
C The Incas
D The Sumerians

3 Generally thought to be **blind**, this **Greek poet** wrote two epic poems about the legendary Greek war against the **city of Troy**. What was his name?

4 The **stern-mounted rudder** was invented **2,000 years ago**. Which people invented it?

5 Roman merchant **ships** were usually **safe from attack**. Why?

A Because the Romans had cleared all the pirates from the Mediterranean Sea
B Because the ships carried powerful weapons
C Because the merchants were trained fighters
D Because the ships were slow and hardly ever made it too far from the harbor

6 In the middle ages, **windows** in **farmhouses** did **not** have **glass**. Why?

A Glass wasn't invented back then
B It was too expensive
C It made the farmhouse too hot

7 **Match the arms** used by **Mongol archers** to their **names**:

1   **A** Dagger

2   **B** Scabbard

3   **C** Quiver

4   **D** Bow

8 In the 14th century, some **doctors** wore **birdlike masks**. What was the purpose of these masks?

A To make it easy for people to identify them
B Stuffed with herbs, the masks were believed to ward off the plague
C Doctors who were ill wore these masks to prevent the infection from spreading

9 This is a **knife** used by the **Aztec priests**. What was it used for?

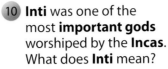

- **A** Cleaning their fingernails
- **B** Cutting out the hearts of prisoners of war
- **C** Chopping fruits and vegetables
- **D** Stoking a sacrificial fire

10 **Inti** was one of the most **important gods** worshiped by the **Incas**. What does **Inti** mean?

- **A** The Sun
- **B** The Earth
- **C** The Moon
- **D** Fire

11 This belt, known as a wampum, was used instead of money by **Native American** tribes. What was a **wampum** made of?

12 In **ships** like these, **explorers** discovered the **sea route** to **India**. What were these ships called?

- **A** Clippers
- **B** Galleons
- **C** Caravels
- **D** Merchant ships

13 This is a **shako**, a **hat** used during the **Napoleonic wars**. It gave little protection, so what was its other purpose?

- **A** A gun was kept under it to use in an emergency
- **B** It showed the soldier's rank
- **C** The soldier could pull it down to cover his eyes
- **D** It made the soldier look taller

14 Built in 1813–14, I am the world's **oldest** surviving **steam locomotive**. What is my name?

15 Between 1918 and 1920, a **terrible pandemic** claimed the lives of 50–100 million people around the world. The disease **still exists** today. What is it?

FAST FACTS

An early **writing system called cuneiform** was developed in **Mesopotamia** (part of modern-day Iraq) around **3,100** BCE. It was written by making wedge-shaped marks on clay tablets.

Modern humans settled in **Australia** at least **10,000** years before they reached Europe.

King Pepi II became **king of Egypt** in **2,275** BCE at the age of just **six**. He ruled for **94 years,** until his death at the age of **100**.

The minimum period of service for legionaries in the Roman army was 25 years.

The **first** ever female head of state was **Queen Merneith**, who ruled **ancient Egypt** around **3,000 BCE.**

The **Roman Empire** reached its greatest extent in **117** CE, when it stretched from Britain in the northwest to the Persian Gulf in the southeast.

The Roman **legal system is the basis for the laws of all countries in** Europe **and** Latin America.

The gladiator **Spartacus** led a revolt of more than **100,000 slaves** against the army of the **Roman empire** in **72** BCE.

The Islamic calendar started in 622 CE. It uses a year that is 11 days shorter than a full solar year.

Greenland was given its name by **Viking chieftain Erik the Red** around **1000** CE in an attempt to attract settlers.

About **2,000 years ago**, traded goods from **China** began to reach **Europe** and **Africa** along a route that became known as the **Silk Road** because silk was one of the goods traded.

14th-century Arabian explorer **Ibn Battuta** traveled **73,000 miles** (117,000 km) and visited every **Islamic country** in the world.

In the census called the **Domesday Book** carried out in 1086, **10 percent** of the population of **England** was listed as **slaves.**

Polynesian sailors crossed the Pacific Ocean 1,000 years ago, using charts made of sticks to find their way.

In 1519, the **Aztec capital Tenochtitlán** had a **quarter of a million** inhabitants. It was five times larger than London at the time.

Of the **270** *crew members who set out from Lisbon with* **Ferdinand Magellan** *in 1519 to sail around the world, just* **18** *completed the journey. Magellan himself died halfway through the trip.*

The Inca thought of gold as the **sweat** of the **Sun, and silver** as the **tears** of the **Moon.**

The **Inca empire** covered **350,000 sq miles** (900,000 sq km). In 1532, it was conquered by Spaniard **Francisco Pizarro** and just 168 men.

The Aztecs used cocoa beans as a form of money.

English explorer **Mary Kingsley** climbed *Mount Cameroon* in Africa on her own in 1895 when local guides refused to take her.

The first English-speaking colony in North America was set up in 1585 in Roanoke in North Carolina. It only lasted one year.

The **ancient Chinese invented** many things. The so-called *"Four Great Inventions of Ancient China"* were *paper*, the *compass*, *printing*, and *gunpowder*.

Between 1760 and 1840, **4,300 miles** *(7,000 km) of* **canals** *were built in* **Britain** *to carry goods from the new factories around the country.*

Zimbabwe is named after the **ancient city** of Great Zimbabwe in southern Africa, **built of stone** between the 11th and 15th centuries, but then **mysteriously abandoned.**

People first settled in **North America** around **20,000 years** ago. They walked across a land bridge that connected **northern Siberia** with **Alaska.**

The **Statue of Liberty** was a present given by France to the US in 1877 to mark the **100th anniversary** of the *American Declaration of Independence.*

The United States bought Alaska from Russia in 1867 for $7.2 million.

The earliest written **constitution** still in use in a country today is that of the tiny European state **San Marino**. It dates back to **1600**.

In the first factories and mines of the Industrial Revolution in Britain, children as young as five worked 16-hour shifts.

Japan's **monarchy** dates from **660 BCE** to the present day, during which time there have been **125 emperors.**

The **Hundred Years' War** between **France** and **England** actually lasted **116** years, from 1337 to 1453.

Between **1848 and 1855**, about **300,000** people went to **California** to find their fortunes in the **Gold Rush.**

In the year 1900, **one-quarter** of the population of the **world** lived under **British rule.**

The longest **reigning** head of state is currently **King Bhumibol** of Thailand, who came to the throne in **1946**.

Approximately 13 million soldiers from Russia were killed in World War II, more than all other countries put together. More than 1 million died in the siege of Stalingrad alone.

King Richard II of England (1367–1400) threw extravagant **parties** for as many as **10,000 people** at a time.

One century ago, **Ethiopia** was the only country in **Africa** that was not ruled by a European power. All African countries are now **independent** from Europe.

In the 13th century, **Constantinople** and **Baghdad** were the largest cities in the world, with about **1 million** inhabitants each.

In 1783, a **sheep**, a **duck**, and a **rooster** became the first aircraft passengers when they **flew** in the Montgolfier brothers' **hot-air balloon.**

The *Viking* law court was called *the Thing.*

In medieval European courts, animals could be tried for crimes. A swarm of locusts was once convicted, in their absence, of illegally eating crops.

Between 1793–1794, at least **17,000** people were executed in the nine-month-long **"Reign of Terror"** during the *French Revolution.*

*The **Black Death**, an outbreak of the bubonic plague, reached **Sicily** in southern Europe in **1347**. Less than three years later it had spread to the **Arctic Circle**, 2,200 miles (3,500 km) to the north.*

The toilets of **16th-century English** homes were cleaned by a worker called a **gong farmer.**

The *Great Plague of London* was ended in *1666* by the *Great Fire of London*, which burned down the affected areas.

Of the *seven wonders* of the ancient world, only the *Great Pyramid of Giza* still exists.

Ghamdan Palace in Sana'a, Yemen, built in the **3rd century CE**, may be the world's first **castle.**

The **Great Wall of China**, built to protect China's northern border, is **4,000 miles** (6,500 km) long.

ART AND CULTURE

PICTURE GALLERY
David Teniers' 1651 painting *Archduke Leopold Wilhelm in his Picture Gallery* features one of the greatest art collections of the age, which numbered 1,300 works. The archduke governed Southern Netherlands (Belgium).

ART

Some artists seek to create a beautiful object, others use art to reveal something about the world. In the past, art also served a religious or magical or mystical purpose. Styles of art vary widely, and artists from different cultures have shown the human form in many different ways.

The first art This carving of a pregnant woman, found in Austria, was made 25,000 years ago. Her hair is shown in detail, yet she has no facial features.

Tomb art Egyptian painters showed each part of the body from its most distinctive angle. Heads and limbs were viewed from the sides, with eyes and torsos shown from the front.

Mona Lisa With her mysterious half-smile, this is the world's most famous work of art. It was painted in 1503–7 by Italian artist Leonardo da Vinci.

Royal portrait German artist, Hans Holbein, was court painter to Henry VIII of England. His 1539 portrait of Henry's son, Edward, shows the clothing in great detail.

Self-portrait Dutch artist Rembrand van Rijn (1606–69) painted 60 self-portraits to experiment with techniques and to document his life.

Indian art This painting, made in 1770, is not a realistic image, but follows set rules. The athletes' heads are shown in profile while their chests face out.

Emotion art In *The Scream* (1893), Norwegian Edvard Munch aimed to express emotion rather than depict a real scene.

New forms Spanish artist Pablo Picasso (1881–1973) took the human form apart and reassembled it in startling ways.

Art Deco Polish artist Tamara de Lempicka (1898–1980) belonged to the Art Deco movement, which saw art as purely decorative.

Self image Mexican artist, Frida Kahlo (1907–54), painted self-portraits using scenes drawn from fantasy.

Terra-cotta Army In 209 BCE, more than 8,000 life-sized pottery figures of soldiers were buried to guard the tomb of China's first emperor. Every soldier has different features.

Prayer book Medieval European art often served a religious purpose. This illustrated book depicts the Virgin Mary holding the baby Jesus.

African mask These elaborate works of art were worn for ritual dances, when the wearer communicated with spirits.

Japanese print In 1794, artist Toshusai Sharaku made this woodcut print of an actor named Otani Oniji. He is shown performing the role of a villain, grimacing threateningly.

Brush strokes Like Rembrandt, Dutch artist, Vincent Van Gogh (1853–90), painted many self-portraits, 30 of them in the last five years of his life. He had a loose style, with each brush stroke visible.

Impressionism French artist Edgar Degas (1834–1917) founded an artistic movement called Impressionism. Its goal, shown in this painting of ballerinas, was to capture changing light and movement.

Sculptural curves Reducing human figures to simple curving shapes was a specialty of British sculptor Henry Moore (1898–1986).

Pop art Andy Warhol (1928–87) used subjects drawn from popular culture. In 1962, Warhol used a photo of movie star Marilyn Monroe to make this screenprint.

Cartoon art US artist Keith Haring (1958–90) started his career as a graffiti artist, drawing cartoonlike figures.

ARCHITECTURE

The art and science of designing buildings and other structures is known as architecture. From early times, people designed buildings both for practical reasons, such as shelters to live in, and religious reasons, such as stone tombs and places to worship the gods. Over the centuries, architecture has evolved to become an art form using high-quality materials to create ever more daring designs.

Triangular windows set in seven silvery arches under a spire crown the top of the building

1 THE COLOSSEUM

The first permanent amphitheater in Rome, the Colosseum was completed in 80 CE. It is amazing not only for its size but also for its design. Up to 50,000 spectators poured safely in and out of 80 doors to watch all-day gladiator battles and other public spectacles.

2 KUNSTHAUS GRAZ

Nicknamed "the friendly alien" by locals, this Austrian art museum, completed in 2003, has a blue outer skin of acrylic glass that can display images and animations. Inside, two large spaces can be adapted to display different exhibitions.

Nozzles on top of the building let natural light flood the museum galleries

Pointed gables were often decorated with carved crosses and dragon heads, like those on Viking ships

The lower classes sat in the top levels, while the nobles sat close to the action on the lower level

The church is coated with a mix of tar and oil to preserve the wood

In 2005, some panels were sanded down after nearby residents complained about the glare and heat of reflected light

A coated fabric "sail" keeps the sun out in the day. At night it is lit with colored lights

3 HEDDAL STAVKIRKE

As 12th-century Norwegians turned away from Viking beliefs to follow Christianity, they built a thousand beautiful wooden stave churches along trade routes in Norway. Carvings of animals often decorated the door frames.

4 DISNEY CONCERT HALL

This striking home for the Los Angeles Philharmonic Orchestra took 16 years to complete from design to opening night in 2003. Its striking exterior is made of stainless-steel curves. The wood-paneled main auditorium features state-of-the-art acoustics.

5 CHRYSLER BUILDING

This 1920s skyscraper in New York City remains the tallest brick building in the world at 1,047 ft (319 m). It was designed to house the Chrysler automobile company, and the gargoyles that jut from the building were designed like car mascots.

6 DJENNE MOSQUE

The largest mud-brick building in the world, the present mosque in Mali dates from 1909. The thick walls are coated with a smooth layer of plasterlike mud to even out the surface. Palm wood supports help people scale the walls to repair them each spring.

7 REICHSTAG

This building housed the German Republic parliament from 1894 until it burned down in 1933. When Germany reunited in 1990, the Bundestag (the new parliament) returned to Berlin. The original building was gutted and a new home built inside the old walls.

Visitors travel up a spiral walkway in the huge glass dome to take in a panoramic view of the Berlin skyline

Three massive towers are topped with oval spires shaped like ostrich eggs, which symbolize purity

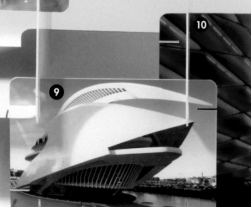

8 BURJ AL ARAB

Designed to resemble the sail of an Arabian dhow boat, this 1,035-ft- (321-m-) high luxury hotel in Dubai is one of the tallest in the world. Built on an artificial island off the coast, the Burj features a pair of wings spread into a V-shape to resemble a ship's mast.

9 EL PALAU DE LES ARTS

This Spanish opera house is part of a complex of museum buildings near Valencia. It is set within landscaped gardens with reflecting pools and interlinked paths. The roof is made from a pair of curving steel shells clad in concrete and mosaic tiles.

10 ALLIANZ ARENA

This soccer stadium is located in Munich, Germany, and is the only stadium in the world that can change its exterior color. Opened in 2005, the stadium holds nearly 70,000 spectators. Some locals nicknamed it the "inflatable boat" due to its unusual shape.

The opera house has been compared to an ocean liner, with its sleek exterior and shiplike decks inside

Some 3,000 air-filled foil panels that form the exterior can be lit from within to match the home team's colors

SYMBOLS

From a fire-breathing dragon to a four-leaf clover, people use symbols—images, objects, and figures—to represent abstract ideas or concepts. Symbols can best be described as something visible that represents something invisible. We use them every day without thinking about it. For example, our written language and numbers are made up of symbols.

GOOD LUCK

People hoping to protect themselves from misfortune or evil may carry a good-luck symbol. It could be a trinket, a piece of jewelry, or something from nature. Many symbols are lucky only to a particular culture and the superstition can stretch back centuries.

RELIGION

Followers of different faiths can express religious concepts, such as their idea of god, through symbols. Religious symbols have many meanings and uses and may be used in places of worship or as part of other religious practices.

Star and Crescent These are linked with the Islamic faith and appear on the flags of many Muslim nations.

Fu Thought to bring good fortune, this Chinese symbol decorates envelopes given to children for Lunar New Year.

Saint Christoper Some Christians wear pendants showing the patron saint of long journeys to protect them when they travel.

Apsaras This supernatural being represents the female spirit in Hindu mythology.

White heather Regarded as a symbol of good luck in Scotland, some say heather grew on battlefields where no blood had been shed.

Yin Yang This symbol of the Taoist belief represents harmony and unity in the universe.

Four-leaf clover Most have three leaves, so superstition has it that finding one by accident brings good luck.

Wheel of Law The eight spokes of this Buddhist symbol represent the eight paths to enlightenment.

Horse shoe In Europe and the US, hanging a horsehoe by the front door will bring good fortune.

Star of David Named for King David of Israel, this has been a symbol of the Jewish faith since medieval times.

Crucifix This shows Jesus Christ's death on the cross—a reminder to Christian worshipers of his sacrfice.

Evil eye This symbol is meant to block a curse sent by the nasty stare of an envious person.

Anubis The ancient Egyptian god of the dead, Anubis led the mummification process and protected the dead.

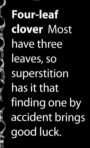

MYTHICAL BEASTS

These creatures only existed in myths and legends, but they hold real symbolic meaning for many people. They may be created from parts of different animals, or mixes between human and animal forms. Sometimes they can take the form of animals with incredible powers.

Salamander This creature is linked with fire and may represent the righteous who have escaped the flames of hell.

Centaur In Greek mythology, this half-man, half-horse beast symbolizes the instinct of an animal with the judgment of a human.

Minotaur This ferocious creature from Greek mythology has the body of a man and the head of a bull. It is a symbol of conflict between reason and animal instincts.

Unicorn A horse with a twisted horn appears in the legends of many cultures. In China, it represents gentleness.

Makara An aquatic creature from Hindu mythology, makara is part fish, part crocodile. It symbolizes love.

Dragon This giant beast, which features strongly in Chinese mythology, is a symbol of power. It is said to be able to spit fire.

NATURE

In many cultures across the world, members of the animal kingdom are chosen as symbols of a particular quality people would like to have. When animals are used in this way they are known as totems.

Eagle Seen as wise and majestic creatures, a cry from these usually silent birds is said to foretell a big event.

Owl A symbol of death in some parts of the world, in other cultures owls are linked with wisdom.

Snake Regarded as a symbol of evil in many cultures, it can also represent rebirth since it sheds its skin.

Carp This fish is a symbol of strength in Japan and other parts of Asia, perhaps because it swims against the current of the river.

Dolphin These are seen as symbols of joy, love, and happiness.

Beetle Amulets carved to resemble scarab beetles were the most powerful symbol in ancient Egypt and were thought to give the wearer eternal life.

Toad The Aztecs thought the toad was a powerful symbol of life and rebirth, while the Chinese associate it with wealth.

Monkey Three Japanese monkeys symbolize the principle "See no evil; hear no evil; speak no evil."

LANGUAGE

People communicate through language, whether the words are spoken or written down. Today, there are some 6,800 different languages spoken around the globe. Many more languages were spoken in the past, which have now been forgotten. The languages of the most powerful economic and political nations are spoken by millions of people.

5 HINDI

The family of languages spoken in northern and central India is known as Hindi. As well as 300 million native speakers, there are many Indians who use Hindi as a second language.

6 PORTUGUESE

This Romance language originated in Portugal, but spread to parts of South America in the 16th and 17th centuries. Today, it has 230 million speakers worldwide.

1 CHINESE

More than a billion people are native speakers of one of the family of Chinese languages. Some 880 million people communicate in Mandarin Chinese, a group of dialects (language variations) from northern and southwestern China.

2 GREEK

This ancient language has used the same alphabet since the 9th century BCE. Today, about 25 million speakers in Greece and Greek communities worldwide keep this language alive.

3 HEBREW

The holy language of the Jewish faith, Hebrew is spoken by 15 million people around the world. Many religious texts are written in an ancient form of Hebrew, in use from the 12th to the 6th century BCE.

4 ARABIC

Some 246 million people communicate with a dialect of Arabic, a family of very old languages closely related to Hebrew. The Qu'ran, the holy book of the Islamic faith, is written in Arabic.

In early Greek writing, there are no gaps between individual words

The Hebrew alphabet uses 22 characters, written from right to left

Around 4,000 characters are used in everyday written Chinese

In this Hindi script, symbols are joined together by a horizontal bar

7 JAPANESE

Used by 130 million people, the Japanese language can be adapted by the speaker to show respect to someone, according to their age and social status.

8 FRENCH

Spoken by 350 million people worldwide, French is an official language of the United Nations. It is one of the family of Romance languages that developed from Latin.

9 BENGALI

Also known as Bangla, this language is India's second most spoken language. Bengali is also used in other parts of southern Asia, with 230 million native speakers.

10 SPANISH

Originating in northern Spain, this Romance language has 400 million speakers. It is widely spoken in Central and South America. Today, Mexico has the most Spanish speakers.

11 LATIN

The language of the Roman Empire, Latin developed into the family of Romance languages, as well as lending its vocabulary to a number of other languages.

12 RUSSIAN

With 160 million native speakers and many more using it as a second language, Russian is an important language in Europe and one of six official languages of the United Nations.

13 ENGLISH

This widely spoken language went global through British colonization. Today, there are 400 million native speakers, and it is the most used language on the internet.

Portuguese writing has 26 letters and five accent signs

Written French has five accent marks to indicate pronunciation

In traditional written Spanish, 28 letters are used

Many Bengali characters stand for a combined consonant and vowel sound

Written Russian uses the Cyrillic alphabet, a medieval system named after its inventor, St. Cyril

LITERATURE

Any form of creative writing is called literature. It includes fiction, such as novels, poems, and plays, and nonfiction, including reference books, diaries, letters, and autobiographies. In all these literary forms, writers use their imagination to shape their material. They set out to convey information, ideas, or feelings in a clear and informed way that will interest and engage the reader.

▲ NONFICTION

Writing that is based on fact is called nonfiction. Authors need to research and understand their subject thoroughly so they can bring to life actual events—historical, political, and personal. Nonfiction titles also include biographies (accounts of people's lives) and autobiographies (authors' accounts of their own lives).

Anne Frank wrote about her experiences as a Jewish girl hiding from the Nazis in World War II

Crime and Punishment is a novel by Russian writer Fyodor Dostoevsky

Romance This popular fiction focuses on a love story between two people, usually with a happy ending. It may take place against a modern or historical setting.

Crime This type of fiction covers the exploits of criminals and their crimes, and follows the detectives who crack cases and foil their plans.

▲ FICTION

Authors who write fiction create events, settings, and characters from their imaginations. Although writers may base their stories on true events, there are always some elements that are made up. Works of fiction can include short stories, novels (long stories containing at least 60,000 words), poems, and plays.

Science fiction Authors may use scientific fact and modern technology to explore and imagine an alternative world, set now or in the future.

ФЕДОР
ДОСТОЕВСКИЙ
Преступление и наказание

АЗБУКА-КЛАССИКА

▶ DRAMA

Stories written for an audience fall into the category of drama, which may be performed in a theater, on radio, television, or the movies. The audience watching a drama expect something to happen, so writers use language to create characters and situations that will hold their interest.

English playwright William Shakespeare is considered the world's most successful dramatist

When a book is a success, the author may follow it up with one or more sequels to create a series

J. K. Rowling
Harry Potter
ET LA COUPE DE FEU

ALD DAHL
he BFG

by Quentin Blake

▲ CHILDREN'S BOOKS

Today, young readers enjoy a huge range of literature, both fiction and nonfiction. Writing for children is a specialized area, and authors often work alongside illustrators to get the story across effectively. In general, children's books follow the adventures of a main character who is a similar age to the reader. The storyline may also introduce the reader to challenges in their own lives, such as bullying or a bereavement.

BEST SELLERS

Hugely popular books that sell to vast numbers of readers are referred to as best sellers. The biggest seller of all time is the Bible, with approximately 6 billion copies sold. Former Chinese leader Mao Zedong's Quotations from Chairman Mao sold some 900 million copies. The holy book of Islam, the Qur'an, is close behind with 800 million copies. One of the most important works of Western literature, the Spanish novel Don Quixote by Miguel de Cervantes Saavedra, has to date sold about 500 million copies.

- More than 2 billion copies of Agatha Christie's crime novels have been sold worldwide.
- The best-selling playwright is William Shakespeare, with an estimated 4 billion copies sold.
- The seven books in J. K. Rowling's Harry Potter series have sold more than 500 million copies.
- The Count of Monte Christo by Alexandre Dumas has sold more than 250 million copies.
- The Bible has been translated into more than 2,000 languages.

◀ POETRY

In contrast to prose, poetry is often written in lines rather than paragraphs. Poets chose words in a way that will best express an image, an idea, or a feeling. Some poetry rhymes, but not all. An ancient form of poem is the Japanese haiku, which requires the poet to use words made up from 17 syllables (single units of speech) to convey an idea or image.

Basho (1644–94) was Japan's most famous haiku poet

◀ FOLKTALES

These magical stories usually feature fantastic characters facing near impossible challenges, set in an unspecific time in the past. The original tales, found in every culture, have no known authors. They were first intended for a general audience, but now folktales are often thought of as children's books. They are usually beautifully illustrated with images of the people and places.

Exquisitely illustrated Russian folk tale

MEDIA

The many ways people seek to communicate information to a large audience are known as the media. This communication can be in written, spoken, printed, or digital form. Throughout history, leaps in technology from the invention of printing to growth of the internet have led to better, faster ways of reaching people. Today, information can be relayed around the globe in seconds.

3 CONVERGENCE

Media technology tends to overlap, or converge, so that one device is able to do several jobs. Cell phones, for example, also play music, take photographs, play games, and connect to the internet.

1 DIGITAL MEDIA

The word "digital" refers to the way that information is turned into number-based codes before being sent or stored via electronics. The internet is the key form of digital media and has opened up mass media to the individual. Anyone with a blog or website can express opinions to a huge audience.

2 NEWSPAPERS

Published daily or weekly, newspapers contain news, information, feature stories, and advertising. China leads the world with 93.5 million newspapers circulating daily. Today, many papers are available to read online.

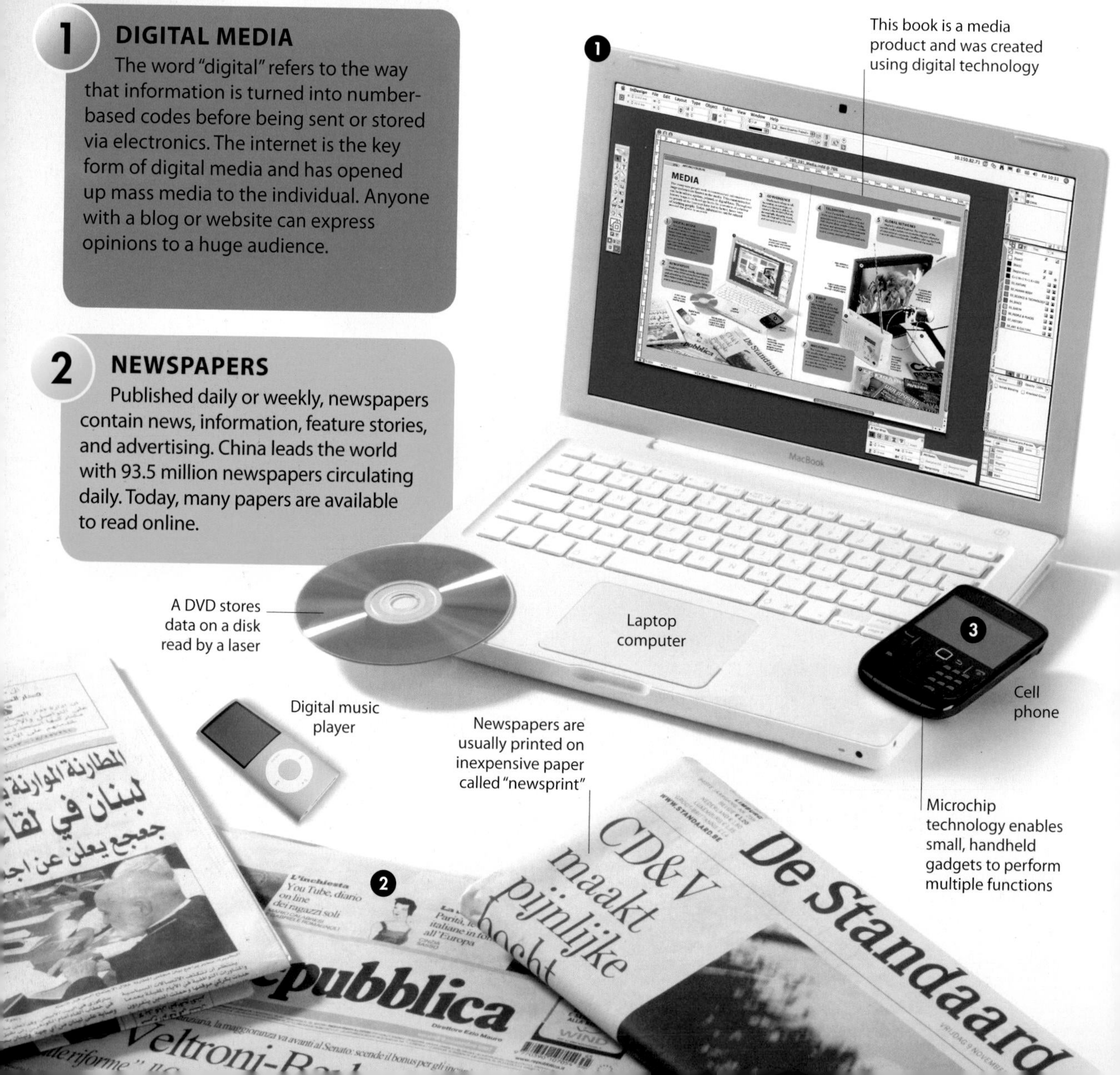

This book is a media product and was created using digital technology
1
MacBook
A DVD stores data on a disk read by a laser
Laptop computer
3
Cell phone
Digital music player
Newspapers are usually printed on inexpensive paper called "newsprint"
Microchip technology enables small, handheld gadgets to perform multiple functions
2
De Standaard
CD&V maakt pijnlijke

4 TELEVISION

Since the early broadcasts of the 1930s, television has brought news and entertainment to a wide audience. Today, DVD players allow people to watch movies at home, and viewers can chose between hundreds of television channels and record, pause, and rewind live broadcasts.

5 GLOBAL NETWORKS

Media is a global business. The majority of the world's media outlets are controlled by just a handful of international companies. Satellites orbiting the Earth transmit television broadcasts around the world.

Satellite dish

High-definition flat-screen TV

6 RADIO

In 1938, a radio dramatization of *The War of the Worlds* in the United States convinced many listeners that an actual Martian invasion was in progress. Today, radio stations still fill the airwaves with music, talk, news, and drama.

A satellite dish attached to a building receives signals from an orbiting satellite

Digital radios deliver high-quality sound through a digital signal

PURE

ONE

Magazines are usually printed on glossier paper than newspapers

7 MAGAZINES

The content of a magazine does not usually date as quickly as that of a newspaper. Magazines may cover current events or they may be aimed at a specific audience, for example, movie or music fans.

LE FIGARO MAGAZINE

SCIENCES ET AVENIR
Novembre 2007

60 GRANDES QUESTE
Le temps existe-t-il
La fin des civilisations
Le réchauffement climati
9 milliards d'hommes sur la
Décrypter le cerveau
Avant le Big Bang
La vie extraterrestre

CAR OF T
WHO WINS TH
GRADE A
ERCARS

DER SPIEGEL
Geboren am 9. No
Die Kinder des Ma

NORD DU NORD
NOS REPORTERS
AU CŒUR
DU PAYS

PHOTOGRAPHY

Photography is a method of making pictures of the real world by capturing light from objects. Light can be captured on film—a sheet of plastic coated with light-sensitive chemicals—or by an electronic sensor. Since cameras were invented, in the early 19th century, photographers have changed the way we see the world. They have shown us the wonders of nature, microscopic bacteria, the horrors of war, distant galaxies, sporting triumphs, and family portraits.

The speed of the shutter catches individual drops of water

▲ ACTION

Modern cameras are very sensitive and can open and close their shutters in a fraction of a second. This allows them to freeze a moment in time, showing a soccer player scoring a goal or a swimmer powering through the water.

▲ ADVERTISING ART

The photos we see most often are ads, blown up on street billboards and in glossy magazines. These photos are often "retouched" so that the models look more perfect. In a lipstick ad, teeth can be whitened and lips made to shine.

Sepia, a brown pigment derived from cuttlefish, made printed photos more durable

▶ PORTRAITS

Before photography was invented, only the very rich could afford to have portraits painted by artists. In the early days of photography, people wore their best clothes to strike a pose in a photographer's studio. Today, family photo albums chronicle birthdays, vacations, weddings, and everyday life.

Collapsible bellows allow the lens to be folded back into the camera

▶ LENSES

Cameras work by focusing light from objects using curved pieces of glass called lenses. A zoom lens (above) uses an assembly of several lenses. By adjusting their distance from each other, the photographer can zoom in on distant objects.

▲ EARLY CAMERAS

The first cameras, developed in 1839, were large boxes, which had long exposure times (the time needed for photographic film or an image sensor to be subjected to light). Early sitters look stiff and uncomfortable, as they often had to hold a pose for up to 20 minutes. Over time, cameras became smaller and more sensitive to the light.

▶ MACRO

This type of photography uses a special lens to take close-up pictures of tiny objects, such as flies. A macro lens can only focus on a limited area of an object. While this fly's eyes are in sharp focus, its body is blurred.

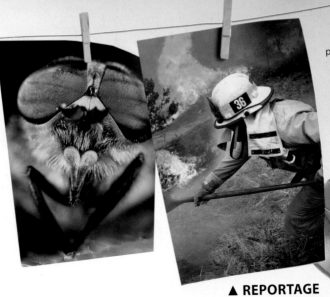

In a studio, a photographer can control how a shot is lit

▼ LANDSCAPES

Like painting, photography is used to record beautiful and often dramatic scenery. Some of the best landscape photographs are taken either in the hour after sunrise or before sunset. The Sun, low in the sky, bathes the world in a warm golden glow.

▲ REPORTAGE

Photojournalists are reporters who use pictures, rather than words, to tell news stories. Armed with their cameras, they visit war zones and scenes of natural disasters, such as floods and fires, often risking their lives to bring back photographs that will tell an accurate story.

Lights on stands can be raised and set at different angles

▼ DIGITAL CAMERAS

Modern cameras contain computers, which record images electronically rather than on film. Photographers with digital cameras can take as many pictures as they want without wasting film. Images can also be sent easily over the internet from one computer to another.

This "portrait" view is unusual for landscape photography, which gave its named to horizontally oriented photos

▲ FILM CAMERAS

Early cameras used heavy metal or glass plates. The roll of film, invented in 1888, made cameras both smaller and cheaper. The image was captured on the film in reverse, as a negative, which was used to print positive copies on paper.

THEATER

Theater has its origins in ancient Greece, where performances included singing and dancing as well as acting. In medieval times, plays were based on religious stories and were staged on large wagons in public places. It was not until the 17th century that theaters were built with raised, framed platforms and curtains that separated the audience from the stage. Today, modern theaters provide the setting for performances of all kinds, from plays and pantomimes to opera and ballet.

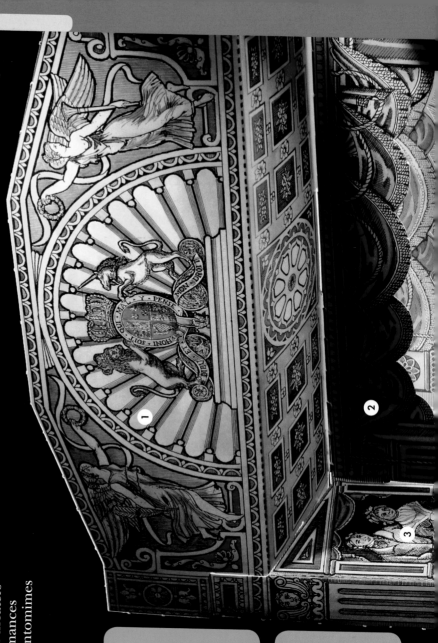

1 PROSCENIUM

The decorated arch that divides the stage from the audience is known as the proscenium. It acts as a picture frame for the performance on stage. This type of arch was invented in Italy in 1618, although many modern theaters now have an open stage without a curtain.

2 CURTAIN

Made from heavy cloth, such as velvet, the curtain screens the stage from the audience while stagehands change the scenery. The flameproof safety curtain prevents fire from spreading from the stage to the rest of the theater.

BOX

The auditorium, where the audience sits, is made up of private boxes, tiered seats called the stalls, the dress circle, and the upper circle. Private boxes contain the most expensive seats and usually have the closest view of the stage.

WINGS

The offstage areas on each side of the curtain are called the wings. Concealed by the proscenium, the actors wait in the wings before they make their entrance on stage.

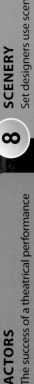

9 STAGE

In the theater, the stage is the platform where the performance takes place. Traditionally, the stage is made from wooden boards and often contains a trapdoor through which performers and scenery can be raised and lowered.

8 SCENERY

Set designers use scenery to create atmosphere, set the location of the story, and give the illusion of distance and space on stage. Above the stage is a "fly" space in which scenery and equipment hang. A complex system of pulleys hoists heavy pieces of scenery to and from the stage.

5 COSTUMES

The actors' costumes are the responsibility of the wardrobe department. The wardrobe manager researches, designs, and looks after the costumes and helps the actors change outfits between scenes.

6 ORCHESTRA

Beneath the front of the stage is the orchestra pit, where the musicians and sound technicians sit. The conductor stands facing the stage to coordinate the music in time with the actions of the singers, dancers, and actors.

7 ACTORS

The success of a theatrical performance often depends on the skills of the actors, who use facial expressions, tone of voice, and gestures to make the audience believe what is happening on stage. The first recorded actor was a Greek poet named Thespis who was writing and acting out his own plays in the 6th century BCE.

▼ SILENT

Until the late 1920s, the technology to add recorded sound to movies did not exist. Instead, bits of dialog or key story points appeared as words on screen, and actors relied on body language. Live piano music helped to set the mood.

▼ WESTERN

Set in the tough American West, these movies captivated huge audiences in the 1950s and '60s. Westerns tell of cowboys, outlaws, gunslingers, and good guys as they faced the challenges of frontier life.

MOVIES

From 1895, when the Lumière brothers first delighted French audiences with their "moving pictures" to today's multibillion-dollar film industry, movies have become a popular type of entertainment, an important art form, and a way to shape people's opinions. The "magic" of movies is that they are created from a series of individual images shown in rapid sequence.

▼ HORROR

These movies are created to terrify and shock the audience. In a typical horror film, characters must overpower evil—be it a monster, a ghost, or a serial killer. Horror movies are usually violent and gory.

▲ SCI-FI AND FANTASY

Imaginative and visually stunning, science fiction and fantasy allow filmmakers to explore future worlds, use special effects, and speculate about our relationship with technology.

▲ ACTION-ADVENTURE

These movies often follow the exploits of a hero, with plenty of fast-paced stunt work, chases, fistfights, and shootouts. From intrepid crime-fighters to special agents, these daring heroes always save the day.

▲ ANIMATION

These movies are created when a rapid sequence of drawings (or models) is run together to give the illusion of movement. Animation also uses computer-generated images (CGI).

▼ BOLLYWOOD

From the early 1900s, Hollywood has been the center of moviemaking. Today, more than 1,000 films a year are made in India. Many are lavish, colorful Bollywood musicals (the name is from the "B" in Bombay, the old name for Mumbai).

▼ COMEDY

From slapstick to spoofs, audiences have always loved comedy films. Some rely on the dialog for the laughs, others on physical quirks of the actors—or a combination of both. These films often have happy endings, even if they explore the darker side of life.

▼ DISASTER

Asteroids hurtling to Earth, shipwrecks, and earthquakes have all been subjects of disaster movies. Since the 1990s, the introduction of CGI special effects has made it easier to create visually spectacular disasters.

▲ THRILLER

Action-packed and fast-paced, thriller movies create audience tension as the hero tries to outwit an evil adversary. Some thrillers feature plenty of action, while others rely on creating an atmosphere of suspense.

▲ MARTIAL ARTS

These Asian-based action films feature spectacular fight sequences using one or more of the martial arts. Among the martial artists who became stars due to their skills are Bruce Lee and Jackie Chan.

▲ MUSICAL

Featuring singing and dancing as part of the storytelling, musicals are often adapted from stage productions. Recently, Hollywood musicals have played to wide audiences in a revival of the genre.

DANCE

Energetic or graceful, dancers use athletic skill and flexibility to perform a series of movements, often in time to music. Dancing is a form of expression that may be a type of performing art, part of a special ritual, or a fun social activity. The earliest dancers used movement to worship gods and spirits and to act out stories. In performances, dancers often follow a pre-planned series of steps and movements devised by a choreographer.

Arm movements are coordinated with the legs for balance and effect

▶ BALLET

Ballet is a theatrical dance with graceful moves. Dancers undergo rigorous training and wear special hard-toed ballet shoes in order to dance *en pointe*— on the tip of their toes.

◀ DISCO

In the 1970s, pop songs with strong dance beats ruled the airwaves and people gathered in clubs to disco dance. Some dances had set steps; others were created by the dancers themselves, perhaps inspired by the film *Saturday Night Fever*.

The dragon is a symbol of power and strength. The longer the dragon, the more luck it will bring

Bamboo poles help the dancers to move the dragon in a realistic way

▶ CHINESE DRAGON DANCE

In this ceremonial dance, dating back to the Han Dynasty (206 BCE–220 CE), a team of performers carries a colorful dragon, held up with poles. They lift and lower the poles to make the dragon dance. This dance is a key part of Chinese New Year celebrations.

▶ BHARATA NATYAM

In ancient times, Hindu temple dancers in south India performed a set of moves and postures to tell the stories of the gods. These evolved into the Bharata Natyam dance style. In this dance, certain poses—especially hand gestures—are held to represent different meanings.

◀ TANGO

This dramatic dance for couples began as a street dance in Argentina and Uruguay during the mid-1800s. With hands tightly clasped, dancers either face each other, or look in the same direction, as they move to the beat. Tango is also the name for the music associated with the dance.

▶ CAN-CAN

This high-kicking, cartwheeling dance began in Paris in the 1830s, and was originally for couples. French dance troupes soon took up the can-can in music halls, where chorus lines of girls performed the energetic dance.

Dancers swirl their skirts and petticoats as part of the performance

Castanets were not originally part of "true" flamenco, but were introduced to add drama

◀ TRIBAL DANCE

These traditional African dances, often performed to the beat of a drum, are important parts of many ceremonies, both joyful (weddings and coming-of-age celebrations) and sad (funerals). Tribal dances help to unite and uplift the community.

Touching the limbo pole means the dancer is out of the competition

Flamenco dress features a tight-fitting bodice with a layered skirt for easy movement

▶ LIMBO

The limbo was created in the Caribbean Islands. Performers have to dance under a horizontal pole without touching it or losing their balance. The pole is lowered after each round until one limbo champion dancer remains.

▲ FLAMENCO

With its roots in small villages of the Andalusian region in Spain, flamenco is a passionate style of music and dance with a strong, powerful rhythm. Dancers extend their arms and stamp their feet to match the drama of the guitar music.

MUSIC

Music is a performance art created by the sounds of singers and instruments and covers an incredible range of styles. It can be enjoyed live or through various media forms from television and radio to the internet. Music has always been written and performed, but it was not until the 20th century, when new technology to record and share music developed, that musicians could become global stars.

1
A disco ball hung over the dancefloor was a regular feature of discotheques

Touring provides a major income stream for today's global pop stars, such as Justin Timberlake

1 DISCO

In the 1970s, pop music with a dance beat known as disco (from discotheque, a French word for nightclub) filled dance floors across the globe. Disco music topped the charts and created major stars, but it faded from popularity in the 1980s.

2

A score (manuscript of musical notes) is used by classical musicians so they can keep track of which parts they play

2 CLASSICAL

Classical music is a general name for the various types of music written to be performed in a concert hall. It may be composed for the instruments of an orchestra (either a full symphony or a small group of players), or written for a choir or opera company. The music of composers like Bach and Beethoven is still popular centuries after it was written.

A relatively modern instrument, the saxophone became key to the emerging jazz sound

Turntables and vinyl records are used by DJs to create and mix live music

3 MUSIC AND VISUALS

From the late 1970s, bands made short music videos to accompany and promote their songs. The arrival of music video networks and the internet has created a huge boom in this area. The virtual band Gorillaz, which previously only existed as cartoon animations in music videos, turned the form on its head in 2005 when it performed live as a normal band.

5

Rapping evolved when DJs used microphones to talk—or "rap"— over music

GORILLAZ

3

From the 1980s onwards, CDs became the standard way to store and sell recorded music, with more than 200 billion sold worldwide by 2008

4 POP

This type of rock music is aimed mostly at a young audience. Pop songs can be fairly simple in their structure, with lots of repetition in the lyrics, so it's easy to sing along. Today's major pop stars reach an international audience with their hit songs.

5 DANCE

The popularity of electronic instruments like synthesizers, and the ability to use computers to make music, led to a new generation of music written to fill the dance floors. DJs became stars, using turntables to mix live music.

6 JAZZ

Jazz was born in early 20th-century America, when elements of European music were blended with the rhythmic music brought by African slaves to the South.

7 ROCK

In the 1940s and 50s, rock'n'roll music sprang up in the United States. It was played on electric guitars, bass guitars, and drums, and featured exciting vocals, catchy tunes, and a strong beat. This evolved into rock music, a group of many diverse styles that remains popular worldwide.

Rock band The Killers have sold over 10 million copies of their first two albums

Female singers, such as Beyoncé, are among the world's top-earning pop stars

8 R&B

Rhythm and blues, or R&B, music started in the United States in the 1940s, originally performed by and for a mainly African-American audience. Today's version of the style is closely related to disco and dance music, but is smoother and features softer vocals.

9 REGGAE

This style of music originated in Jamaica in the 1960s. It has a characteristic rhythm style and a slow and steady tempo (speed). The bass guitar keeps the rhythm and is the most prominent instrument. Reggae is associated with the Rastafarian religion.

Jamaican music legend Bob Marley is the most famous reggae star

Many country music stars have adopted the cowboy image

Portable media players can be plugged into docks so the music plays on speakers

The electric guitar is the main instrument in many musical styles, especially rock

Digital audio formats, such as MP3, can be downloaded from the internet and music can be stored on portable media players

10 COUNTRY

Mixing the traditional music of the Southern states of the US with rock-and-roll and other musical styles, country music is one of the largest-selling music genres today, with major stars, huge record sales, and enormously successful tours.

ORCHESTRA

An orchestra is a large group of instrumental musicians playing together under the direction of a conductor. Orchestras usually include four sections: percussion, brass, woodwinds, and strings. Players of similar instruments sit together, with the conductor keeping time up front.

Glockenspiel

Trumpet

Cymbals

Snare drum

French horn

Triangle

① Bass drum

Clarinet

Flute

Oboe

Piccolo

Xylophone

Bass clarinet

When blown through its reed—a very thin piece of wood—the bass clarinet makes a rich, full sound

Viola

⑥

Harp

⑦

Violin

Most orchestras have one or two harps

The conductor has a complete orchestral score (written music) for all the instruments

1 PERCUSSION
These instruments make sounds when struck, and include items that can be tuned to different notes (glockenspiels and xylophones) as well as those which cannot (drums, cymbals, and triangles).

2 LOW BRASS
Trombones, bass trombones, and tubas play the middle to lower brass notes in the orchestra. The trombone has a slide that moves up and down to change the note. The tuba plays the lowest notes, which boom out from its bell-shaped end.

5 TIMPANI
These percussion instruments are giant copper bowls with skinlike heads struck by wool-topped sticks. They are also called kettledrums.

3 BRASS
Blowing air through hollow brass tubes produces sound in instruments such as trumpets and French horns. The note is changed by pressing down valves.

4 WOODWINDS
This section of the orchestra includes piccolos, flutes, clarinets, bass clarinets, oboes, English horns, bassoons, and contrabassoons. Players blow air over a hole or through a reed to make notes.

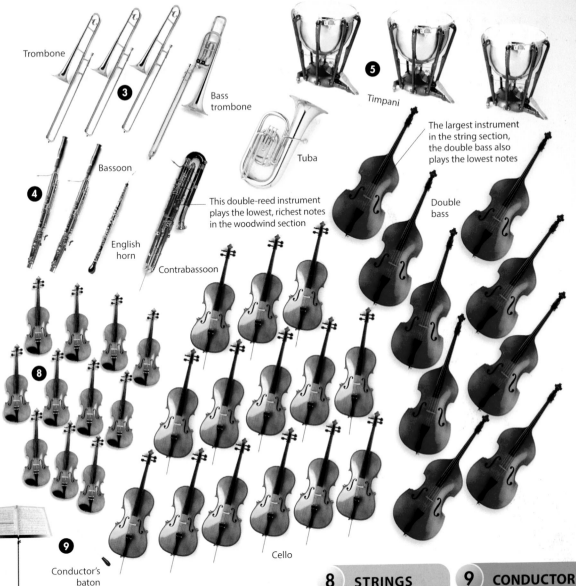

Trombone

3

Bass trombone

Bassoon

4

English horn

Tuba

Contrabassoon

This double-reed instrument plays the lowest, richest notes in the woodwind section

5

Timpani

The largest instrument in the string section, the double bass also plays the lowest notes

Double bass

8

Conductor's baton

Conductor's stand

9

Cello

6 HARP
A harp has a triangle-shaped wooden frame with 47 strings attached. The harpist plays the high notes on thin strings and the low notes on thicker ones.

7 VIOLIN
There are more violins than any other instrument in the orchestra, and it is the smallest member of the string section. Players make notes by moving a bow across its strings.

8 STRINGS
The strings often carry the melody (tune), and there are more string instruments than any other type in the orchestra. The section includes violins, violas, cellos, double bass, and harps.

9 CONDUCTOR
The conductor stands on a raised platform in front of the players. The conductor's main tasks are to lead the orchestra and keep everyone in time by waving a baton to the beat of the music.

SPORTS

Many sports developed from ancient times, when running and throwing skills were essential to survival. Any activity governed by rules and requiring physical ability is considered a sport—and at the heart of many sports is a ball.

1 FOOTBALL
Points are scored by players carrying or throwing an oval ball into the opposing team's area.

2 NETBALL
Based on basketball, this team sport is played on courts and is most popular with women in Australasia.

3 AUSSIE RULES FOOTBALL
Players pass the oval-shaped ball to teammates by kicking or throwing it. To score, they must kick the ball between four posts at each end of the field.

4 SOCCER
The world's most popular sport involves two teams of 11 players trying to score goals in the opposing team's net. Each game lasts 90 minutes.

5 GAELIC FOOTBALL
With its roots in an ancient Irish game called *caid*, players score by kicking or hitting the ball through H-shaped goals.

6 HOCKEY
In this game, two teams armed with hockey sticks try to score by smashing a ball into the opponent's net.

7 SHOTPUT
Players compete to throw a 16 lb (7 kg) metal shot as far as possible.

8 BASEBALL
This sport is very similar to softball, but played with a smaller, harder ball.

9 CRICKET
A bowler throws the ball at a wicket (set of wooden poles), which is defended by a batsman.

10 GOLF
A club is used to hit a small ball a long distance to get it into, or as near as possible to, each hole on a course.

11 RUGBY
Players attempt to gain points by landing the oval ball beyond the other team's goal line or kicking it over a high H-shaped goal.

The ball used in netball is smaller than the one used to play basketball

Modern soccer balls have 32 stitched panels

12 SOFTBALL

In this team sport, players use a bat to whack a ball as far as possible to give them time to run around four bases.

13 TABLE TENNIS

This sport began in Victorian England, when dinner guests turned their table into a mini tennis court. Champagne corks were used as balls.

14 TENPIN BOWLING

Players hurl a heavy ball down a wooden lane to knock down the 10 pins.

15 BASKETBALL

The game was first played using peach baskets on poles for hoops. If a team scored, the referee climbed a ladder to get the ball.

Hollow table tennis balls are hit with bats called "paddles"

13

Three finger holes are drilled into a bowling ball so it can be gripped

16 VOLLEYBALL

Two teams of six players compete to pass a ball over a high net using only their hands. If the ball touches the ground, the other team gains points.

17 BEACH VOLLEYBALL

First played on California's sandy beaches in the 1920s, this sport can now be played on artificial sand courts.

18 CROQUET

French peasants in the 14th century used wooden mallets to whack a wooden ball through hoops crafted from bent branches, inventing the game of croquet.

14

19 SQUASH

Inside a walled court, players take turns smashing a rubber ball with a racket against the wall.

20 TENNIS

Played on grass or clay courts, two players (singles) or four players (doubles) use rackets to hit a felt-covered ball over a net.

21 BOULES

Very popular in France, players compete to throw heavy balls at a much smaller ball, called a jack.

15

22 BOWLS

On well-maintained lawns, players try to roll balls closer to a small target ball than their opponents.

23 SNOOKER

Using sticks called cues, two players attempt to pot 15 red balls and six different-colored balls into six pockets on a special felt-covered table.

A beach volleyball is softer and larger than a regular volleyball

Rugby balls are oval shaped to make them easier to hold against the upper body while running

23

22

18

16

17

21

20

19

QUICK QUIZ

What can you remember about Art and Culture?
Jot down your answers, then check them on pp.296–97.

1 **Sepia** made early **printed photos** more durable. What is sepia?
- Ⓐ A photography technique
- Ⓑ An extract from fig leaves
- Ⓒ A type of coated photo paper
- Ⓓ A brown pigment from cuttlefish

2 This building, called **Kunsthaus Graz**, is an **art museum** in Austria. What have the locals **nicknamed** it?
- Ⓐ The friendly fish
- Ⓑ The blue monster
- Ⓒ The friendly alien
- Ⓓ The spiny alligator

3 In 1938, a **US radio dramatization** of which book convinced many listeners that **Martians** were **invading** the Earth?
- Ⓐ *Mars Attacks*
- Ⓑ *The War of the Worlds*
- Ⓒ *The Martian Chronicles*
- Ⓓ *Invaders from Mars*

4 **Match** the **mythical beasts** to their **names:**
- ❶ — Ⓐ Unicorn
- ❷ — Ⓑ Minotaur
- ❸ — Ⓒ Makara
- ❹ — Ⓓ Centaur

5 In which game do players take turns smashing this **rubber ball** against the walls with a **racket**?

6 This is a **woodcut print** of an actor named **Otani Oniji** made by **Toshusai Sharaku** in 1794. Which country is the artist from?
- Ⓐ China
- Ⓑ Japan
- Ⓒ Philippines
- Ⓓ Honolulu

7 **Match** these **famous buildings** to their **names**:

1

2

3

4

A Colosseum
B El Palau de les Arts
C Heddal Stavkirke
D Djenne Mosque

8 **Reggae** music **originated** in **Jamaica** in the 1960s. Which **religion** is this style of music associated with?

9 Which **language** is **rarely spoken** today, but its alphabet is the **most widely used** across the globe?

10 In an **orchestra**, why does the **conductor** wave a **baton** to the beat of the music?
A To keep the musicians entertained during a lengthy performance
B To keep himself busy while the musicians are playing
C To inform the audience about the notes being played
D To lead the orchestra and keep everyone in time

11 The centre of the **Indian movie industry** is called **Bollywood**. How many **films** are made in Bollywood **in a year**?
A At least 1
B At least 10
C More than 1,000
D About 10,000

12 I am the **smallest member** of the string section in an **orchestra**. What am I?

13 What is this **man** doing?

A Reaching up to turn on the lights
B Disco dancing
C Asking a question
D Playing statues

14 The goal of the artistic movement called **Impressionism** was to capture **changing light** and **movement**. Which **French artist** founded Impressionism?

15 Which **sport** began in **Victorian England**, when dinner guests turned their table into a **mini playing court**?

16 This **writing** is in an **ancient language** that has used the **same alphabet** since the 9th century BCE. What is it called?

17 I am a **symbol of death** in some cultures and of **wisdom** in others. What **animal** am I?

ΣΟΦΟΥΠΑΡΑΝΑΡΟΙ ΤΡΟΣΔΕΧΟΥΣΥΛΒΟΥΑ
ΙΜΗΤΙΑΣΙΝΕΙΚΗΤΟΙΣΦΙΛΟΙΣΠΙΣΤΕΥΕΤΑ

FAST FACTS

The first apartment buildings were built in **Rome** in the 1st century BCE.

Eleven Christian **churches** were carved out of solid rock at Labilela in **Ethiopia** in the 12th century CE. They took **24 years** to complete.

The **first skyscraper** was the **10-story**-high Home Insurance Building, built in **Chicago** in **1885**.

In 1923, **marathon dancing** competitions became popular in the US after Alma Cummings danced for **27 hours** without stopping.

After a performance of the opera **Otello** in Vienna, Austria, in 1991, starring Spanish tenor **Placido Domingo**, the audience applauded for **1 hour 20 minutes**.

Irish-born James Devine is the world's fastest **tap dancer**. He made **38 taps per second** in a performance in Sydney, Australia, in 1998.

Ancient Greek theaters were open-air. The biggest could hold 10,000 spectators.

Agatha Christie's whodunit play **The Mousetrap** has been playing in London's West End since 1952. There have been more than **25,000** performances so far.

The **"Whirling Dervishes"** of the Sufi order of Islam perform their **spinning dance** as an aid to religious **meditation**.

In the Mayan **ballgame court** at Chichen Itza, the acoustics are so good that a **whisper** at one end of the court can be heard at the other end **500 ft** (150 m) away.

The **marble** and precious stones used to build the **Taj Mahal** in Agra, India, were carried there by **1,000 elephants**.

In 2005, China had 39,425 movie theater screens—more than any other country.

The first modern novel was called **The Tale of Genji**, written **1,000 years ago** by Japanese author Murasaki Shikibu.

By the age of **65**, the average American has spent nine years watching television.

The film **Gandhi** had **294,560 extras.**

The **Harry Potter** novels by J. K. Rowling have been translated into **72** languages.

Playing cards date from **12th-century Persia** and **India**, when a pack contained **48 cards.**

The most **expensive film** ever made was the 1968 Russian epic **War and Peace**, which cost the equivalent of **$560 million** to produce.

The world's biggest movie theater screen is the **IMAX** in Sydney, Australia. It is as high as an **eight-story** building.

On average, it takes **eight weeks** to shoot a **Hollywood feature film**. Editing and adding special effects takes many months more.

French author Marcel Proust's novel **In Search of Lost Time** contains just under 1.5 million words.

The epic ancient Indian poem **The Mahabharata** is four times longer than the Bible.

The **deputy electrician** on a film set is called the "**best boy**," even when she's a girl.

The **biggest library** in the world is the Library of Congress in Washington, D.C., which has more than **30 million books**.

The **Asterix** books, by French duo René Goscinny and Albert Uderzo, have sold 320 million copies worldwide.

English playwright **William Shakespeare** (1564–1616) is credited with inventing **1,700** new words.

The most prolific **novelist** in history was South African writer **Mary Faulkner**, who wrote **904 books**.

The **Codex Leicester**, one of **Leonardo da Vinci's** notebooks, was bought by US billionaire **Bill Gates** in 1994 for **$29 million.**

In May 1990, Dutch artist **Vincent van Gogh**'s painting *Portrait of Dr. Gachet* sold for **$82.5 million.** In his lifetime, he was unable to make a living from his art.

Italian artist **Michelangelo** spent **five years,** between 1536 and 1541, painting Biblical scenes on the walls of the **Sistine Chapel** in Rome.

In 1872, Austrian composer **Johann Strauss** conducted an orchestra of **987 musicians** and a choir of **19,000 singers** in Boston.

The slowest musical tempo is called **larghissimo,** Italian for as slow as possible. The fastest is **prestissimo,** meaning as fast as possible.

The first permanent **photograph** was taken by **French inventor** *Nicéphore Niépce* in **1826.** It needed eight hours of exposure time.

The first museum to open its doors to the public was the **Uffizi Gallery** in Florence, Italy, in 1591.

In December 2006, the **Netherlands** became the first country to **switch off** its analog **TV** signal, forcing everyone to use digital receivers.

In the 1930s, German company Blütner made a **baby grand piano** out of **aluminum** and **pigskin,** so that it would be light enough to be carried in an **airship.** It weighed **397 lb** (180 kg).

The best-selling album of all time is *Thriller* by US pop star Michael Jackson, with estimated sales in excess of 59 million.

The lowest voice in opera singing is called a *basso profundo*, Italian for "deep bass."

The term for actor, **thespian,** comes from the first actor known to history, Thespis from ancient Greece.

The first **compact disc** went on sale in 1982.

An estimated 1.5 billion people watched the 1985 charity concert Live Aid on television.

The drawings of animals on cave walls in Chauvet, France, are 32,000 years old.

A **giant reclining** Buddha in China is the world's **largest statue.** Carved from stone, it is 1,365 ft (416 m) long. It was finished in 2004.

*The fastest ball game in the world is **pelota,** played in the Basque region of northern Spain and southern France. The ball can move at up to **185 mph** (300 km/h).*

La Scala opera house in Milan, Italy, has **3,600** seats.

It is now possible to watch more than 2,000 different TV channels from around the world online.

The practice of awarding **caps** for international sports appearances started in England in **1886.** Soccer players in their first international event were presented with a white **silk cap** with a red rose on the front.

Track and field was the first sport to hold organized **competitions.** The first such event probably took place in ancient Greece **5,000 years ago.**

Seattle-based artist **No Clue** is officially the **fastest rapper** in the world. On January 15, 2005, he rapped **723** separate syllables (parts of words) in **41.27 seconds.**

Walt Disney was nominated for **64 Oscars** and won **26,** more than anyone in history.

The highest paid sportsman of the **21st century** is *Tiger Woods*, with earnings of around **$100 million** per year.

Over its **20** separate stages, **15 million** people come out to watch the ***Tour de France*** bicycle race pass by.

On December 31, 1994, British pop singer **Rod Stewart** played a concert on *Copacabana Beach,* Rio de Janeiro, Brazil, to an estimated **3,500,000** New Year's Eve revelers.

The **marathon** is a race run over a distance of **26.218 miles** (42.195 km). This is the distance Greek soldier *Pheidippides* ran without stopping from the town of Marathon to Athens in 490 BCE to announce victory in battle over the Persians.

The English language has about **500,000** words, compared to **185,000** in German and **100,000** in French.

QUIZ ANSWERS

NATURE

1. D 5,000 years **2.** The age of the tree **3.** Water
4. C Holly **5.** 1B Iguana 2D Salamander 3C Octopus 4A Tiger
6. A Petal B Filament C Ovary D Anther **7.** D Once or twice a year
8. Scavengers **9.** A Norwegian wasp **10.** B To deter predators
11. Ostrich **12.** A The queen **13.** C Toucan **14.** Six **15.** C So it
can turn its back to look fierce when attacked **16.** D Squid
17. A Pig **18.** 1C Hamster 2A Armadillo 3B Badger
19. C Woodlouse **20.** D Food

HUMAN BODY

1. B Fight disease-causing germs **2.** In the bone matrix **3.** A Phalanges B Tarsals
4. C 20 per cent **5.** B Twelve **6.** B They are carried in blood through the
umbilical cord **7.** Windpipe **8.** C Muscles **9.** 1C Skin 2A Hair 3B Fingernail
10. 1D Stethoscope 2C Laryngeal mirror 3A Otoscope 4B Opthalmoscope
11. Nerve cells **12.** C Sixteen **13.** A Stomach B Large intestine C Small
intestines **14.** D Tongue **15.** C Our genes **16.** Dark blue, Broca's area
17. A Two **18.** Blood cells

SCIENCE AND TECHNOLOGY

1. B White **2.** A It is acidic **3.** Kevlar **4.** A Alkali neutralizes the acid injected by the bee **5.** Ozone
6. Phenols in apple oxidize when exposed to air and turn brown **7.** D Microwaves **8.** B Pale blue
9. A You are bringing like poles together **10.** Copernicus **11.** D It is lighter than air, so the balloon
floats upwards **12.** B Passengers **13.** 1C Methane 2D Water 3B Ammonia 4A Sulphur
14. B By using an X-ray telescope to detect the X-rays the black hole emits **15.** C 3 km
(2 miles) **16.** It emits radiation **17.** A Red **18.** 10 kg (22 lb) **19.** C An apple falling from a tree

SPACE

1. Ganymede **2.** Andromeda galaxy **3.** A Inside vast clouds of hydrogen gas
4. C Dennis Tito **5.** The Sun **6.** C There is methane gas in its atmosphere
7. Gemini **8.** B Titan **9.** A Laika **10.** B Sirius **11.** C A meteor
12. 1B Callisto 2C Europa 3D Io 4A Titan **13.** B A huge explosion in the
universe that occurred about 13.7 billion years ago **14.** 1B Esquel 2A Thiel
15. A Neptune **16.** C Mars **17.** A Valentina Tereshkova **18.** C It uses
a lens or mirror to collect light and bring it to a focus

EARTH

1. A Cloud piercer **2.** B The first fossil specimen of this dinosaur was found on a nest of dinosaur eggs **3.** B Graphite **4.** C Oceans becoming warmer **5.** A *Archaeopteryx* **6.** B The Red Sea **7.** Flash flood **8.** 1D Silver 2C Platinum 3A Copper 4B Gold **9.** D Tectonic plates sliding past each other **10.** Mont Blanc **11.** 1C Eurasian 2B Australian 3D African 4A Pacific **12.** B 9.5 **13.** C *Homo habilis* **14.** Topaz **15.** B Pulses **16.** C By wind picking up grains of sand and hurling them against bare rock **17.** Terra Nova

PEOPLE AND PLACES

1. B A Vietnamese beef noodle soup **2.** A They gather here to offer their prayers **3.** 1D Jimmy Carter 2A George W. Bush 3B Ronald Reagan 4C John F. Kennedy **4.** A By water and ice over millions of years **5.** B Republic **6.** C A hat worn by a bishop in the Roman Catholic Church **7.** Paella **8.** The Three Sisters **9.** C Maori **10.** B On board the cruise ships they travel in, because there are no resorts **11.** Vatican City **12.** 1A Germany 2C Kenya 3D Jamaica 4B Spain **13.** C Day of the Dead **14.** D Australia **15.** B Ostrich eggs **16.** Ivory Coast **17.** Greece **18.** Mount Rushmore

HISTORY

1. B Stainless steel **2.** D The Sumerians **3.** Homer **4.** Chinese **5.** A Because the Romans had cleared all the pirates from the Mediterranean Sea **6.** B It was too expensive **7.** 1D Bow 2C Quiver 3B Scabbard 4A Dagger **8.** B Stuffed with herbs, the masks were believed to ward off the plague **9.** B Cutting out the hearts of prisoners of war **10.** A The Sun **11.** White and purple clam shells **12.** C Caravels **13.** D It made the soldier look taller **14.** Puffing Billy **15.** Flu

ART AND CULTURE

1. D A brown pigment from cuttlefish **2.** C The friendly alien **3.** B *The War of the Worlds* **4.** 1C Makara 2D Centaur 3A Unicorn 4B Minotaur **5.** Squash **6.** B Japan **7.** 1B El Palau de les Arts 2D Djenne Mosque 3C Heddal Stavkirke 4A Colosseum **8.** Rastafari **9.** Latin **10.** D To lead the orchestra and keep everyone in time **11.** C More than 1,000 **12.** Violin **13.** B Disco dancing **14.** Edgar Degas **15.** Table tennis **16.** Greek **17.** Owl

Bold page numbers
refer to main entries

A

Aboriginals 210, 211
acid rain 193
acids **96–7**
actinides 92, 93
actors 280, 281
advertising 278
Africa 169, **200–1**,
    267, 285
Agrippina 243
AIDS 258
airplanes **120–1**, 259
air resistance 105
Alaska 166, 168, 169
albatrosses **8–9**, 43
Alexander the Great 242
algae 20, 41, 48
alkalis **96–7**
    metals 92, 93
Allianz Arena 269
aluminum 177
alveoli 71
Amazon River 206, 207
Americas see
    Central America;
    North America;
    South America;
    United States of America
ammonia 95
Ampère, André Marie 122
amphibians **32–3**, 34
analgesics 84
Andes 168, 206, 207
Andromeda galaxy 132–3
Angel Falls 186, 206
animals 16, 17
    in ancient civilizations
        241
    around the world 201, 202,
        205, 206, 210, 212
    attack and defense **36–7**
    earliest 131
    endangered 193
    feeding **28–9**
    life cycles **34–5**
    movement **46–7**
    relationships **48–9**
    skulls **54–5**
    sleep **52–3**
    as symbols 271

see also amphibians; birds;
    crustaceans; fish; insects;
    mammals; mollusks;
    plankton; reptiles
animation 282
Antarctica **158–9**, 169, 171,
    212–13
anteaters 29, 55
antelope 55
antibiotics 84
antlers 55
ants **23**, 48, 49
apartheid 259
apes 51
aphids 48, 49
Apollo space missions 150,
    151, 152
apples 98
Arabic language 272
architecture **268–9**
Arctic 188, **230–1**
Arctic Ocean 171
armadillos 54
armor 250
art 209, 210, **264–7**
Art Deco 266
arteries 72
artists 266–7
Asia 180, **202–3**
asteroids 141, 146, 150, 151
astronauts 105, **152–3**
astronomy 122, 123
    see also space, outer
Athens 228, 242
Atlantic Ocean 170
atmosphere 120, **161**
atoms **94–5**, 98, 100–1
Augustus, Emperor 243
auk, great 44
Australasia **210–11**
    see also Australia;
        New Zealand
Australia 184, **210–11**,
    214, 230
Aztecs **246–7**

B

babies, human 52, **80–1**
baboons 55
bacteria **255**
badgers 54
ballot boxes 221
bananas 16, 191

barnacles 30
barracudas 55
Barringer Crater **146–7**
basalt 164, 165
bases **96–7**
bats 36, 50, 52
batteries 122, 123
bears 29
bees **23**, 96, 191
beetles 23
Bengali language 273
berries 13, 16, 17
Big Bang 130
birds 8–9, **42–3**, 210
    color vision 14, 16
    eggs **44–5**
    feeding 28, 29
    pollination by 13, 14, 48
    skulls 54
black holes **105**, 135
bladder 66, **69**
blood **72–3**
    cells **60–1**, 62, 63, 68, 72–3
blowpipes 230–1
body, human **60–85**
    blood **60–1**, 62, 63, 68,
        72–3
    brain 68, **76–7**, 80, 81
    genetics **82–3**
    health **84–5**
    muscles **66–7**, 70
    nutrition 85
    reproduction **80–1**
    respiratory system 68,
        70–1
    senses 76, 77, **78–9**
    skeleton **64–5**, 70
    skin, hair, and nails **74–5**
    systems and organs **68–9**
    water content 101
    see also cells, human
Bollywood 203, **283**
bomb disposal 119
bones **64–5**, 70, 80
    see also skulls
Book of Hours **244–5**
books 247, 267, **274–5**, 276
boomerangs 230
bows and arrows **250**
boxfish 26
brain 68, **76–7**, 80, 81
Brazil 206, 229
bread 99
Britain see United Kingdom
Broca's area 76

bromine 93
bronchial tree 70–1
bronze 239
Buddhism 203, **224**, 270
buildings 216, **268–9**
Bunsen burner 122
Burj al Arab 268, 269
burning (chemistry) 98
butterflies **22**, 25, **35**, 202
Byzantine Empire 236–7

C

caecilians 33
Caesar, Julius 243
calcite **172**, 173
calculator, mechanical
    122, 123
calendars 247
California 12, 166, 184
    see also Los Angeles;
        San Francisco
camels 231
cameras **278–9**
camouflage 37, 251
Canada 192, 204, 205,
    226, 231
Canis Minor and Major 136–7
canyons **185**, 205
capillaries 72
caravels 248
carbon 95, 102
carp **27**, 271
cars 105, 106–7, **120**, 202,
    208, 259
cartoon art 267
    see also animation
castles 244–5
catalysts 99
caterpillars 22, 35
cats 53
CDs (compact discs) 286
cell phones 276
cells, human **60–3**, 68, 70
    blood **60–1**, 62, 63, 68,
        72–3
    reproduction 80, 81
Cenozoic era 179
Centaur 271
Central America **204–5**, 246–7
ceramics 102, 103
cerebellum 76, 77
cerebrum 76
cerium 93

chameleons 38
charts, navigation 217
cheetahs 47
chemical hazard symols 96
chemical reactions **98–9**
Chile 166, 206, 207, 221
chimpanzees 152
China **202**, **203**, 221, 276
    Dragon Boat Festival
        226
    dragon dance 284
    giant panda 193
    junks 249
    landscape 185, 187
    language 272
    money 256, 257
    space program 152
    symbols 270, 271
    tea 190
    Terra-cotta Army 267
chitin 19
chlorophyll 11
chocolate 190, 209
cholera 254, 255
Christianity **224**, 226, 227,
    229, 268, 270
    Bible 275
Christmas 226
chromosomes 82, 83
Chrysler Building 268–9
churches, Norwegian 268
cichlids 27
cinema 203, 204–5, 258,
    282–3
cities 192, 203, 209,
    228–9
citizenship 220
citric acid 96
civilizations, early **240–3**,
    246–7
clams, giant 40–1
cleaning fluids 97
cliffs 184
climate see weather

clipper ships 249
clothing 231, 241, 250–1, 252
cobras 39
cocoa **190**, 201
coconuts 191
coffee 191
Cold War 258
collision, inelastic 107
Colosseum 268
color **114–15**
colubrids 38
Columba 136–7
Columbia space missions
    150, 151
comets **144–5**, 150, 151
communism 258
compass 109
computers 259
concrete 102
constellations 136–7
consumer goods 219
continents 160, 161
conurbations 228–9
cooling 100
copepods 21
Copernicus 123
copper **93**, 98, **176**,
    210, 239
coral 48, 192–3
corn **190**, 201, 207
cotton **103**, 201, 252
cotyledons 10–11
cowrie shells 256, 257
crabs 20, **30**
credit cards 256, 257
crocodiles 39, 54
crops **190–1**, 200, 201, 206
crustaceans **30–1**
crystals 100, 172, 173, 174–5
cuckoos 45, 49
Curie, Marie 122
cuttlefish **41**, 46
cyanobacteria 20
cycling 193, 208

D

dance 203, 206, **284–5**
dance music 286, 287
Day of the Dead 226
deer 55
deltas 187
democracy 221
dermis 74, 75
deserts 184, **188–9**,
    201, 205
    living in **230–1**
dhows **249**, 269
diagnosis 84
diamonds **95**, 200
diaphragm 71
diatoms 20
diet see food
digestive system 69
digital technology
    276, 279
dinosaurs 178–9, **180–1**
disco 284, 286, 287
disease see health
Disney Concert Hall 268
displacement 98
Diwali 227
Djenne Mosque 269
DNA (deoxyribonucleic acid)
    82, 123
dogs **34**, 53, 54, 152, 153
dolphins **51**, 271
domestic life 218, 258
Don Quixote 275
Dragon Boat Festival 226
dragons 271, 284
drama 275
drugs, medical 84
drupes 17
Dubai 203, 269
durian fruit 16, 17
DVDs 276
dyes 98, 99
dynamics **106–7**

E

eagles **42**, **44**, 271
ears 77, **78**, 80, 84
Earth **140–1**, 150, **160–1**
    atmosphere 112, **161**
    beginnings 131
    gravity 104
    magnetism 108–9
    water 101, 161
earthquakes 161, 162, 163,
    166–7
Easter 227
echidnas **50**, 53
economy **218–19**, 256–7
eggs
    birds' **44–5**
    human 80
Egypt, ancient 191,
    201, 239
    art 266
    money 256
    ships 248
    symbols 270, 271
Eid al-Fitr 227
Einstein, Albert 105,
    122, 123
electricity **110–11**,
    122, 123
electromagnetic spectrum
    112–15
elements **92–3**
elephants 50, 53
embryos 80
emus 42
energy 98, 99, 100
    electromagnetic 112–13
    kinetic 106–7
    solar 138
    see also electricity
English language 273
environment **192–3**
enzymes 69, 99
epidermis 74, 75

INDEX

epithelial cells 63
Eridanus 137
erosion **184–5**
esophagus 69
estuaries 187
ethanol 94
eucalyptus trees 210
Europa 142, 143
Europe 169, **208–9**
evaporation 100, 101
exoskeletons 30, 31
eyes 77, **78**, 82, 83,
    84, 115
    insects' 24

F

factories 252–3
farmhouses, medieval
    245
farming **190–1**, 201,
    210, 218
    ancient 238, 241
    see also crops
fat cells 63
fatty acids 85
fava beans 17
fertilization
    humans 80
    plants 14, 15
festivals 204, **226–7**
fetus 81
feudal system 244
films see cinema
fingers and fingernails
    75, 81
first aid 84
fish 21, **26–7**, 37, 46,
    47, 55
    in the diet 85
fishing 208,
    230, 241
flags **214–15**
flamingos 43
flies 22, 29
floods 182
flowers 13, **14–15**, 97, 208
flu pandemic 254
folk tales 275
food 85, 259
    crops **190–1**, 200, 201, 206
    for festivals 226–7
    international 200, 203, 204,
        207, 209

forceps fish 26
forests 188, 189,
    193, 208
fossils **178–9**,
    180–1, 200
foxes 53
France 209, 251,
    285, 291
    see also Paris
Franklin, Benjamin 123
French language 273
frogs **32–3**, 34, 54,
    206, 230
fruits 13, **16–17**,
    85, 191
    citrus 96
    oxidation 98
fungi **18–19**

G

galaxies 128–9, 130,
    132–3
Galileo 122, 123
gall bladder 69
galleons 248
Galvani, Luigi 122, 123
gamma rays 112
Ganymede 142, 143
gases 92, 93, **100**, 101
gears 116, 117
geckos 38
Gemini 136
gems **174–5**
genetics **82–3**
geology **172–3**,
    184–5, 217
Germany 208, 209, 214,
    215, 269
Gila monsters 38
giraffes 28
glaciers **185**, 186, 213
glass 102
global warming 192
gold **176**, 200, 210
good-luck symbols 270
gorges 185, 187
gorillas 51, 53
governments 220–1
gramophones 258
granite 103, 172,
    173, 184
grapes 16, 17, 191, 245
graphite 95, **172**

grasslands **189**, 201, 205,
    206, 207
gravity **104–5**
Greece, ancient 228,
    242–3, 271, 272, 280
guns 251

H

hailstones 182
hair 74, **75**
Halley's Comet
    144–5, 150
halogens 92, 93
hares, mountain 37
Harry Potter books 275
Hawaii 164, 165, 169, 170
hay fever 14
health **84–5**
    and diet 85
    in history 253, **254–5**
hearing 77, **78**
heart 66, **68**, 72, 73,
    80, 81
heat (in chemistry) 98,
    99, 100
Hebrew language 272
hedgehogs 53, 54
helicopters **120–1**
helium **93**, 130, 138
Himalayas 168
Hindi language
    272, 273
Hinduism 203, **225**,
    270, 271
    dance 284
    Diwali 227
hippopotami 51
Homer 242
Hong Kong 203, **228**
horses 52, 53
House of Commons 220
houseflies 29
hummingbirds 14, 43,
    45, 49
hunter-gatherers 238
hunting 230–1, 244
hurricanes 183
hydrangeas 97
hydrocarbons 94
hydrochloric acid 96
hydrogen **92**, 96, 130,
    134, 138
hygiene 255

I

Iapetus 142, 143
ice **100**, 101
    effect on landscape
        185, 213
    see also Antarctica;
        Arctic
ice storms 183
icebergs 213
Iceland 208, 209
iguanas 38
illness see health
impala 49
Impressionism 267
Incas 207, **246**
inclined plane 116, 117
India 168, 190, 202,
    203, 229
    art 266
    Bollywood 203, **283**
    flag 214, 215
    language 272, 273
Indian Ocean 171
Indonesia 167, 202, 203
Industrial Revolution
    252–3
industry 119, 200, 202,
    203, 208, 210
inertia 106
infrared rays 113
inhalers 84
insects 14, 15, **22–5**
insulators 110
internet **276**, 286, 287
intestines 69
Io 142, 143
Iraq 202, 240
Ireland 214, 215
iron 98, 99, 108,
    177, 210
Iron Age 239
Islam 203, **225**, 270
    Djenne Mosque 269
    Eid al-Fitr 227
    Mecca 228
    Qur'an 272, 275
Italy 209, 229

J

Jamaica 215, 287
Japan 202, 203,
    228–9, 257

art 267
earthquakes 167
haiku 275
language 273
Jefferys, Alec 123
jellyfish 36
Judaism (Jewish religion) **224–5**, 227, 270, 272
judges 221
Jupiter **140**, 141, 151
moons 142, 143

K

kangaroos **47**, **50**, 210
karst 185
Kenya 201, 214, 215
keratin 74, 75
Kevlar 102
kidneys **69**, 80
kiwis 45
knights 245, **250**, 256
koalas 53, 210
Korea, South 202, 214
Kunsthaus Graz 268

L

langoustines 30
language 198, **272–3**
lanthanides 92, 93
larvae 20, 21, 23, 24
Las Vegas 229
Latin language **273**
law 221
lead 176
leaves **10–11**, 12, 13
leeches 28
legislature 220
Lepus 137
levers 116, 117
ligaments 64
light 110–11, 112, 114–15
lightning **111**, 123, **182**
limestone 97, **172**, 173
limpets 40–1
lions 28, 29, 36, 52, 54
liquids 100, 101
literature **274–5**
see also books
liver 63, **69**, 73, 80
lizards **38–9**, 210

lobsters 31
lodestone 109
London 208, **228**
Los Angeles 192, 268
lungs **68**, **70–1**, 81
lycra 103
lymphatic system 68
lymphocytes 62, 72

M

machines **116–17**, 252–3
macrophages 62, 72
Madagascar 201
magazines 277
magnesium 92
magnetism **108–9**
Makara 271
mammals 34, **50–1**, 202
Mandela, Nelson 258–9
Mao Zedong 275
Maori 210
maps **216–17**
Mars 140, **141**, 150, 151
marsupials 210
see also kangaroos
martial arts 202, 283
mass **104**, 134
materials **102–3**
insulating 110
magnetic 108
matter, states of **100–1**
Mayan civilization **246–7**
media 258, **276–7**
medical instruments 84, 85
medicines 84
Mediterranean region 171, 188, 192, 209
melanin 74
mercury (metal) 177
Mercury (planet) **140**, 141, 150, 151
mesas 185
Mesopotamia **240–1**, 256
Mesozoic era 178
metals **92–3**, 102, 108, **176–7**
meteorites **146-7**
methane 94
Mexico 193, 204, 214, 215, 226, 266
Mexico City 166
mice 50
microwaves **113**, 130

Mid-fall Festival 227
Middle Ages **244–5**, 250, 267, 280
Milky Way **131**, 136
minerals **172–5**, 200, 210
Minotaur 271
molecules **94–5**, 98, 99
moles 51
mollusks **40–1**
momentum 107
Mona Lisa 266
monarchy **221**, 266
money **256–7**
Mongolia 202, 250
Monoceros 136–7
Moon (Earth's) 104, 131, **142**, **143**, **161**
space missions to 150, 151, 152, 153
moons (of other planets) **142–3**
Morocco 200, 201
mosaics 236–7
mosquitoes **24**, 230
moths **22**, 24, 25
motion, laws of 106–7
motorcycles **120**
mountains **168–9**, 188, 205, 206, 213
movies see cinema
MRI (magnetic resonance imaging) scan 109
muscles **66–7**, 70
mushrooms **18–19**
music **286–7**
ancient 241, 246
international 200, 203, 204–5, 206
orchestra 286, **288–9**
theater and film 281, 283
Muslim religion see Islam
mussels 41
mycelium 18, 19
mythical beasts 271

N

nails 74, **75**, 81
navigation 217
nebulae **135**, 148–9
nectar 14, 15, 22, 23
Neptune 140, **141**, 143, 151

nerve cells 62
nervous system **68**, 80
neutrophils 62, 72
New York 204, 268–9
New Zealand 169, 186, **210–11**
newspapers 276
Newton, Isaac 104, 106–7, **122**
newts 32
nickel 177
Nigeria 187, 200
nitrogen dioxide 99
North America 180, 181, 184–5, **204–5**, 226
see also Canada; Mexico; United States of America
Norway 208, 209, 227, 266, 268
nuclear reactions 138, 160
nutrition see food
nuts 13, **16**
nylon 103

O

oceans 20–1, 161, 162, **170–1**
octopuses 40, **41**, 46
omnivores 29
Oort Cloud 144
opossums 37
oranges 16
orchestras 286, **288–9**
organs **68–9**
Orion **136–7**, 148
Orion Nebula 148–9
osteocytes 63
ostrich eggs **44–5**, 231
ovules 14, 15
owls 43, 47, 54, 271
oxidation 98, **99**
oxpeckers 49
oxygen **94**, 98, 99

P Q

Pacific Ocean **170**, 183, 210, 211, 256
paleontology 179
Palau de les Arts, El 269

Pampas 206, 207
pancreas 69
pandas 52, 53, 193
paratroopers 251
Paris 209, 254
parrots **28**, 43, 54
Pascal, Blaise 122, 123
Passover 227
passports 220
peaches 17
peacocks and peahens 42–3
pelicans 43
penguins 42, 44, 46, 212
Pericles 242
Peru 187, 206, 207, 246
petrochemicals 102, 103
pH scale 96
photography **278–9**
photosphere 138
photosynthesis 11
pigs 52
pike 27
pine trees 12, 13, 18
piranhas 27, 206
pivots 116
plague, bubonic 254
planets 101, 104, 105,
    134, **140-1**
    moons **142–3**
    space missions to
        150, 151
plankton **20–1**
plants **10–11**, 95, 210
    earliest 131
    relationships **48–9**
    see also flowers;
        fruits; trees
plasma 72
plastics 102
plate tectonics **162–3**,
    164, 166, 168, 170
platelets 72
platinum 176
Pluto 141, 151
poetry 275
poison dart frogs
    32, 230
polar regions 188
poles 108–9
politics 220–1
pollination **14**, **15**, 49
pollution 192, 193
Pop art 267
population 259
porcupines 37

portraits 266, 267, 278
Portugal 208, 248,
    272, 273
potassium 92
potassium permanganate
    99
potatoes 190
power plants 110–11
Prague 209
prairies 205
praying mantis 36
prehistory **238–9**
presidents 221
    US **222–3**
production 218
protests **220**, 258
puffballs 19
pufferfish 26
pulleys 116
pulsars 135
pupae 22, 35
Puppis 136–7
Pythagoras 242
pythons 36, 38
quails' eggs **44**

R

rabbits 52, 54
radar systems 113
radio 258, **277**
radio waves 113
radioactivity 92, 93, 122
railroads **120–1**,
    252–3
rain 101
    acid 193
rainbows 115
rain forests **188**, 193, 201,
    206, 207, 210
    living in **230–1**
rapping 286
rattlesnakes 39
raw materials 219
rays (fish) 26
refrigerators 258
Reichstag 268–9
relativity 122
religion 203, **224–5**,
    246–7, 270
    see also Buddhism;
        Christianity;
        Hinduism;
        Islam; Judaism

remoras 48
reproduction, human
    80–1
reptiles 35, **38–9**
republics 221
respiratory system 68,
    70–1
rice 190
Richter Scale 166
Rio de Janeiro 229
rivers 185, **186–7**, 201,
    240, 241
robots **118–19**
rocks **172–3**, 184–5,
    211, 217
rodents 50
Roman Catholic Church
    224, 229
Rome, ancient **242–3**, 249,
    268, 273
roots 10–11
rubber 103
Russia 209, 255, 274
    language 273
    space program 150,
        151, 152

S

Saint Lucia, feast of 227
salamanders **32**,
    33, 271
salmon 27
salt 94
San Andreas Fault
    163, 166
San Francisco 166, 193
sandpipers 45
sandstone **173**, 184
satellites 150, 151, 183,
    216, 277
Saturn **140–1**, 143, 151
Saudi Arabia 202, 228
scallops 41
science fiction 274, 282
scientists **122–3**
scorpions **36**, 205
screw mechanism 116
sculpture 267
sea anemone 46
seahorses 26
seals 52, 53, 212
seeds 10, 13, 16, 17
senses 76, 77, **78–9**

sewers 255
Shakespeare, William 275
sharks 28, 48
sheep 52, 53, 210–11
ships 121, 248–9
    charts 217
shrimp 31
sidewinders 46
silicon 93
silk 102, 103
silver **176**, 210
skeleton **64–5**, 70
skin **74**, 79
skulls **54–5**, 64, 178–9
skunks 37
sleep **52–3**
sloths, two-toed 52–3
slugs **40**, 41
smallpox 254, 255
smell 79
snails **40**, 46, 47
snakes 36, **38–9**, 46,
    205, 271
soap 97
Socrates 242
soil 10, 11
solar system 123, **131**
    comets **144–5**, 151
    meteorites **146-7**
    moons **142–3**
    Sun 112, 123, 131, 134,
        138–9
    see also Earth; Moon
        (Earth's); planets;
        space, outer; stars
solids 100, 101
solutions 99
South Africa 200,
    201, 259
South America 168, 186,
    187, 190, **206–7**
    see also Brazil; Chile;
        Peru; Venezuela
Southern Ocean 171
soybeans 190
space, outer 100, 104–5,
    128–53
    universe **130–1**
    see also astronomy;
        solar system; stars
space exploration **150-1**
    astronauts 150,
        152–3
    robot craft 119
    zero gravity 105

Spain 209, 266, 269, 275
  flag 214, 215
  flamenco 285
  language 273
sparrowhawks 44, 45
sperm 80
spiders 152, 153, 210
spinal cord 68
spleen **68**, 73
spores 18, 19
sport 202, 204, 208, 210,
  290–1
squid **40**, 46
stamens 14
starfish 47
stars 104, 105, **134–5**
  constellations **136–7**
  galaxies 128–9,
    130, **132–3**
state, the **220–1**
steam engines 252–3
steel 177, 208, 253
sticklebacks 27
stings 25, 96
stomach 69
stone 102, 103
  see also rocks
strangler vines 49
submarines and submersibles
  121, 177
sugar, dietary 191
Sulla 243
sulfur **95**, 98, 99
Sun 112, 123, 131, 134,
  138–9
  see also solar system
sunflowers 191
supernovas 135
surgery **85**, 118, 255
sweat 74
Sweden 208, 227
swifts 43
swords 250, 251
symbols **270–1**
syringe, hypodermic 84

T

tadpoles 33, 34
Tanzania 201
tapeworms 29
taste 78–9
Taurus 136–7
tea **190**, 201

tektites 147
telephones 259
telescopes 122, 123,
  148–9
television 258, **277**
tendons 66, 67
Thanksgiving 226
theaters **280–1**
thermite 98, 99
thunderstorms **182**
tides 104
tigers 51, 53
tin 93, **177**, 210
Titan **142**, **143**, 151
Titania 142, 143
titanium 177
toads **32**, **37**, 271
toadstools 19
Tokyo 228–9
tomatoes 17, 190
tools, prehistoric
  238–9
tornadoes 182
toucans 43, 206
touch 75, 76, 77, **79**
tourism 201, 211,
  212, **259**
towns 253
  see also cities
trachea 70, 71
trainers 85
trains see railroads
Trajan 243
transpiration 11
transportation **120–1**,
  216, 259
  see also airplanes;
    cars; motorcycles;
    railroads; ships
tree frogs **32**, 206
tree rings 13
trees **12–13**, 14, 49,
  207, 210
Triton 143
tropics 188, 189
Tsunami **167**, 171
tuataras 39
tundra 188
Tunisia 200, 201
turtles **35**, **39**
twentieth century
  258–9
twins 83
typewriters 259
typhoons 183

U

ultraviolet rays 112
umbilical cord 81
UNESCO (United
  Nations Educational,
  Scientific and Cultural
  Organization) 229
Unicorn 271
uniforms 251
United Kingdom 208, 209, 220
  see also London
United Nations (UN) 229, 258
United States of America
  204–5, 214, 215, 220,
  221, 226
  buildings 268–9
  Declaration of landscape
    184, 187
  pollution 192, 193
  presidents **222–3**
  space program 150, 151,
    152, 153
  see also California;
    Las Vegas;
    Los Angeles;
    New York;
    San Francisco
universe **130–1**
  see also solar system;
    space, outer
Ur **240–1**
Uranus **140–1**, 143, 151
urinary system 69
uterus 80, 81

V

vaccination 255
valleys 187
Van Gogh, Vincent
  209, **267**
Vatican City 229
veins 72
Venezuela 186, 206, 207
Venus **140–1**, 151
vertebrates 26, **54–5**
videos 277, 286
Vikings 248, 268
vinegar **96**, 98
vipers 39
vision 77, **78**
  color blindness 115
vitamins 94

volcanoes 160, 161, 162,
  164–5, 169, 209, 213
  lava 164–5
  pumice 172, 173
Volta, Alessandro 122, 123
votes **221**, 258
vultures 29

W

walkmans 258
warfare 119, 250–1, 258
wasps 23, 24–5
water 95, 97, 100, **101**, 131
water striders 46–7
wavelengths, electromagnetic
  112–15
weapons 230–1, 250–1
  prehistoric **238–9**
weather **161**, **182–3**
  Antarctica 213
  climate zones 188–9
  extreme living 230–1
  forecasts 113, **183**
wedding, traditional 198–9
wedges 116, 117
weight 104
Wernicke's area 77
whales 28, **51**, 212
wheat 190
wheels 116, 117
whelks 40, 41
windpipe see trachea
wolves 52
women's rights 259
wood 102
woodlice 31
woodpeckers 43
wool 102
work and workers 241,
  258, **259**
World Heritage Sites 229
World War I 258
World War II **258**, 274
worms 21, 29
writing 247, 272–3

X Y Z

X-rays 105, 112, 149
Yin Yang 270
zebra finches 42
zinc 177

ACKNOWLEDGMENTS

DK would like to thank:
Antara Moitra for editorial assistance; Anjana Nair and Chhaya Sajwan for design assistance; Ben Hung for DTP assistance; Adam Shorrock for creative retouching assistance; Caroline Gates for loaning knitted body parts; David Donkin for the machine model; Nikid for digital artworks; Tall Tree for supplying the reference section; Jackie Brind for the index; Jenny Finch and Henry Fry for proofreading; Nigel Sapp and the Ocular Prosthetics Department, Moorfields Eye Hospital; Jamie Owen and the Natural History Museum; Dr. Tony Irwin, curator of natural history, Norwich Castle Museum and Archaeology Service; William Edwards and the Gordon Museum, Guys Hospital; Hanh Thi Luc for assistance with props; Zygmunt Podhorodecki for supplying and handling wasps and bees; Pia-Henrike Böttger, Cladia Vasconcellos, and Riley's Snooker Club, Walthamstow, for supplying props.

The publisher would like to thank the following for their kind permission to reproduce their photographs:

Key:
a–above; b–below/bottom; c–center; f–far; l–left; r–right; t–top

The Advertising Archives: 255tl (Advertisement), 258cra; **akg-images:** 274tr, Johann Brandste 104tc; **Alamy Images:** ArkReligion.com 270cr, Auscape International 210cl, Bill Bachmann 205bl, J. R. Bale 106-107, Brett Baunton 188clb, Pat Behnke 202bl, blickwinkel 48c, Tibor Bogna 169fcr, Paul Chauncey 205bl, CW Motorsport Images 105tr, David Noton Photography 169cr, Kathy deWitt 221tc, Dennis Frates 204-205, Interfoto 209tc, Sean Justice 230-231 (Background), Kim Karpeles 112-113cb, Iain Masterton 283cb, Eric Nathan 200-201c (background), Ron Niebrugge 168clb, M. Timothy O'Keefe 35crb (Green Sea Turtle Hatchlings on Beach), Pictorial Press Ltd. 283crb, Christopher Pillitz 218tr, The Print Collector 242br, Helene Rogers 210-211c, Alex Segre 282-283c, Jeff Smith 147cr, vario images GmbH & Co. KG 118bc, Visual Arts Library 7tl, 236-237c, David Wall 186br, 211cr, Sue Walsham 223crb, 297crb, Andrew Woodley 229cr, World Religions Photo Library 270br; **Andy Rouse Wildlife Photography:** Andy Rouse 4tl, 8c; **the-blueprints.com:** Onno van Braam 120tl, 120bl, 120-121t, 120-121c, 120-121b, 121tr, 121br; **The Bridgeman Art Library:** Bibliotheque Nationale, Paris, France, Archives Charmet 254tc, 260br, British Library 267cl, 292bl, English School / Private Collection 253tr, Guildhall Library, City of London / Shepherd, Fred 255clb, The Estate of Keith Haring / Deichtorhallen, Hamburg / Wolfgang Neeb 267br, Louvre, Paris, France, Giraudon 243crb, National Portrait Gallery, London, E. Seeman (after) 122c, Peter Newark American Pictures / Private Collection 222cl, 222-223t, 223c, 232cr, 232c, Skelton, William / Bibliotheque de la Faculte de Medecine, Paris, France, Archives Charmet 254br, Vatican Museums and Galleries, Vatican City, Italy 243tl, Victoria and Albert Museum, London 244t, 244b, 245t, 245b; **By permission of The British Library:** 274cl, 274-275bc; **The Trustees of the British Museum:** 239r; **Bryan And Cherry Alexander Photography:** articphoto / Troels Jacobson 212bl; **Corbis:** 207br, Peter Adams / zefa 269c, 293tl, London Aerial Photo Library 228b, Albright-Knox Art Gallery / © DACS 2008 266fbr, Theo Allofs 206bl, 212-213 (background), Mario Anzuoni / Reuters 287cl, The Art Archive 123bc, 243tr, 243c, Yann Arthus-Bertrand 6tl, 158-159c,

211tr, Asian Art & Archaeology, Inc. 275br, Simon Baker 210-211tc, Beateworks / David Papazian 219c, Nathan Benn 207tl, Bettmann 122cr, 123c, 166t, 222tr/3 (all Harrison items), 222ca (Garfield campaign medal), 222cr (Truman), 223tl, 223tc/3 (McKinley items), 223tr/2 (Roosevelt items), 223cra, 255tr, Jonathan Blair 146-147c, Gene Blevins 153cb (17), Georgina Bowater 269clb, Gary Braasch 187cl, Tom Brakefield 29tl, 51cl, Burstein Collection / The Munch Museum / The Munch-Ellingsen Group / © DACS 2008 266fbl, Christie's Images / © DACS 2008 266br, Tim Clayton 211tl, Ashley Cooper 166-167c (background), Richard Cummins 229cb, Tim Davis 37bl, Michael DeYoung 184br, DLILLC 200tr, Momatluk-Eastcott 212cb, epa 167cl, epa / Jon Hrusa 258-259cb, epa / Larry W. Smith 183bl, epa / Marcelo Sayao 192c, epa / Valdrin Xhemaj 6tr, 198-199, Eurasia Press / Steven Vidler 205tr, Macduff Everton 203ca, Warren Faidley 182cl, Michael & Patricia Fogden 33cl, David J. & Janice L. Frent Collection 223cl/2 (Eisenhower items), 223clb, Paulo Fridman 229cl, The Gallery Collection 7tr, 264-265c, Lynn Goldsmith 287fclb, Michael Goulding 279tr, Darrell Gulin 184c, Robert Harding World Imagery / Occidor Ltd. 185tr, Rune Hellestad 209crb, Chris Hellier 254cl, Jon Hicks 229tl, 268-269t, Fritz Hoffman 259crb, Robbie Jack 209cr, Peter Johnson 213tr, Wolfgang Kaehler 231bl, Ed Kashi 200tl (Oil Platform), Karen Kasmauski 229bl, Brooks Kraft 223bc, 232cl, Kurt Krieger 268cb, Frans Lanting 187br, 206cl, Charles & Josette Lenars 268clb, 292tc, Liu Liqun 187bl, Araldo de Luca 242tl, 242c, 242bl, 260tr, Joe Macdonald 37crb, Jamed Marshall 186tr, 206clb, Leo Mason 208tl, George McCarthy 37tc, Gideon Mendel 119tr, Minden Pictures / Michael & Patricia Fogden 184bl, Momatiuk - Eastcott 186tl, NASA 183cr, 187cr, Eric Nguyen 182tr, Nightlight / zefa 182bc, James Noble 110l, Kazuyoshi Nomachi 200tc (sand dune), 228cr, Charles O'Rear 200br, Owaki - Kulla 184cr, Miyoko Oyashiki 118cr, Paul Hardy 26-27b, 269cl, PoodlesRock 166cl, Jim Reed 182tl, Reuters 166b, 193cr, 208tc (cyclists), Reuters / Jim Ruymen 286-287tc, Lynda Richardson 49t, Galen Rowell 212tl, Pete Saloutos 184-185tc, Kevin Schafer 35clb (Green Turtle Hatching), Joseph Sohm; Visions of America 221fclb, Paul Souders 36cb, George Steinmetz 213tl, STScI / NASA 51tr, 128-129, 130ca, Jim Sugar 122-123bc, 164-165, Paul J. Sutton 278tc, Swim Ink 2, LLC 282cla, Gustavo Tomsich 209cb, TWPhoto 167t, Ultimate Chase / Mike Theiss 183cl, Alessandro Della Valle / Keystone 269cb, 293ftl, Francesco Venturi 271fcl, 292cr, 297br, Philip Wallick 182br, Michele Westmorland 48t, Nik Wheeler 192cl, Dennis Whitehead 192-193 (All Placards), Haruyoshi Yamaguchi 118l, zefa / Frank Krahmer 50bc; **Dorling Kindersley:** Academy of Motion Picture Arts and Sciences 205ftl, Angus Beare Collection 51cr, Archaeological Receipts Fund (TAP) 228cl, Australian Museum, Sydney 230tr, Birmingham Buddhist Vihara 203br, Geoff Brightling / Peter Minister 36tr, The Trustees of the British Museum / The Trustees of the British Museum 238br, 239bc, British Museum 230-231c, 242tr, 246cra, 246clb, 247tl (Gods), 256bl, 257bc, 257br, 271cra, 271c, 271crb, 292crb (Minotaur), British Museum / Chas Howson 256tl, 256tr, 256cla, 257cra, 257c, 257c, 257bl (Thai ring coin), 257fcr, 257fcrb, British Museum / Museum of Mankind 210ca, British Museum / Museum of Mankind / Kate Warren 257tr, 257bl, 261ca, IFREMER, Paris / Tina Chambers 177tl, Charlestown Shipwreck and Heritage Centre, Cornwall / Alex Wilson 257tc, Conaculta-Inah-Mex. Authorized reproduction by the Instituto Nacional de Antropologia e Historia 246cl (Knife), 246bl,

246br (Plate), 246-247t, 246-247b, 247c, 247crb, 247bl (Funerary urn), 247bc, 247br (Sacrificial Knife), 261tl, © Crown copyright material is reproduced with the permission of the Controller of HMSO and Queen's Printer for Scotland. 220cla, David Edge / Geoff Dann 241bl, Dinosaur State Park, Connecticut 179bl, Eden Camp Museum 258ca, Linda Esposito 200tc (Jump Dance), Football Museum, Preston 272-273 (Futebol poster), Glasgow Museums 267tr (Grass-skirted mask), Gordon Museum / Guy's, King's and St. Thomas' School of Medicine 76-77 (human brain), Rowan Greenwood Collection 212cra, Henry Moore Foundation (The work illustrated on page 255 is reproduced by permission of the Henry Moore Foundation) 267bl, Jamie Marshall Collection 270cl, Kröller-Müller Museum 267c (Van Gogh), Lindsey Stock Collection 51tr, National Maritime Museum, London / James Stevenson and Tina Chambers 249cr, 249br, National Maritime Museum, London / Tina Chambers 160-161bc, 248bl, Judith Miller / Bibliophion 275cla, Judith Miller / Cooper Owen / © DACS 2008 267bc, Judith Miller / JYP Tribal Art 210tc, Judith Miller / Lyon and Turnbull Ltd. 166-167, Judith Miller / Nigel Wright Collection 271crb (Dolphin), Moorfields Eye Hospital, London 82-83c, Musée du Louvre 266fcl (Mona Lisa), Courtesy of the Museum of London / Courtesy of the Museum of London 239bl, Museum of London 238cra (Adze), 238cl (Flint), 238cl (Iron pyrite), 239cr, 272-273c, 293b, National Maritime Museum, London / James Stevenson 123bl, Natural History Museum, London 54 (8 Skulls), 54tl, 54tr, 54ca (Merganser), 55tr, 178cra, 178bc, 179tl, 238c, 266tc (figurine), Vincent Oliver 220br, Liberto Perugi / Museum of Natural History of the University of Florence, Zoology Section 'La Specola' 66c, 66cr, 67c, 67cr, Pitt Rivers Museum, University of Oxford 238ca, 238l, Pitts Rivers Museum, University of Oxford / Dave King 257cla, Rough Guides 229br, 233tc, Courtesy Science Museum, London 252-253bs, 261tr, Science Museum, London 259bc (Commodore Computer), Scottish United Services Museum, Edinburgh Castle / National Museums of Scotland / Geoff Dann 251c, 251bl, South West Shopfittings Ltd. 224-225 (Background), Tap Service Archaeological Receipts Fund, Hellenic Republic Ministry Of Culture / Tap Service Archaeological Receipts Fund, Hellenic Republic Ministry Of Culture 239cla, The Science Museum, London / John Lepine 253br, University Museum of Archaeology and Anthropology, Cambridge 238cb, 239cl, 239cl (Bronze-Age Pin), 239c, Wallace Collection / Geoff Dann 250cr, Jerry Young 50clb, Michel Zabe 271tc; **Dreamstime.com:** Svenler 276clb; **FLPA:** Nigel Cattlin 152br (11), Mike Lane 42-43t, Minden Pictures / Gerry Ellis 210c, Minden Pictures / Jim Brandenburg 169bc, Minden Pictures / Suzi Eszterhas 47bl, Sunset 279tc; © **Transport for London:** 07 / 1010 / LS 216clb; **Galaxy Picture Library:** 135tl, 144tc, 144tr, 144cl, 144-145c, 144-145cb, 144-145b, 145tc, 145ca, 145cra, 145br; **Getty Images:** 119cr, 153crb (19), 193br, 252tr, 258tr, AFP 152 (Yang Liwei), 206tl, 220cra, 221clb, Steve Bonini 136-137b, Bridgeman Art Library 221br, S. Brimberg & C. Coulson 169cl, Peter Dazeley 286-287c (background), David De Lossy 62-63, Phil Degginger 208clb, DigitalGLobe 167cr, 167b, Dave Hogan 286bc, Frank Micelotta 287fcl, National Geographic / Gordon Wiltsie 169c, Dana Neely 123crb, Bob O'Connor 286-287t, Panoramic Images 184tl, 195bl, Petrified Collection 259cla, Andy Ryan 182-183c, Time & Life Pictures / Nat Farbman 166cr, Time & Life Pictures / Terry Ashe 222clb, 222cb,

222crb, 222fclb, 232cl (Ronald Reagan), 232fcl, Time Life Pictures 254bc, Untitled X-Ray, Nick Veasey 65ca, 65cb; **Hutchison Library:** J. Wright 230tc; **courtesy Intel Corporation Ltd.:** 5tl, 88-89; **iStockphoto.com:** 286crb, Linda Bucklin 76-77, 87bl, Marc Dietrich 220cr, Shaun Lowe 230cl, Gytis Mikulicius 230clb, James Steidl 221cla; **The Kobal Collection:** Dreamworks / LLC 282crb, Universal 282cb, Warner Bros. / DC Comics 282cb; **Lebrecht Music and Arts:** Chris Stock 287cr; **Leeds Library and Information Services, McKenna Collection:** 253tl; **Lumigenic Media / Marc Shargel:** Marc Shargel 35bc; **Duccio Malagamba:** 269crb; **Museum of London:** 259bl; **NASA:** 92tr, 104cl, 119cla, 130cb, 131cra, 132-133cl, 134 (All images except cb), 135 (All images except tl), 138-139c, 148tc, 148-149cla, 149tr, 149crb, 149br, 149ftr, 153cb (18), 154tr, 154cr; **National Geographic Stock:** David Liittschwager 20-21; **Natural Visions:** Soames Summerhays 35clb; **naturepl.com:** Juan Manuel Borrero 49cla, John Cancalosi 49c, Jim Clare 49b, Hans Christoph Kappel 35cla, Kim Taylor 48br; **NHPA / Photoshot:** Bryan & Cherry Alexander 46cr, Linda Pitkin 28tc, Andy Rouse 205crb, T. Kitchen & V. Hurst 37cra; **Photolibrary:** Gerard Soury 35crb; **PunchStock:** Stockbyte 64c; **Richard Revels:** 35tc, 35ca; **Rex Features:** 20th Century Fox / Everett 283cra, Peter Brooker 221cb; **rogersmushrooms.com:** Roger Phillips 18-19; **The Ronald Grant Archive:** 282ca, 282cr, 282clb, 283ca; **Science Photo Library:** 63bc, 123cl, Agstockusa / B. W. Hoffman 10-11, Anatomical Travelogue 75cl, 86br, Andrew Lambert Photography 92ca, 92c, 93cra, 93cr, Julian Baum 105cr, Chris Bjornberg 112bl, Martin Bond 184-185cb, British Antarctic Survey 212-213bc, BSIP, Cavallini James 109cl, BSIP / Kretz Technik 81bl, Jean-Claude Revy, A. Carion 146ca, 155fclb, 296br, Jean-Claude Revy, A. Carion, ISM 147tr, Lynette Cook 131br, Kevin Curtis 72-73, Custom Medical Stock Photo / Richard Rawlins 80tr, Charles D. Winters 92-93c, Eeleman 80bl, 80bc, 80br, 81tl, 81tc, Eurelios / Karim Agabi 212tc, Eye of Science 4ca, 29tc, 60-61, 62br, Mark Garlick 130-131, 131cl, Genesis Films / Neil Bromhall 81tr, Pascal Goetgheluck 118tr, Steve Gschmeissner 62bl, 67cla, 67cl, 74tc, 86bc, 87tr, Gustoimages 112bc, Innersrace Imaging 70-71, Mehau Kulyk 64ftr, 64fbr, 105br, 125cr, Veronique Leplat 112br, Living Art Enterprises 64cr, Living Art Enterprises, LCC 64tr, 64br, 65cra, Jerry Lodriguss 146cl, 155cra, George Mattei 65crb, 86cl, David McCarthy 62-63b, Will McIntyre 193cl, Professors P. M. Motta, P. M. Andrews, K. R. PORTER & J. VIAL 63c, 67tl, Mount Stromlo and Siding Spring Observatories 134cb, Dr. Yorgos Nikas 80cl, Susumu Nishinaga 62-63t, NOAA 113bl, David Nunuk 148bc, Sam Ogden 118cb, 119bl, Alfred Pasieka 64cl, Prof. P. Motta 78-79t, Publiphoto Diffusion, P. G. Adam 112r, Victor de Schwanberg 113cb, 130l, Volker Steger 118br, Andrew Syred 75tc, 83bl, 86fbr, Richard Wehr 74br, F. S. Westmorland 113cr, Charles D. Winter 93c; **SeaPics.com:** 192cr; **Sony Pictures:** SLB 283cla; **South American Pictures:** Tony Morrison 230-231b; **Specialist Stock:** Norman Benton 168-169cb, 195tr; **SuperStock:** Carmel Studios 205cra; **The Art Archive:** Marco Polo Gallery, Paris / A. Dagli Orti 266fcr, Museo del Prado, Madrid / A. Dagli Orti 266cr, National Gallery of Art, Washington 266cl, Pierpont Morgan Library / A. Dagli Orti 267cr, Tate Gallery, London / Eileen Tweedy / © DACS 2008 266bl; **TopFoto.co.uk:** A© Photri 255bc, 243clb

All other images © Dorling Kindersley
For further information see:
www.dkimages.com